002544

Welfare of the Poor

Mary Bryna Sanger

Graduate School of Management and Urban Professions
Department of Urban Affairs and Policy Analysis
New School for Social Research
New York, New York

HV
95
.S25
WEST

ACADEMIC PRESS

A Subsidiary of Harcourt Brace Jovanovich, Publishers

New York   London   Toronto   Sydney   San Francisco

ASU WEST LIBRARY

ACADEMIC PRESS, INC.
111 Fifth Avenue, New York, New York 10003

United Kingdom Edition published by
ACADEMIC PRESS, INC. (LONDON) LTD.
24/28 Oval Road, London NW1 7DX

Library of Congress Cataloging in Publication Data

Sanger, Mary Bryna.
    Welfare of the poor.

    Bibliography: p.
    Includes index.
    1. Welfare recipients––United States. 2. Public
welfare––United States. 3. United States––Social
policy. 4. Unemployed––United States. I. Title.
HV95.S25   362'.973   79–20923
ISBN 0–12–618650–2

PRINTED IN THE UNITED STATES OF AMERICA

79 80 81 82   9 8 7 6 5 4 3 2 1

Contents

Preface

Public officials and social scientists have been talking about welfare reform for more than three decades. Welfare families have been researched almost continually; existing programs have been tinkered with almost since their development as part of the Social Security Act of 1935. Nevertheless, welfare remains perhaps the most misunderstood topic on the agenda of social policy—it is an endlessly controversial public issue.

Social planners really cannot state with any confidence what makes people poor or what makes some poor people turn to welfare while others do not. Despite abundant literature and research, valid data on the characteristics and behavior of the welfare poor are few, and important gaps exist. Previous research requires updating, and conclusions need reconsideration.

The early part of this decade saw considerable funding from the Department of Health, Education and Welfare (DHEW) and the Department of Labor (DOL), both of which financed many new studies. In addition, city and state governments have been noticeably eager in recent years to support research on the unprecedented growth of welfare caseloads, especially where there are high concentrations of welfare families. The big industrial states—New York, California, and Illinois among them—and their major cities financed much important work during this period. Several major sources of longitudinal data, such as negative income tax (NIT) experiments and the University of Michigan's Panel Study on Income Dynamics (PSID), have permitted new analyses of the welfare poor, particularly of their behavior. Longitudinal data bases have permitted analysts to address questions related to changes in the status and circumstances of families over time. The findings have profoundly altered earlier concepts of a static welfare population. Because decisions are necessary regarding welfare reform legislation, this new body of literature should be evaluated, and efforts should be made to resolve the many apparent contradictions. This monograph attempts to serve that purpose. In addition to reviewing new research, it deals in detail with a variety of areas on which welfare research has not recently focused.

Since the erosion of the social initiatives of the 1960s and the winding down of the War on Poverty, most researchers have centered their attention on developing new strategies for a national system of income transfers for the poor. However, without general agreement on strategy, research efforts have addressed the specific issues of program design rather than the strategies. Though much can be learned from the literature on these efforts, there is a pressing need to examine the special requirements and circumstances of the welfare poor as they relate to important social institutions. In addition to reviewing research findings on the status, behavior, and attitudes of welfare families in relation to a variety of social and economic institutions, this monograph restates several fundamental policy issues for welfare reform. The discussion limits itself, when data permit, to the population covered under the welfare program known as Aid to Families with Dependent Children (AFDC). This program received national sanction with the passage of the Social Security Act in 1935. Along with several others, the AFDC program authorized temporary cash assistance to certain categories of the poor who qualified for it upon determination of need. A partnership exists between state and federal governments such that partial federal financing follows upon the state's fulfillment of certain federal administrative regulations.

The AFDC program originally served families in which children were deprived of support through a parent's death, disability, or absence from the home. In addition, a federal option allowing the inclusion of families headed by unemployed fathers in a program known as AFDC–UF has been exercised in 26 states. (This federal option was legislated in the 1962 amendments to the Social Security Act.)

The AFDC program (including AFDC–UF) is the most significant national income assistance program. It has grown from less than 1 million recipients in 1936 to more than 11.4 million in 1975 (U.S. DHEW, 1977). Over 80% of the AFDC families have female heads. Almost 50% of all female-headed families are poor, and almost an equal number spend some time on welfare (Ross & Sawhill, 1975).

The increasing number of families of this type and their continued presence among the welfare and nonwelfare poor have made the AFDC program one of the most controversial and debated targets of social inquiry. Because of these developments, this monograph focuses on the population of the AFDC program. Since AFDC recipients are the largest group receiving cash transfers, research on these families and the impact of this program on the recipients is likely to reveal important dimensions of the entire poverty population. Indeed, new evidence indicates that though some of the poor initially come on welfare as intact families, in time many of them become female-headed families.

Throughout, it will be important to include findings on other groups of welfare recipients and on the nonwelfare poor. Indeed, these groups are "at risk." The population at risk may be described as all those families or individuals who are poor at a given time or who, over some longer time frame, are in danger of becoming poor because of their personal characteristics. At any point in time the proportion of this population which is on welfare may be quite small. However, over some longer time frame the probability of a large portion appearing on welfare is quite high. In the chapters that follow, the term *welfare* will denote AFDC unless otherwise indicated. When data specific to the welfare population are not available, data for the larger poverty population will be used.

Growing concern about the rise in welfare recipiency and the escalating costs of welfare budgets at all levels of government has created renewed interest in the study of the characteristics and behavior of this population. Data from the past have indicated that these characteristics and behavior patterns differ from those of the nonpoor population. Responsible approaches to reform require a verification of earlier assumptions and an empirically founded explanation for these differences.

Renewed research activity over the last decade and the availability of new and better data bases permit a reconsideration of earlier assumptions. This monograph is motivated by a desire to reconsider previous conclusions and research findings on the welfare poor in light of the growth in research activity. Furthermore, it is the implicit assumption of this work that the status of welfare families cannot be viewed in isolation from the major institutions that bear on their lives. These institutions include the labor market, the family, the health care system, and the educational system. Later chapters attempt to review the explanatory models previously used to predict the relation of the poor to these institutions and the impact these relations have on the status of the poor.

Many models exist to explain welfare dependency. In the grossest sense they can be distinguished by two extremes. One extreme holds that the status of the welfare poor is a function of their personal characteristics (i.e., human resources), and the other stresses the importance of institutional factors or arrangements outside the control of individuals. Any successful attempt to decrease poverty and dependency ultimately rests on the appropriateness of its underlying theoretical explanation about what makes people poor, what makes them turn to welfare, and what influences their tenure and experience on welfare. This monograph assesses the current state of the art. It will evaluate, where data permit, the importance of models based both on personal characteristics and on institutional factors and arrangements in order to determine their relative explanatory power.

The book is divided into six chapters. Chapter 1 draws together research findings on the size and stability of the welfare caseload. This includes a consideration of how the caseload can be characterized regarding the nature, length, and patterns of welfare dependency of different cases. For example, special attention is directed toward estimating the median length of time a case remains on the rolls, the degree of case turnover, and the incidence of multiple spells. Studies of case records are reviewed to reveal the correlates of case behavior. Recent methodological refinements that provide a new and more accurate description of case behavior are identified.

Chapter 1 introduces the range of current explanations regarding the existence of a dependent population; the usefulness of these notions is evaluated in Chapter 2, where the determinants of work and welfare patterns are investigated based on a variety of research approaches and data bases. Chapters 3, 4, and 5 follow from the findings in Chapter 2 that family composition, health, and education are important intervening variables in predicting welfare status. Chapter 3 asks whether family breakups, illegitimacy, and fertility result in economic dependency and welfare receipt, or whether the welfare system itself induces such behavioral responses. Competing theories are investigated.

In Chapters 4 and 5 the inadequacy of the health and educational status of the poverty population is recognized and confirmed, and an explanation is offered of how personal characteristics and institutional constraints are related to this inadequacy. Through a critical assessment of recent research, both chapters conclude that research approaches stressing institutional factors offer considerable promise for increasing the explanatory power of existing models. They also underscore the weaknesses and dangers of overestimating the independent importance of personal characteristics.

Chapters 3, 4, and 5 deal with intervening variables that affect poverty and dependency in both direct and indirect ways. There is a recognition throughout that these variables are also related to one another. For example, poor nutrition and health often affect school performance and, therefore, chances for employment. Similarly, early motherhood often results in unstable marriages and divorce. Such factors can inhibit educational attainment, favorable employment experiences, and economic independence. Although each of these issues is treated separately, there is always a recognition that they may have more than a single direct effect on poverty and dependency.

The book concludes with a discussion of the political and methodological weaknesses of the prevailing approaches in poverty research. It is suggested that recent research findings are challenging previous theories of the welfare poor and that alternative paradigms may be more successful in directing public policy.

Acknowledgments

Historically, the Center for New York City Affairs of the New School for Social Research has had a considerable research commitment to the study of welfare. Blanche Bernstein's pioneering efforts in this area provided a stimulating intellectual climate as well as institutional support for the study of this highly controversial area of social policy. In particular, Henry Cohen, Dean of the Center, is to be thanked for providing personal and institutional support and an environment of intellectual freedom—for all undertakings of this kind and especially for this one. David Rose is thanked for his financial support.

Many individuals helped by providing a forum for a rigorous exchange and discussion of ideas. David Lyon at the Rand Corporation, Leonard Hausman at Brandeis, Norman Fainstein at the New School, and Thomas Glynn have given of their time to analyze and debate many of the critical empirical and theoretical questions in the study of welfare policy. To all of them I owe a considerable debt.

For much of the review of the literature in the chapters on health and education, I am grateful to my research assistants Nancy Kulina and Catherine Johnson. Thanks are due to Peter Skinner for skilled editorial assistance. Diane Sanger's critical review of early drafts was most helpful. The final preparation of the manuscript could not have been completed without the valuable research assistance of Tom Reed and the typing endeavors of Robert Rivelli. Finally, I am deeply indebted to my husband, Harry Katz, for his unwavering patience and support throughout the duration of this project.

Most of the research funding was provided through a grant from the Ford Foundation. To all of the above I offer my thanks. The responsibility for all the remaining efforts and shortcomings, however, must be accepted by the author.

1

Welfare Caseload Dynamics

CASELOAD VARIATIONS: CONCEPTUAL
ISSUES AND METHODOLOGICAL
TECHNIQUES

Much of the current interest in welfare policy is a direct response to
the significant growth of the Aid to Families with Dependent Children
(AFDC) program; the number of recipients rose from 2.9 million in 1960
to 7.3 million in 1969, leveling off in 1975 at 11.4 million (U.S. Department of Health, Education and Welfare [DHEW], 1977). Though it is
now known that changes in administrative regulations, eligibility requirements, and benefit levels caused a considerable part of this
growth, many officials viewed it with apprehension. Expenditures
rose from $1 billion in 1960 to $9.2 billion in 1975. Thus, even apart from
the moral difficulties many have with such a large dependent population, the size and cost of the AFDC program justify its claim for special
research.

Welfare was initially envisioned as an emergency cash program for
those temporarily in financial difficulty. Planners expected that general
economic conditions would govern, to a large extent, the size of the

1

welfare population. However, during the 1960s many observers were confused by the seeming lack of association between the growth of the AFDC rolls and the level of aggregate unemployment. Indeed, the unemployment rate, after a brief increase to 6.7% in 1961, fell below 4% in 1965 and remained at about that level until 1970 (U.S. Department of Labor [DOL] & U.S. DHEW, 1978). At exactly this time, the national welfare caseload began its steep rise. Because the traditional relationship no longer held, caseload growth became a topic of public policy interest. A prevalent American suspiciousness of people who receive cash assistance from the government heightened this concern (Williamson, 1974).

Because the "culture of poverty" was seen as a legacy, handed down from generation to generation, the growth in the welfare caseload was viewed as the growth of a permanent welfare population. In fact, welfare was seen as a way of life for an increasingly large percentage of the population. Though many researchers hypothesized that this view of the welfare population was not accurate, existing data were not convincing enough to alter it. At best, several studies on intergenerational dependency among current welfare recipients failed to turn up support for the contention that welfare recipients had, in general, come from families who had also received welfare (Greenleigh, 1969; Lowery, 1967; Podell, 1969). More recent analyses of the University of Michigan's Panel Study on Income Dynamics (PSID) data reveal that children of welfare families were no more likely to become welfare recipients than those of nonwelfare families (Ryan, n.d.).

The paucity of available data makes it difficult to test hypotheses regarding the nature, length, and patterns of welfare dependency. Most data on welfare families were derived from point-in-time or cross-sectional surveys, and studies which reviewed case records provided additional data. While such data have severe limitations regarding validity, many estimates derived from cross-sectional surveys have influenced assumptions regarding the length and patterns of dependency that characterize welfare cases. Reviews of a sample of case records attempt to find out how long (since its most recent opening) the median case has been on the rolls. Results from cross-sectional studies based on this type of analysis suggest that the median range falls between 2 and 3 years (Ketron, 1973; Ostow & Dutka, 1975; Rydell, Palmerio, Blais, & Brown, 1974; U.S. DHEW, 1974, 1977). Estimates of the average length of time a welfare case remains on the rolls in any given spell varies according to the sample; no studies support the view that most AFDC cases are permanent.

Cross-sectional studies are likely to overrepresent long-term cases.

Lyon argues that point-in-time surveys tend to underrepresent short-term cases and fail to distinguish between intermittent episodes and uninterrupted episodes; the former characterize a large portion of the caseload (Lyon, 1977). Thus the results obtained from analyses of length of stay on welfare will differ significantly depending on how the base group of recipients is chosen:

> [The choice may reflect] cases on welfare in a given month, cases on welfare in a given year, or perhaps all cases ever on welfare. The longer the time frame, the higher the fraction of cases with a temporary attachment to welfare and the lower the fraction of cases with a continual attachment, the closer the composition and the sample to a random sample of families ever on welfare [Lyon, Armstrong, Hosek, & McCall, 1976, p. 112].

The Rydell et al. 1974 study of welfare dynamics illustrated the importance of the time frame. The authors compared the percentages of caseloads on welfare for various periods of time, using several different time frames. Table 1.1 demonstrates the effect of the time frame in determining the conclusions that can be drawn. In short, caseload descriptions based on cross-sectional data tend to underestimate grossly the mobility and change of the caseload over time. Traditional dependence on cross-sectional data has drawn a picture of a significantly more dependent population than more recent research validates. The study (though exclusively on New York City's caseload) is an important contribution to our improved understanding of the patterns and length of welfare dependency.

Perhaps the most important aspect of the Rydell et al. study was use of a longitudinal data file on an opening cohort, that is, a specific group of recipients whose cases were all opened at the same time. This prevents the kind of distortions that result from evaluating the welfare histories of a sample over time because such a sample may include cases that moved on to welfare at the end of the study period or that had been on for some time before the beginning of the study period and closed sometime during it. Although this study (Rydell et al., 1974) follows the welfare history of all case types, the groups of interest here can be presented separately by length of dependency and incidence of recidivism.

The findings of the Rydell et al. study of this opening cohort for 1967–1972 distinguish between case types. Though evaluations of these distinctions will be presented more fully in the next section, certain differences are noteworthy here. In general, the majority of families on welfare are not long-term cases. The proportion is actually quite small

TABLE 1.1
Comparison of Percentage Distributions of Welfare Case Histories, 1967–1972, for Cases in Opening Cohorts and Cases at a Point in Time

	Distribution of opening types of assistance							
	AFDC cases, 2+ children (%)		AFDC cases, 1 child (%)		AFDC cases, no adults (%)		AFDC-UF cases (%)	
Welfare history, 1967–1972	Point in time	Opening cohort	Point in time	Opening cohort	Point in time	Opening cohort	Point in time	Opening cohort
Short term (one time on welfare, less than 1 year)	1.0	10.2	3.4	14.9	1.2	16.7	1.8	19.6
Intermediate term (one time on welfare, 1–3 years)	4.8	8.5	10.3	12.8	13.6	16.7	7.7	7.2
Long term (one time on welfare, over 3 years)	68.6	47.5	63.6	36.9	66.5	43.1	52.3	20.3
Multiple times (all durations)	25.6	33.8	22.7	35.4	18.7	23.5	38.2	52.9
Total	100.0%	100.0%	100.0%	100.0%	100.0%	100.0%	100.0%	100.0%

Source: From *Welfare Caseload Dynamics in New York City* by C. P. Rydell, T. Palmerio, G. Blais, and D. Brown, New York: The New York Rand Institute, 1974, Tables 2.9 and 2.10, pp. 20–21.

for AFDC-UF, cases with unemployed fathers. In addition, the incidence of multiple spells within this period is quite substantial for the AFDC-UF caseload, characterizing more than one-half the cases. Among the AFDC cases, long-term histories predominate among families with two or more children. These show fewer multiple episodes than families with only one child.

Other longitudinal studies provided similar results. The Boskin and Nold (1975) longitudinal study in California covered 5 years for 440 AFDC families headed by females and entering the caseload in 1965. Although these cases were not necessarily all first-timers, the findings indicate a mean period on welfare of 16 months, while the median was only 14 months. About 75% of the sample had only one period on welfare (of an average duration of nearly 2 years) during the study period. This finding, though not exactly comparable to those of Rydell *et al.*, certainly supports their basic conclusions.

Among the most recent efforts to reevaluate these findings are the analyses of the PSID. This massive and continuing study has been collecting comprehensive and detailed longitudinal data on the social and economic status of 5000 American families since 1968. Work is in progress by Rein (1977) and others at the Harvard–MIT Joint Center for Urban Studies on the income dynamics of families headed by women aged 25–55 who have been on welfare at some time during this period. Early findings strongly suggest that the conclusions of Rydell *et al.*, Boskin and Nold, and others are correct. Preliminary findings reveal far fewer long-term cases over the study period than data derived from cross-sectional studies would suggest. Furthermore, the Rein study found that only 30% of the cases exhibited intermittent or chronic dependency. *Nearly 40% had short-term dependency of 1 year or less.*

In general, all the studies that were reviewed, particularly those that used longitudinal data, confirm that the welfare caseload is not characterized by long-term dependent families; for large portions of the caseload, welfare episodes are short term. Further, the studies showed relative differences among case types in duration and patterns of dependency.

Turnover, or the movement of families on and off the welfare rolls, is another important concept in understanding the nature of the welfare population. The longitudinal studies of the lengths and patterns of dependency (cited above) reveal a considerable amount of caseload turnover. For example, if the median length of stay on welfare over a given time frame is not generally long term but the welfare caseload remains constant or grows, then it follows that the number of families that have been on welfare within that period is larger than the number on welfare at any given time. Indeed, turnover is often measured by the percentage of new cases replacing old cases in a given period. A high turnover rate suggests that the idea of a static and entrenched welfare class is errone-ous. It suggests that a far greater population of low-income people is at risk; *more* of them will enter the welfare rolls at *some time* than will be receiving assistance at *any given time.*

Determining caseload turnover by assessing the percentage of new cases replacing old ones presents difficulties regarding interpretations. The percentage of new cases replacing old ones may merely reflect the reopening of previously closed cases. To distinguish between genuinely new cases and merely reopened old ones, Rydell *et al.* refer to "tempo-rary" and "permanent" turnover in the study for New York City (see Table 1.2). Permanent turnover is based upon cases closed permanently and replaced by cases never on welfare before. Both rates are calculated separately.

Examining caseload turnover for the full 6 years of the study, Rydell *et al.* found that more than 50% of the cases on the rolls were simply replacing former cases which had previously been on welfare but had closed permanently. Quint and Brown's (1974) study of a 1-year period in New York City provided further evidence of this nature. The new data available from longitudinal data files on caseload turnover help enlarge and modify the traditional picture that emerged from studies of welfare dependency patterns. A high degree of mobility both on and off the welfare rolls over time was strongly indicated; further, the popula-tion at risk at a given time is far larger than is suggested by those actually receiving welfare at that time.

The data on caseload turnover and from studies of income dynamics suggest far more constant and substantial change in the welfare popula-tion than was suggested previously; nevertheless, the enduring nature of dependency, even though its incidence appears to be altered substan-

TABLE 1.2
Average Monthly Turnover Rates, 1972

Type of case	Percentage of turnover per month		
	Permanent	Temporary	Total
AFDC	.8	.78	1.64
AFDC-UF	2.12	2.69	4.31

Source: From *Welfare Caseload Dynamics in New York City* by C. P. Rydell, T. Palmerio, G. Blais, and D. Brown, New York: The New York Rand Institute, 1974, Table 3.12, p. 44.

tially over a longer time frame, remains problematic. Furthermore, even though the proportion of long-term dependents is far smaller than was originally supposed, questions about the reasons for its existence remain.

Rein (1977, p. 2) asks why a class of individuals has become permanently entrenched (chronically dependent) in welfare. He suggests that the first step in understanding this concept of a "welfare class" is to be aware not only of the nature of individuals' attachment to welfare, but also of all the possible reasons for this long-term attachment. Rein distinguishes between several causes of dependency and points out that given a welfare dependent population, a choice among policy options will be determined by the particular cause. Several possible explanations (deviating somewhat from Rein's typology) suggest themselves both logically and in the literature.

First to be considered are the *personal resources and human capital* (or their lack) that the welfare or potential welfare recipient brings to the labor market. These include personal disabilities, such as, physical and emotional illness, inadequate skills, and a deficiency in the ability or *will* to get and keep a job[1] (Rein, 1977). These personal disabilities can be compounded by a general lack of human capital such as in education, job training, and experience. Rein suggests that persons so afflicted may be seen as representing the social work paradigm of the multiproblem family, whose members suffer from a variety of social and personal difficulties such as family disruption and disorganization.

Second among possible explanations is a group that is welfare dependent as a function of the *labor market structure and performance*. In his study, Rein calls such groups "the exploited"; those workers no longer needed by the economy. When demand for their labor is low, such persons are provided with income support to allow them to subsist until their labor is in demand again. The normal cyclical performance of the economy together with the structural segmentation of the low-income labor market tends to govern their dependency. These labor market factors are exogenous to these individuals, outside their control. The structure of the economy defines their position as marginal. As a result, they move back and forth from work to welfare.

Economic rationality is a third view, according to which, the existence of the dependent population is a function of economic choice. The theory of individual choice posits that potential welfare recipients with their given skills and desires compare the benefits from employment with benefits they would receive if not working. If working provides

---

1. *Will* includes ambition to work and commitment to the middle-class work ethic.

income (plus nonincome benefits) equal or nearly equal to what they would receive if not working, economically rational individuals will choose welfare rather than work.[2] Included in this group are people who consciously make themselves eligible for welfare through family breakup (feigned or real), illegitimate births, or mere voluntary unemployment. Rein includes in this category "entrepreneurs," hustlers who exploit weaknesses in the system, failing to report income from work or changes in their circumstances that would make them ineligible for welfare.

Though causes differ, these theories attempting to explain dependency clearly need not exclude each other. The typology, in fact, represents the range of popular notions, and the data will show that certain elements of each model will be useful in explaining observed patterns of dependency.

An additional element is that the welfare program itself may have characteristics that reinforce dependency. Several design features of the program provide work disincentives (e.g., tax rate, guarantee level, accounting period, multiple benefits); and these have to be considered in conjunction with the argument of individual economic choice. Opposed to this is the "settling-in" hypothesis. Based on studies of welfare dynamics (e.g., Rydell *et al.*, 1974), this hypothesis empirically demonstrates that the longer a case remains on welfare, the less likely it is to move off the rolls. It lends support to those who see a dependent population, settled into and adapted to a life on welfare.

VARIATIONS WITHIN THE WELFARE POPULATION

Recent evidence on the length and patterns of welfare dependency and caseload turnover reveals that cases vary greatly. The welfare population appears, in fact, to be quite heterogeneous in its characteristics, circumstances, and reasons for being on welfare.

Some of the recent research approaches have enabled analysts to begin to identify the correlates of welfare patterns and duration on the rolls. Additional evidence from studies on the reasons for case openings and closings will help distinguish between the various factors distributed among the welfare population that govern moving on or off the rolls.

2. Nonincome benefits include personal satisfaction, social solidarity in the work place, self-esteem derived from community and family, etc.

Mayo's study of welfare families in Cook County, Illinois, followed cases over a 3-year period (1975b). She distinguishes between the welfare experiences of the sample over the study period in the following manner: nonmobile continuous cases, which appeared on the rolls for the entire study period; off-mobile cases, which moved off the rolls during the study period; and on-mobile cases, which moved on to welfare during the study period. The on-mobile group comprised by far the largest part of the sample (62.7%). Chi-squares were then calculated to explain the relationships between a recipient's characteristics and welfare experience. Several interesting findings emerged from the analysis. Continuous cases were generally those with the most fundamental disadvantages. These recipients included the oldest, the most rural, and new immigrants from the South. In addition, they were most likely to have profound constraints on their activity: They had the largest number of children; they and their children had the largest number of health problems; and they had the lowest employability.[3] They were most likely to have been raised in a household with a single parent and to have had only a grammar school education. In short, the continuous cases had characteristics that posed the greatest difficulties in achieving independence.

The new cases clearly held most promise for independence; they were likely to be the youngest and best educated, with the fewest health problems; they were the most employable and had fewer children and the smallest number of limitations on their activity. The only major limitation appeared to be the presence of preschool children. These cases were also the most likely to have come from families that were intact.

The mobile cases represented a rather mixed group; some had moved off AFDC permanently, and some had basic employment and family characteristics that rendered them extremely unstable. The latter group usually had the lowest educational attainment and the fewest number of jobs, compared with all other groups. These families generally had come on AFDC at a younger age than the other two groups and appear to represent "a northern, urban underclass of very poor, residentially mobile women [Mayo, 1975b, p. 57]."

Rydell *et al.* (1974) analyzed the relationship between the case type and the nature of its welfare dependency.[4] Several general findings seem

---

3. The measure was an index of seven variables including work experience, training, age, health, and education.

4. Rydell considered five case characteristics: (*a*) amount of nonwelfare income in the household; (*b*) existence of employment income in the household; (*c*) whether payee is available for employment; (*d*) age of the payee; and (*e*) number of children in a case.

noteworthy. Despite the obvious finding that the more nonwelfare income a family has, the less it depends on welfare, the study stated that
more of the long-term dependent cases were households with income
than were the short-term cases.[5] The authors conclude: "Partial or low-
wage employment is not necessarily a stepping stone to self-sufficiency,
but it is compatible with long-term dependence on welfare [p. 51]."
Additional findings revealed that long-term cases are more likely to
include more children than are short-term cases. In addition, long-term
cases were more likely to have had older payees than were short-term
cases.

    Further insight into the relationship between the characteristics of
cases and the length and patterns of dependency is provided by a recent
cross-sectional analysis of welfare families in New York City headed by
males and females (Ostow & Dutka, 1975). Though the study found
considerably less turnover in the sample than would have been expected
on the basis of the Rydell analysis, significant behavioral differences by
case type were found in the duration of dependency. In keeping with
the Rydell *et al.* findings, families with female heads showed a far
higher incidence of chronic dependency than did those with male
heads. This finding was true of hardcore dependent families (10 years or
more on welfare) as well. Women who had a husband present were
likely to have somewhat shorter periods of dependency than those who
had never married or whose husbands were no longer with the family.
The presence of a husband, even if he is an incapacitated or long-term
unemployed person, appears to curtail the length of dependency. Perhaps this suggests the value of family stability in promoting independence.

    An important consideration in comparing the results from different
studies is that researchers use varying definitions of long-term and
short-term dependency. Some define short-term spells as 1 year or 2;
others as inclusive of 3 or 4 years. Obviously, the correlates of dependency will reflect alternative specifications of the dependent variables.

    In addition, the welfare experience itself may effect the length of
stay on welfare (and movement from welfare to work). Rydell *et al.*
(1974) refer to the "settling in" hypothesis. Stressing a significant fact—
that the longer a case remained on welfare, the less likely it was to
close—the study posits a hypothesis. Finding that even when case
characteristics were held constant, closing rates diminished with the
increase in case age, he concluded that no evidence existed to contradict

    5. Long-term ("extended dependency") are those on welfare 6 years or more; short-
term ("limited dependency"), 2 years or less.

this "settling in" hypothesis. Levy, in two separate studies for Ketron, (1973), demonstrated that the movement from welfare to nonwelfare status depended on the duration of the current spell of a given case as well as on the number of the previous episodes. Thus, the inherent nature of the welfare experience influences whether people go on or off the rolls.

Alternative hypotheses are, however, consistent with these findings. If case closing rates decline with case age that may be merely the recognition that two different types of cases move onto the rolls; the movers who stay only a short time and the stayers who stay a long time (Lyon, 1977). It may also be that cases which stay are systematically selected for long stays by their preferences or by characteristics which have yet to be empirically identified. Though no research has yet refuted the "settling-in hypothesis," additional empirical evidence would be necessary to conclude with certainty that families adapt to welfare over time.[6]

The bulk of these findings on the relationship of case characteristics to welfare behavior stress the importance of personal resources and human capital in different subsets of the welfare poor. Such characteristics appear to influence the length and nature of the dependency of these populations and the likelihood of recidivism. They also influence the probability of a family going on welfare initially and later going off the rolls.

Evaluation of the reasons for case openings and closings aid in an analysis of variables affecting welfare caseload levels. What principal factors enable a family to leave welfare? Tables 1.3 and 1.4 list the categories for case openings and closings of New York City's welfare department and present an average, by month, over the period January through September, 1972.

It is immediately obvious that the reasons for case openings are not the opposite of those for case closings and that the reasons for openings and closings differ markedly depending on whether the families are headed by males or famles. Although unemployment accounts for the overwhelming majority of case openings in AFDC-UF, it accounts for a very small percentage of case openings in female-headed AFDC cases. Changes in family composition are the dominant reason for case openings; they do not govern case closings. A major finding of the Quint and Brown (1974) study on reasons for caseload turnover is the dominance of

6. Lyon (1977) cited an unpublished finding by Wiseman and Levy at the University of California, Berkeley: The number of months on welfare was insignificant in predicting closing rates for the Alameda County Caseload.

TABLE 1.3
Percentage Distribution of Average Case Openings per Month by Reason for Opening

Reason for case opening	AFDC (%)	AFDC-UF (%)
Unemployment	13.4	67.6
Reduction in nonwage income	3.2	8.0
Medical	17.5	2.8
Change in household composition	45.6	6.8
Contact reestablished	7.7	6.8
Administrative	4.8	2.8
Other	7.7	5.2
Total	100.0%	100.0%

Source: From *Welfare Caseload Dynamics in New York City* by C. P. Rydell, T. Palmerio, G. Blais, and D. Brown, New York: The New York Rand Institute, 1974, Table 5.5, p. 61.

administrative factors, including changes in welfare department regulations, which often make income documentation or work registration requirements more stringent. Failure to comply with such administrative regulations may result in temporary case closings for a rather significant number of cases.

Quint and Brown have termed these often short-run factors in case closing as "administrative churning." Though employment accounts for

TABLE 1.4
Percentage Distribution of Average Case Closings per Month by Reason for Closing

Reason for case closing	AFDC (%)	AFDC-UF (%)
Employment	11.4	28.9
Increase in nonwage income	3.0	4.0
Death	.2	—
Change in household composition	8.5	.4
Contact lost	35.3	19.3
Administrative	17.5	27.6
Other	24.0	19.7
Total	100.0%	100.0%

Source: From *Welfare Caseload Dynamics in New York City* by C. P. Rydell, T. Palmerio, G. Blais, and D. Brown, New York: The New York Rand Institute, 1974, Table 5.6, p. 62.

more than 10% of the case closings for AFDC and 28% in AFDC-UF, the administrative categories predominate. Even when administrative factors are excluded, only 12.2% of the AFDC cases and 31.9% of the AFDC-UF cases are closed because of employment. An additional 8.8% of the AFDC cases are closed because of changes in family composition (presumably marriage to a male head) or ineligibility of children because of age.

In his study of case turnover in California, Wiseman (1976) cites factors that can cause measures of case closings to be misleading. Arguing that moving off welfare can mean different things at different times, he illustrates from his data that a change in employment status or other income, which would have moved a case off welfare under one payment and eligibility calculation might not do so under another. Moreover, leaving welfare is not necessarily the same as leaving poverty or leaving dependence.[7]

> Families leave welfare, among other things, because the youngest child reaches 18 and leaves school, because they move to another state to assume welfare there, because they are transferred to another aid program, and because the mother is killed in an automobile accident and the children are transferred to foster care. These reasons are not atypical. They do not constitute the type of "closures" that are generally what people have in mind when they analyze welfare turnover. [p. 23].

In the Mayo study of welfare mothers in Cook County, reasons for case openings recorded in case records were compared to the individual responses reflected in the survey made of 400 female household heads receiving welfare. The individual responses proved to be generally consistent with administrative categories; however, the details provided by the respondents themselves tended to provide a richer understanding of the factors that cause case openings. By far the most significant factor was loss of employment or inadequate income from work, a reason in 21.6% of the case openings. Following closely was pregnancy, a reason in 17.8% of the case openings. Interviews with the mothers revealed that pregnancy as a cause was often complicated by a broken marriage in the past or the loss of a job because of pregnancy. Some women who had received support from relatives prior to pregnancy found themselves without support after the child was born. Sometimes the birth of

---

7. From the studies of Alameda County, California, for example, it was revealed that if an AFDC-UF case were followed over 1 year, family breakup would move the case to AFDC in about 20% of the cases. Followed over 2 years the probability would increase to 40%. Thus, the close of the AFDC-UF case would not indicate leaving poverty or leaving dependence (Doolittle, Levy, & Wiseman, 1977).

a second child created additional financial burdens without an increase in financial help from relatives. Of the women in the sample who came to welfare as unwed mothers, 62.3% did not enter the case rolls with the birth of their first illegitimate child. "A woman's current arrangements for economic survival—her own employment, living with her boyfriend—may be threatened by a pregnancy which temporarily incapacitates her and places additional financial and emotional burdens on anyone who may be supporting her [Mayo, 1975b, p. 34]."

Quint and Brown's study (1974) of the New York City welfare rolls indicated that marital dissolution was a primary reason for case openings among AFDC mothers. In fact, 45.6% of the AFDC cases opened because of change in family composition. However, only about 18% of the respondents in the Mayo study in Cook County said marital breakup was their primary reason for going on AFDC. Since 78.1% of the sample had been married at one time, marital dissolution remains an important factor in women's decisions to turn to welfare. However, a considerable time lag may occur between marital breakup and turning to welfare. Though marital dissolution was cited as the *precipitating* factor in only 18% of cases, the percentage of the sample at some time married (78.1%) and the percentage of cases opened because of change in family composition (45.6%) clearly showed marital breakup to be one of several factors leading to welfare receipt. This can be reliably inferred from another cited reason for initial case openings. In 8.7% of the cases, mothers said they had been receiving general assistance (GA) or AFDC-UF while married but had turned to AFDC when they separated from their husbands. Additional factors included loss of financial support from former husband, child's father, or boyfriend (9.5%) and from relatives (6.6%); appointment as guardian of dependent children (6.5%); being an intergenerational AFDC household in which a daughter bears an illegitimate child (5.7%). "All other reasons" accounted for 6% of case openings.

CONCLUSION

Causes of case openings and subsequent case closings as indicated by welfare records do not reflect the dynamic interaction of a number of variables that result in a family's movement on and off welfare. Survey data have begun to identify, to a limited degree, the many factors operating in a family's decision to apply for welfare. Administrative factors seem to explain a large amount of caseload turnover. Recent data about caseload behavior have at least been able to dispel many earlier misconceptions about the welfare population.

There is no evidence that the majority of welfare families are permanent, entrenched welfare dependents. Longitudinal studies reveal that the median period on welfare is somewhat less than 2 years and probably closer to 1 year. Welfare families show considerable variation in the length and patterns of their dependency, with many families exhibiting interrupted and multiple spells of welfare receipt over a 6-year period. The research evidence indicates that certain case characteristics can explain some of the variations among lengths and patterns of dependency. Most important in explaining these variations are differences in personal and family characteristics, which provide clues to the probable causes of the differences in the degree and nature of welfare experiences, but do not lead to any definitive conclusions. As Rydell and his colleagues (1974) conclude:

> Our analysis also shows that even though financial and demographic case characteristics provide additional explanatory power, there are still case-history differences that they cannot explain. It seems, therefore, that *at the current state of knowledge about welfare dependency, chance events play a large part in determining whether a welfare case is a short-term or a long-term one.* If we knew more about the health, job skills, ambition, or personality of welfare recipients, then we might be able to reduce the behavior that is now lumped under "chance" [p. x].

Chapter 2 will explore the employment and employability of welfare families and the relationship of these factors to their welfare experience. The three models discussed earlier as explanations of welfare dependency will be evaluated. Later chapters will explore in greater depth many of the apparent precipitating and underlying factors related to welfare receipt. The remainder of the monograph explores the critical social and economic factors associated with poverty and the risk of welfare dependency.

2

Employment

In order to explain the existence and nature of the welfare poor, this chapter will explore in greater depth the typology presented in Chapter 1. Generally, families move on to welfare when adequate means for self-support are precluded by circumstances such as inability or lack of desire to work and inadequate wages or work hours.[1] Central to understanding distinctions in circumstances is the concept of employability. Since employment is the "solution" to welfare dependency most consistent with American values and policy, this chapter will focus on the relationship between work and welfare. Many variables intervene between work and welfare, altering the probabilities that certain population subsets can or will make the transition from welfare to work. Later chapters will consider more fully how certain intervening variables such as family composition, health, and education operate to change these probabilities. The relevance of each variable will be clarified in the paragraphs that follow.

1. Theoretically, eligibility of "able-bodied" household heads for AFDC requires registration and availability for work. Requirements include acceptance of "suitable work." As will become clear, however, "able-bodied" and "suitable work" are not easily defined or enforced.

MEASURING EMPLOYABILITY

The concept of employability became popular among welfare analysts and policymakers in the 1960s. Most of the policies aimed at solving poverty stressed disabilities of personal resources and human capital inherent in the poverty population; and estimates of employability were made, in part, to evaluate policy options designed to move people from welfare to work. Traditionally the sources of data used to measure employability were surveys of a sample of welfare families at one point in time. Cross-sectional data, however, tend to underestimate grossly the importance of work to large segments of the welfare population; while at one point in time the percentage of recipients who are working might be quite low, data based upon tracking recipients over an extended period have revealed a consistently more active relationship with the labor market than could be inferred from data collected at any one point in time.

Discussions of employability have often failed to distinguish among several fundamental issues. They seldom separate the questions of who *can* and who *should* work. For example, are female heads of families with preschool children at home to be considered employable (Levitan, 1977)? The employability of a welfare recipient is a function of several interrelated factors, not the least of which may be the person's potential for and motivation to work (Lyon, 1977). Every individual's likelihood to work is influenced by many labor market factors as well as his or her personal characteristics. Mayo (1975b) recognizes that a high degree of subjectivity occurs in defining employability:

> People who are "unemployable" under one set of market conditions may be highly "employable" under another. Employability is clearly a continuum, not an either/or proposition; people vary widely in the degree to which and the circumstances under which they are employable [p. 21].

Although the amount of variation in the degree to which welfare recipients are considered employable depends upon the definition used, evidence indicates that in such a heterogeneous population recipients will still vary substantially among themselves in their employability, regardless of the definition selected. Many researchers have developed scales that include all variables (e.g., personal and labor market factors) thought to predict the probability of employment for an individual with a given set of characteristics. Key among personal characteristics are age, sex, education, previous work experience, job training, family composition (number and ages of children), and health of recipients and family members. Such measures, along with labor

market conditions and motivation, are the principal predictors of employability. However, the population at risk is diverse with respect to
many of these measures. For both analytic and policy purposes, distinctions must be made between several subsets of the welfare population
in terms of their relative employability. It is also important to evaluate
the welfare population's employment assets or handicaps against those
of the rest of the low-income population with whom welfare recipients
compete for employment.

EMPLOYED RECIPIENTS

Identifying those who already work assists significantly in evaluating
the relative employability of welfare recipients. As noted earlier, re-
liance on cross-sectional data has led to many misconceptions about the
relationship of the welfare poor to the labor force. Conclusions based on
a point-in-time description of families on welfare have usually
obscured the significant degree to which a greater proportion of the
caseload than is usually recognized participates in the labor force.
Point-in-time survey data tend to conceal the considerable degree of
mobility whereby a good portion of the caseload moves from welfare to
work and work to welfare more quickly and more often than has been
commonly acknowledged.

An initial analysis of any data on the work experiences of the welfare poor indicates that the circumstances and behavior of female-
headed families differ significantly from those of male-headed families
(the latter are usually intact). Eighty percent of all families participating
in the AFDC program have female heads. Compared with the participation rate of women in the regular AFDC program, the rate of participation among eligibles in AFDC-UF programs is far lower. (Only 26 states
and Washington, D.C., operate AFDC-UF programs.) Because of apparent differences in the characteristics of the labor force and the obstacles
to independence as regards these two groups (and because of policy and
analytic demands), they must be considered separately in this analysis.
AFDC fathers resemble in many ways the male heads of families in
poverty of the larger population. Thus, a consideration of AFDC fathers
provides a basis for understanding the characteristics of many poverty
families who may receive welfare in the future through loss of the male
head or through unemployment.

EMPLOYMENT STATUS AND EXPERIENCE OF AFDC FATHERS

To become eligible for AFDC, the male head of the household must
be disabled; or, in states offering AFDC-UF, he must be unemployed for
a substantial period of time, with unemployment benefits exhausted. In

1975, 10% of all AFDC families had a father present; but 47.3% of these men were disabled.[2] Under current regulations, to remain eligible for AFDC benefits, a male household head may not be employed for more than 100 hours a month.

It is not surprising, therefore, that the participation of male heads of AFDC families in the labor force can appear to be quite low at a given point in time. In 1975, during the month of a U.S. DHEW (1977) survey, 12% of the AFDC fathers were employed, 8% working full time and 4% part time. An additional 25% reported that they had been actively seeking work or awaiting recall from a layoff. Of the remainder, neither employed nor looking for employment, 47% were incapacitated, 7% were not actively seeking work and 2% were reportedly needed at home as homemakers full time. An additional 2% not employed were attending school or participating in a work training program at the time of the survey. Thus, at one point in time, 37% were either employed or strongly connected to the labor force (U.S. DHEW, 1977).

The attachment of these fathers to the labor force is not reflected in the data on their current work status; but it becomes evident when their experience is viewed over a period longer than one month. Using data from a 1973 AFDC study, Friedman and Hausman (1975) attempted to characterize the employment history of welfare fathers over a longer period. Though lack of complete data was a problem, they were able to estimate that only 1% of all AFDC fathers had never been employed, whereas 82.8% of those not employed during the survey month had been previously employed. Of this 82.8%, 55% had been employed within the previous 2 years and 33% within the past year.[3]

The dominance of female family heads in the AFDC program means that most data on the work experience of welfare family heads have tended to emphasize the experience of women. However, an abundance of additional information permits certain distinctions between male and female family heads.

EMPLOYMENT STATUS AND EXPERIENCE OF
AFDC MOTHERS

The 1975 AFDC study (U.S. DHEW, 1977) indicated that 16.1% of welfare mothers were employed during the study month. An additional 10% were actively seeking work or awaiting recall from a layoff. Among

2. This includes a natural or adoptive father or legally responsible stepfather.
3. The 1975 AFDC survey confirmed employment histories for only 95% of the sample; information on 4.9% was unavailable.

those not employed 22% were not actively seeking work; 7% were incapacitated for employment; 40% were needed as homemakers full time. The 1975 study suffers from a considerable lack of data on the employment history of AFDC mothers. Data on the length of time since a mother was last employed are missing for 46% of the sample. Nevertheless, on the basis of data that were available, 89% of the cases sampled had some previous work experience; 27% within the previous year, 33% within the past 2 years, and 41% within the past 5 years.

Data from Podell's (1969) study of welfare families in New York City confirmed histories of strong labor force experience among welfare mothers in the sample. Some 80% had some employment experience, though this was generally prior to the birth of the first child; some 50% continued to work afterward. As will be shown later, the time at which the first birth occurs has profound significance for the participation of mothers in the labor force. Perhaps more significant was the high degree of interest among mothers in future work: 70% preferred to work than stay at home; and 66.6% had plans to work in the future. (In later discussions of these mothers' motivation to work, these issues and pertinent data will be explored further.)

Comparisons between data on fathers and mothers show that on the whole AFDC mothers have less recent work experience than do AFDC fathers. Fathers who had been out of work more than 2 years were more likely to be disabled or incapacitated. Although at a point in time more mothers are working than fathers, many more mothers who are out of work have never worked at all. This is not the case for the fathers. Of those mothers not currently working who have previously worked, it is very probably that far more will have been out of work for a longer time than would be the case with a comparable group of fathers.

A national study of AFDC recipients in 1969 (Meyers & McIntyre, 1969) followed the work patterns of family heads over 3 years. Data limited to the active cases showed that 35.6% had at least one period of employment over the 37-month period; 10% had two periods; and 4.7% had three or more periods. Thus, data collected over a longer time frame show that over 50% of AFDC recipients worked at least once.

A different approach, based on a study of income dynamics, revealed a still stronger attachment to the labor force for "ever-welfare" women (Rein, 1977). Looking at the income package (earned, unearned, and transfer income) available to these women over the 7 years of the PSID study, Rein described them as complex and diverse. The extent of their work, he found, was quite substantial for all women except those heavily dependent on welfare. He found evidence for both serial and simultaneous work and welfare mixes.

During the years on welfare, earnings of the family comprise between one-quarter and one-third of the family's income for all patterns
of welfare use, except the continuous long-term welfare families (the
proportion varies between 24 and 37%). It is only for women with
long-term welfare attachment and extensive dependency (50% of their
7-year income comes from welfare) that we find marginal earnings
which account for only 6% of their family income. But this minor
attachment to work applies to only 12% of the ever-welfare women [p.
37].

FACTORS AFFECTING WORK AND WELFARE
PATTERNS

The typology presented in Chapter 1 attempted to characterize the
range of theories currently offered to explain the existence of a dependent population. Each hypothesis considered the factors which inhibited or prevented adequate employment. The remainder of this chapter
will review the usefulness of each component of that typology in explaining dependency. Included will be research findings on the impact
of disabilities in personal resources and human capital; labor market
factors; and the impact of rational economic choice on the work and
welfare patterns of the population at risk.

PERSONAL RESOURCES AND HUMAN CAPITAL

The literature on welfare families is filled with descriptive data on
their demographic and employment characteristics. Many analysts
argue that the multiple characteristics of these families put them at an
extreme disadvantage in generating income from stable employment.
Descriptive data on the incidence of these social and demographic
characteristics follows.

Education. Lack of educational attainment is commonly thought to
erode the welfare dependent's potential for employment. Table 2.1
shows that both male and female AFDC family heads have low educational attainment levels compared to the national labor force. However,
these figures do not show the impact of age on education. Table 2.2,
showing the distribution of the relative age of the national AFDC
caseload, indicates that though the educational attainment of female
heads is far higher than that of male heads, female heads also tend to be
younger. This suggests that in keeping with national trends, younger
welfare family heads, like younger nonwelfare family heads, are likely
to be better educated than older ones. Comparative education data for a

TABLE 2.1
Education of AFDC Family Heads

Years of schooling	AFDC mothers, 1975 (%)	All females in labor force aged 16+, 1977 (%)	AFDC fathers, 1975 (%)	All males in labor force aged 16+, 1977 (%)
Less than 5	4.0	.9	14	1.9
5–8	12.7	6.9	19.4	9.9
9	8.4 ⎫		6.2 ⎫	
10–11	23.3 ⎭	17.0	14.7 ⎭	17.2
12	23.7	44.6	15.6	36.0
More than 12	4.6	30.7	3.2	35.1
Unknown	23.3		26.9	

Sources: U.S. Department of Health, Education and Welfare, *Aid to Families with Dependent Children: 1975 Recipient Characteristics Study*, Part 1, 1977, pp. 57, 68, and U.S. Department of Labor and U.S. Department of Health, Education and Welfare, *Employment and Training Report of the President*, 1978, Table B-9, pp. 248–249.

sample of working heads of welfare families and low-income, nonrecipient family heads in Detroit (Miller & Ferman, 1972) indicated that the educational attainment did not differ significantly between the recipient and nonrecipient low-income groups.

Occupation. The welfare poor look much like the low-income population with respect to education; and they both fare badly in the general labor market. Occupations when working and the industries in which

TABLE 2.2
Age Distribution of AFDC Family Heads

Years of age	AFDC mothers	AFDC fathers
Under 20	8.3	1.6
20–24	22.0	9.6
25–29	21.1	12.8
30–34	16.5	12.1
35–39	11.4	9.5
40–54	15.9	31.6
55+	1.7	14.3
Unknown	3.0	8.4

Source: U.S. Department of Health, Education and Welfare, *Aid to Families with Dependent Children: 1975 Recipient Characteristics Study*, Part 1, 1977, pp. 56, 67.

they commonly work are factors thought to affect the work and welfare prospects of members of the welfare population. Much of the discussion of the disabilities of the welfare poor with respect to their chances for independence has centered around their lack of employment skills and the instability and segmentation of the labor markets in which they work. Though these issues will be explored further in a later section, the descriptive data below will provide the context in which to evaluate the importance of the labor market in the work and welfare behavior of these family heads.

According to the 1975 AFDC study (U.S. DHEW, 1977), in 23% of all cases, the usual occupation of welfare mothers cited is service work. (The occupations of 35% of the sample were not known.) In comparison, only 6.9% of the fathers do service work as their usual occupation. AFDC fathers were generally concentrated in unskilled blue-collar occupations. Of the AFDC fathers, 28.8% were laborers, 12.5% operatives, and 13.2% skilled blue-collar workers (craftsmen or kindred workers). Of the mothers, 6.1% were operatives, and 4% were laborers. The only significant categories mothers cited as their usual occupations were sales, clerical, and kindred workers, which accounted for 13.8%.

When these occupational classifications are compared to those of the labor force as a whole, it is seen that welfare mothers and fathers occupy a disproportionate share of low-wage, high-turnover, unstable jobs. Comparison with low-income nonrecipient family heads in a Detroit sample shows that their status is quite similar (Miller & Ferman, 1972). Welfare family heads, particularly men, tended to have a slightly higher concentration in service occupations than did low income nonrecipient family heads. Female family heads among the working recipient group had somewhat higher concentrations in sales and clerical jobs than did the nonrecipient working women. The nonrecipient low-wage female worker was more likely to be a kindred or blue-collar worker than was the welfare mother.

In general, both male and female welfare family heads tend to work in low-paying occupations and industries. Many of these jobs are unstable. For many of the occupational categories, even stable full-time employment would still leave these families below the poverty line because average wages are very low (Levitan, 1977). Though the differences in the occupational classification among men and women are significant, the differences between the working welfare recipient and the low-wage, nonrecipient are not very great.

Family Characteristics. An earlier section of this monograph identified certain distinguishing family composition variables related to the length and nature of the welfare dependency of a particular case. Clearly, in a population dominated by female single-parent households, the age and number of dependent children influences a mother's avail- ability for work and possibly her ability to sustain stable employment, given normal child care responsibilities. In 1975, a majority of AFDC families had young children. In 58% of the cases, at least 1 child was below preschool age. The average number of children in an AFDC household in the same year was 2.4. Table 2.3 indicates the distribution of welfare families by number of children. Though as many as 37.9% of the families had only 1 dependent child, 26% had 2. An additional 16.1% had 3 children, while 20% had 4 or more children.

Since 80% of AFDC families are headed by females, the family characteristic constituting the biggest single barrier to employment is the presence of young children. In 57.5% of AFDC families, the youngest child was 5 or younger. In their study of low-wage workers, Miller and Ferman (1972) found a significant difference between the recipients and the nonrecipients with respect to family size. Nonrecipients, on aver- age, had far smaller families. Increased family size normally diminishes the adequacy of earnings and imposes child care responsibilities, which frequently interfere with steady work thereby increasing the risk of dependency.

Health. Health factors significantly affect the employability of the welfare population, but they seldom receive adequate treatment in studies. For this reason, later in this monograph we will assess the basic health disabilities of the welfare population, their use of the health care system, and its effects on their well-being.

The reasons for AFDC case openings in the New York City caseload

TABLE 2.3
AFDC Families by Number of Children

Number of children	Percentage of families
1	37.9
2	26.0
3	16.1
4	9.8
5	5.2
6+	5.0

Source: U.S. Department of Health, Education and Welfare, *Aid to Families with Dependent Children: 1975 Re- cipient Characteristics Study*, Part 1, 1977, p. 14.

were presented in Chapter 1; medical reasons were the second most frequent, following changes in family composition. However, in AFDC-UF case openings, medical reasons were considerably less frequent. A more recent study of multiple benefits in New York City (Lyon *et al.*, 1976) indicated that new cases each month on the city's AFDC rolls in 1974 received 54% more medicaid benefits than did previously entered long-term cases. Thus a good many AFDC families may move onto the rolls because of exceptional medical needs that temporarily exceed their financial resources.

A number of surveys of welfare families have indicated that recipients often judge themselves to have medical conditions or disabilities that limit the kinds of jobs they can do. Indeed, a national survey in 1968 (Levinson, 1970) reported that 20% of the mothers said they had health problems that altogether precluded their working. An additional 40% responded that health problems prevented them taking certain kinds of available jobs. Other studies have demonstrated significant correlations between the incidence of illness, perceptions about health, and employment status (Roe & Eickwort, 1974).

In their study of aided and unaided welfare eligibles in New York City, de Ferranti, Leeds, Grundfest, Leach, Parker, and Prusoff (1974) found one of the most significant differences between the two groups to be their reported health status. Those responding positively to questions about the existence of serious health conditions were more likely to be welfare recipients. Miller and Ferman (1972) reported a similar distinction between low-wage workers and working welfare recipients in a Detroit sample.

Relationship of Personal Resources and Employment. No research area on the determinants of dependency has received more attention in the literature than have analyses of the socioeconomic, demographic, and employment characteristics of the heads of welfare families. Research on these issues dominated the efforts of the 1960s; much of the poverty policy since then has been based on the importance of these factors. Several excellent reviews of the literature have been done (e.g., Lowenthal, 1971; Rein, 1974), and this section will be limited to a presentation of the highlights of earlier findings, supplemented by a review of more recent research. The characteristics of the AFDC population described in the previous section are neither new nor startling. The AFDC surveys for 1969, 1971, 1973, and 1975 show an amazing stability in the incidence of these social and demographic characteristics.

Some noteworthy data from a 1977 Rand Corporation study in California will precede our evaluation of the literature regarding the impact of these characteristics on the work and welfare patterns of recipient families. The authors of the study (Abrahamse, de Ferranti, Fleischauer, & Lipson) used an unusual range of data to compare certain social and demographic characteristics of welfare and nonwelfare families. They found that nearly 1 out of every 3 families in California whose head had not finished high school was on welfare; of those heads who had finished, only 1 in 12 families was on welfare. Of all families of the AFDC-FG type in the state with preschool children, over 80% were on welfare as compared with less than 50% for those with no preschoolers.[4] Of those FG-type families whose heads' most recent job was unskilled, 75% were on welfare, as compared with 25% among those whose last job was skilled or semiskilled.

More startling were the following findings. Almost all families of the FG-type in California whose head was less than 25 years old were on welfare. Virtually all FG-type families with heads who had not completed high school or ever worked were on welfare, as were those with preschool children whose heads had not worked recently. Among intact AFDC-U families, those whose heads were 25 or younger were three times as likely to be on welfare than those with older heads. Similarly, those who did not complete high school were five times as likely to be on welfare as those who had.

Most remarkable about these findings is that they were based on a point-in-time study. Had these families been followed over a longer period, the incidence of welfare participation among the entire population at risk (those exhibiting the disadvantaging characteristics) is likely to have been even greater. These data clearly confirm that the disabilities commonly attributed to this population are accurately ascribed.

> Relative to other family heads, recipients: are substantially underschooled, undertrained and underskilled; have much less successful work experiences (i.e., fewer jobs, for shorter periods, at lower pay, and with more frequent turnover), and often, among FG cases at least, have never worked at all. [They] are younger overall, and much more likely to be in the traditionally underemployed "under 25" age bracket; and [they] have larger families and are more likely to have children

4. California's caseload is distinguished by "Family Group" cases and "Unemployed Parent Cases" (FG and U). In this study families in the state are considered FG-type families or U-type families depending upon which component of AFDC they would be enrolled in if eligible. FG cases are regular AFDC cases, generally headed by a woman with a child under 18. (A few have a disabled father present and, rarer still, are those with a father present and a disabled mother or no mother at all.) U-type cases have both parents present and neither disabled. These designations are identical to those of AFDC and AFDC-UF used in other states. (Abrahamse *et al.*, 1977, p. 7).

under 6 or disabled dependents to care for. Also, of course, a substantial majority of AFDC families do not have two adults present in the
home to share responsibilities for earning and child care [Abrahamse *et
al.*, 1977, p. 30].

Levinson (1970) cited major impediments to employment which
affected welfare mothers of both high and low employment potential:
having children at home under 8 years of age, poor or unavailable day
care facilities, and poor health. These impediments are over and above
the variation in employment experience and education that distinguish
the group with high potential from the group with low potential.

A small in-depth study of 75 welfare mothers in California (Opton,
1972) sought to evaluate the effects of a large range of socioeconomic and
employment variables in distinguishing mothers who had substantial
employment experiences from those who did not. Though the sample
was quite small, the analysis suggests the direction of the effects, if not
their magnitude. Only a few of the large number of variables tested for
significant differences between the two groups proved important. Race
proved significant in explaining the differences in the types of jobs and
the extent of employment experiences that the two groups of sample
mothers had. Interviews revealed that all mothers were aware of the
extreme rigidity of segregation by race in job type and experience.

Mothers who had come from the South experienced even greater
employment difficulties, and Opton found them adversely affected by
"cultural disorientation." Being a young mother appeared to be a significant disadvantage. Women who had their first child at a very young
age were among the most disadvantaged with respect to employment.
These early births were generally followed by several others, and these
women had no early opportunity for employment experience or labor
force participation. They were at an extreme disadvantage when compared to the mothers whose previous employment history provided
them with greater potential for continuing and future employment.
Being a deserted mother proved to be a significant determinant of employment disadvantage. There was a clear relationship between marital
status and the likelihood of finding employment. The foregoing factors,
Opton concludes, account for the dominant differences in labor force
participation among his sample mothers. Mothers who had worked less
recorded a multiplicity of characteristics that diminished their
employability.

A more recent study of work and welfare patterns in a sample of
male and female New York City welfare recipients attempted to distinguish the characteristics of those employed, those seeking work, and
those neither employed nor seeking employment at the time of the sur-

vey (Ostow & Dutka, 1975). Male welfare recipients who were working or looking for work were most likely to be heads of intact families in the prime working age group (25–45). Education did not appear to be a significant factor in the work status of men. Those not working or looking for work tended to be older and less likely to be married. They exhibited a striking incidence of health problems.

The findings for women are somewhat different. Those without young dependent children who were working or looking for work were few in number (22% of the sample). However, certain gross distinctions are evident from the data. Those working or looking for work were more likely to be black. Those neither working nor looking for work were more likely to be Puerto Rican, older, and more burdened with health and family problems.

Finally, and perhaps most important, are the characteristics associated with the work behavior of mothers with young dependent children—the dominant case type of AFDC. Though fewer than 13% were reported to have been working or looking for work at the time of the survey, they did have several important characteristics that distinguished them from the overwhelming majority who were not working. Perhaps most striking were the racial differences. Black mothers were far more likely to be working than white mothers; no Puerto Rican mothers were working and very few were looking for work. Indeed, about 90% of the working mothers were black, and 50% of those looking for work were black. For these women, educational attainment appeared to be a good predictor of work status. More than 50% of those who were working had high school diplomas, as compared with 26% for those looking for work and 21% for those not looking for work. Regarding differences in the incidence of personal or family problems, more than twice as many health and family problems were reported in the group not looking for work than among those who were working.

Differences in child care responsibility seemed an important variable in these women's availability for work. Indeed, those who were not working or looking for work tended to be those with younger children and were more likely to be those with larger families. The children of the working mothers were more likely to be of school age than were children of women not looking for work; the latter were usually preschool age.

Harrison and Rein (1976) did a study using longitudinal data from the PSID. Following families headed by males in the first year of study, they were able to develop a model to predict the probability of welfare receipt at least once during the study period (1967–1971). The variables found to be good predictors were: being of minority status, having more or increasing the number of dependent children, living in the northern part of the country and in a county with a high unemployment rate, having the initial male head in a "bad job," and losing the male head later on.[5] These are all variables coincident with those predicting current or potential unemployment status. They are also variables which draw on *both* the human capital and labor market models of dependency. Many other studies have cited the obstacles to employment which plague nonworking heads of welfare families. The critical variables on which many researchers can agree are education; family composition (intact family, numbers and ages of children); immigrant status (see Williams, 1975); health and family problems; age and race; training and work experience.[6] It is important to note, however, that in many cases these factors correlate strongly with one another. Many heads of welfare families are stricken with a multiplicity of these impediments to employment, and these clearly tend to militate even against consistent efforts to become self-supporting.

Mayo (1975b) has drawn such a conclusion. In her study of Cook County, Illinois, she regressed a large number of independent variables, including a variety of recipient characteristics, on the total months worked for the sample mothers. These included measures of generational differences (e.g., rural versus urban origin, immigrant status); characteristics of family orientation; current family situation (e.g., number of children, ages of children, age and employability of recipient, health problems, problems with children); and the situation when the women first went on welfare (e.g., age, education, number of children). After exclusion of a number of nonsignificant variables, the equation was able to explain only 24% of the variance for the entire sample.

The author concludes that although some variables (e.g., employability, problems with a child) may have a significant impact on the work patterns of welfare mothers, the model does not adequately account for these patterns in isolation. The hypothesis is amended, therefore, to include the significance of factors other than the personal charac-

5. The variable, "bad job," is defined by Harrison and Rein as "one paying below the national average for that occupation, with that national occupational average itself paying less than the BLS lower-level budget standard." This variable is hypothesized to be a structural variable, assuming the existence of such jobs as independent of the characteristics of the workers. This factor will be addressed in more detail in sections dealing with considerations of the labor market.

6. Education has not proven to be a stable predictor of employment probabilities for all groups. Most findings for welfare families have revealed that returns to education are more predictable for women in poverty status than for men. Education alone has been able to explain only 7% of the variation in individual income in a variety of studies (Hoffman & Podder, 1976; Mincer, 1974).

teristics and employability of the welfare mother. The author advances critical variables in increasing the exploratory power of the model: institutional factors, such as general economic conditions and those of the local labor market; work disincentives of the welfare system itself; and the length of time a male head supports the family. The contribution of these additional factors is assessed in a later section of this chapter.

ATTITUDES OF WELFARE RECIPIENTS TOWARD WORK

So far this chapter has considered what is known about the impact of personal characteristics on the work and welfare patterns of the low-income population. These factors individually and in combination explained a considerable amount of variation in employment and dependency. However, much interest centers around the importance of work orientation and attitudes as explanations of the nature of the experiences of the low-income population in the labor force. Indeed, the will and desire of the population to work is a major component of the hypothesis of welfare dependency that stresses personal resources and human capital.

In the 1960s, Lewis, an ardent proponent of the then prevalent theory of a culture of poverty, hypothesized that in response to the extreme conditions of material deprivation and instability, poor people had developed cultural adaptations and responses to mitigate their marginal status. Central to this response was a rejection of middle-class values and goals, including the "work ethic" and upward mobility through education and employment. Considerable controversy has always accompanied this theory (see Leacock, 1971). Nevertheless, research continues to show that much of the middle class subscribes to the idea of a culture of poverty (Goodwin, 1972; Williamson, 1974).

The attitudes, values, ambitions, and expectations of potential and current welfare families toward employment have been extensively researched. A number of recent surveys tend to reach conclusions that are in direct contrast to theories of a culture of poverty. The welfare poor, it was found, hold most of the same attitudes and values toward the work ethic as do middle-class workers, and their ambitions and orientations reflect the pervasive American middle-class orientations. A large disparity exists between recipients' prevalent attitudes, values and motivations toward work and upward mobility and their actual expectations based on a realistic assessment of probabilities for success.

These conclusions appear particularly true for men and generally true for women heading poverty households. Women's attitudes toward work and upward mobility are complicated by conflicting societal attitudes about the relative importance of child rearing and work. A study of female-headed families revealed that only 5% of the mothers would think less of someone for receiving welfare. On the other hand, a sizable minority, about 25%, would think worse of a mother who worked rather than stayed at home to care for her children. These responses did *not* vary by economic status (Kriesberg, 1970).

One of the most comprehensive studies of the work orientations of the poor was Goodwin's 1972 study. In his section on the work orientations of mothers, he compared long-term welfare mothers, short-term welfare mothers, mothers participating in the Work Incentive program (WIN), nonwelfare outer-city blacks, and nonwelfare outer-city whites on the basis of nine indices of work orientation. Though Goodwin found these groups to differ significantly among themselves by socioeconomic, demographic, and employment characteristics, in his conclusions about work orientations he states: "These findings do not support the position that there are cultural differences (differences in basic goals or values) between the poor and nonpoor with respect to work [p. 52]." He did find important differences, however, between long-term welfare mothers and outer-city whites in the degree to which they believed their own efforts to find and keep good jobs would be effective. Long-term welfare women lacked confidence in their abilities while outer-city whites felt more secure. The findings also suggest that poor respondents experienced a considerable degree of psychological stress associated with social mobility. Other findings suggest that although all these groups of women adhered strongly to the work ethic, responses to questions about life aspirations suggested a preference for the support of a husband.

In his section on fathers, Goodwin compared white and black welfare fathers participating in the WIN program with outer-city black and white nonwelfare fathers. As with the mothers, socioeconomic, demographic, and employment data for the fathers reflected considerable variety. Nevertheless, the fathers, like the mothers, identified strongly with work, rejected quasi-legal alternatives and, generally, found welfare acceptable when financial need occasioned it. One striking distinction was the extent to which race governed personal confidence. Both poor and nonpoor whites showed higher levels of confidence than black fathers, whether on welfare or not, probably reflecting differences in actual work experiences.

In general, Goodwin's findings, once adjusted for response bias, gave little evidence of significant distortion. The consistent strong work identification, even among those whose attachment to the labor market has been weak and irregular, suggests that it is repeated failure and disappointment in their attempt to secure decent work rather than a negative attitude that result in a lack of confidence in their ability to affect their personal status.

In an earlier study of AFDC recipients in 10 states (Meyers & McIntyre, 1969), an attempt was made to assess the relationship between recipients' self-perceptions and their actual work participation over a previous 37-month period. Several findings were noteworthy. There appeared to be a consistent positive relationship between respondents' levels of self-esteem and employment. This relationship appeared to be stable even when differences in educational attainment were controlled for. Findings showed (as Goodwin did) that welfare did not significantly stigmatize recipients and that those who had worked less or not at all were more likely to feel stigmatized than those who had worked more.

Another study (Davidson & Gaitz, 1974) used data from surveys of 1441 adult respondents, stratified by age, sex, occupational skill level, and ethnicity. Comparison revealed that in ranking life goals, groups of the poor (median family income $1001–2000) and nonpoor ($6001–7001) had the same proportion of respondents ranking "achievement and work rewards" first. Black and Mexican minority respondents showed *greater* attachment to work than did the Anglo nonpoor. No significant differences were found among poor and nonpoor groups with respect to work, leisure, and orientation to present time versus future time.

A study of the hardcore unemployed (Kaplan & Tausky, 1972) produced similar conclusions. Equal numbers of men and women, including many from the minority populations, were surveyed in this study involving 275 disadvantaged enrollees in the Concentrated Employment Program of the Office of Economic Opportunity. Semistructured interviews led to a number of conclusions on work orientations. First, a large majority of respondents attributed importance to work because of the economic function it performs. Second, from comparisons of subjects' responses it was found that commitment to work was as common in the disadvantaged group as among employed workers, both white- and blue-collar. Many respondents indicated feelings of moral indignation toward persons who did not want to work, and many showed a marked tendency to believe that they could gain respectability by holding a job. The authors reported a far greater need among the unemployed to gain respectability and to prove their social worth by working than was evident among employed workers in other studies. The unemployed had a need to be independent, respectable, self-sufficient and productive.

In previous studies, the orientations, expectations, and desires regarding work among welfare mothers were found to be strong. The strength of the work commitment among this population stands in marked contrast to the likelihood of their finding stable and sufficient employment, given a variety of labor market constraints. Podell's study of welfare mothers in New York City (1969) produced similar findings: 70% of the mothers surveyed preferred to work than to stay at home. Of this 70%, 42% cited a desire for greater independence as their reason, and 56% gave financial reasons. Of the 30% who did not prefer to work, 77% gave child-care responsibilities as their reason and 20% gave health considerations. Ethnicity gave rise to interesting distinctions: 80% of the black mothers preferred to work, as compared with 60% of the Puerto Rican mothers and 55% percent of the white mothers. Among mothers with preschool children, 60% said they would prefer to work if appropriate child care arrangements were available; 66% of all welfare mothers planned to work in the future. Regardless of race, this response was far more prevalent among mothers with higher educational attainment than among those with lower levels.

Kriesberg's (1970) study of families headed by mothers (fatherless) found far less variation in respondents' values and beliefs about welfare and work than was found in respondents' circumstances. A variety of factors accounted for the differences in circumstances; particular importance was placed on remaining at home to rear children. Most respondents wanted to be independent of welfare; and they were independent when circumstances made it possible. Kriesberg sees the number and ages of children as important governing factors.

Feldman and Feldman (1972) studied 1325 women, formerly and currently welfare recipients, from a rural poverty pocket. In ascertaining how employment affected the home and personal life of these women and/or how their home situations were barriers to employment, they compared responses to a number of questions on work commitment from several subgroups of the sample: welfare mothers who were working, welfare mothers who were not working, former welfare mothers who were working, and former welfare mothers who were not working. Although all women in the sample felt that employment was important, they had strong competing commitments to their roles as wives, mothers, and homemakers. Among all groups, those on welfare who were working were likely to have the strongest commitment toward work and to feel that work was more important than caring for children at home. However, for all groups, the importance of child rearing and household duties appeared paramount.

Several studies have attempted to evaluate differences between responses of welfare recipients and nonrecipients and of the poor and nonpoor to hypothetical job offers (e.g., Feldman & Feldman, 1972;

Shea, 1973). No study has demonstrated any significant differences in the desire to work, although consistent differences occur between men and women and between members of different ethnic groups. A subset of respondents within a national probability sample of 5083 women aged 30–44 was asked a group of questions to assess the likelihood of their entering the labor force if jobs were offered (Shea, 1973). The sample was analyzed by poverty status and by race. All the women interviewed were out of the labor force and living in families with at least one child. Within the same color group, approximately the same percentage of poor and nonpoor women answered with an unqualified "yes" to a hypothetical job offer: 40% of the black poor and 36% of the black nonpoor; 16% of the white poor and 13% of the white nonpoor.

Among these who gave conditional responses, further questions probed what hourly wage rate would be necessary as a precondition for accepting a job. Poor blacks required the lowest median hourly wage rate (though 24% higher than the existing median rate for poor blacks actually working), followed closely by poor whites. Analyses indicated that women's wage expectations (or requirements) were not out of line with the median hourly wage rates earned by comparable employed women. Further, of those who would not accept the job offer, 20–25% in each color group gave either current pregnancy or the young age of their children as the reason.

The overwhelming preponderance of evidence to date indicates that the work orientations and attitudes of the poor resemble those of the middle class in all important ways. It is impossible to conclude with certainty the degree to which these attitudinal responses can be seen as valid indicators of behavior. Indeed, work is so strongly sanctioned in this society that response bias must be considered in interpretation of the findings. Nevertheless, even taking this into account, the poor, and more specifically the welfare poor, appear to have a strong commitment to work that seems to persist despite severe disadvantages in the labor force and limited prospects for stable and adequate employment.

More significant are the results of an analysis of the first 7 years of the PSID data dealing with the effect of attitudes, motives, and behavior patterns on changes in families' economic well-being (Duncan & Morgan, 1976). Even when the analysis was limited to families that had remained in the bottom quintile for at least 1 year, no evidence could be found to indicate any effect. Data were manipulated in a variety of ways to determine if alternative specifications of the model were likely to produce different results. None were found. The important issue, therefore, is not whether welfare families' attitudes and motivations to work differ (it seems clear they do not), but whether their attitudes and motivations, whatever they are, have the capacity to affect in any way the welfare families' life chances. The most important analysis to date has demonstrated that if there were differences, these would not be meaningful predictions of economic well-being.

STRUCTURE AND FUNCTIONING OF THE LABOR MARKET

Personal resources and human capital variables have been shown to have a major impact on the welfare population's participation in the labor force. Some, such as health status and the presence of young children in a family headed by a female prevent welfare mothers from working. Others, such as the absence of previous employment experience and adequate education, diminish the probability of finding a job and of obtaining employment sufficiently stable to promote financial independence. Studies on their attitudes toward work and their ambitions have revealed no meaningful indication that the poor, or the welfare poor, are unwilling to or undesirous of working. Indeed, the bulk of the evidence on attitudes has confirmed the strong attachment of the poor to traditional American attitudes toward work.

Some of the personal resources and human capital variables do help distinguish between those who do and do not work; but these variables are inadequate to explain much of the wage poverty among the population at risk. The results of studies which have regressed these variables on employment status leave a great deal of the variation in labor force participation unexplained. (Mayo, 1975b). Therefore, other research approaches have been pursued to attempt to increase the predictability of employment status and experience. A growing body of literature has pointed to the importance of certain inherent constraints in the structure and functioning of the labor market itself as a way to explain work and welfare patterns of the population at risk.

For some time it was assumed that the size of the national caseload was tied to the state of the national economy. However, in the 1960s, when the economy was strong, there appeared to be a shift in the relation of size of caseload to national unemployment trends. Given the theory that unemployment creates a demand for welfare, several researchers have tested the relationship between the state of the economy and number of recipients on welfare. In a study of caseload dynamics (reviewed in Chapter 1), Rydell *et al.* (1974) attempted to integrate into their model a consideration of the impact of local unemployment rates on size of welfare caseloads. Unemployment appeared to have only limited explanatory power in the model of caseload size, and then, only for the AFDC-UF and Home Relief (HR) caseloads. It appeared to have little if any impact on the size of the regular AFDC caseload.

Similarly, Saks's study (1975) estimated the impact of aggregate unemployment on the supply of welfare applicants in New York City and was unable to find a significant relationship for the AFDC-UF caseload; in fact, Saks found a significantly *negative* relationship for the AFDC caseload. His interpretation of these findings shows that the relationship may be more complicated than his estimations indicate, that there may be a time lag of some importance that the model does not consider. Nevertheless, it is clear that the aggregate unemployment rate alone at any given time is an insufficient predictor of either the labor supply of welfare family heads or their presence on welfare.

In their study on the microeconomic relations between work and welfare, Harrison and Rein (1976) found (after controlling for all other factors) that households headed by males at the beginning of the study period were 2% more likely to go on welfare some time later if these families were living in a *county* that had a high unemployment rate. Though this local unemployment rate was found to be important, other predictors that measured additional labor market characteristics appeared to represent even stronger explanations for observed work and welfare patterns for both male and female household heads. A variety of researchers are beginning to appreciate the usefulness of this approach.

As part of some larger projects on the determinants of income dynamics, research on the relationship of the labor market to welfare patterns is being done at the Joint Center for Urban Studies (Harvard–MIT). Using longitudinal data from the PSID, the preliminary findings of Harrison and Rein indicate that measures of labor market structure exogenous to the individual appear to have an important causal affect on the probability that a family will go on welfare even after controlling for the differential effects of location, origins, race, human capital, work attachment and changes in eligibility or need.[7] (Harrison & Rein, 1976). Specifically, they found that the variable of "bad job" and "worst job," as well as the unemployment rate in the county, explained to a significant degree the expected relative dependence on welfare over the course of the longitudinal study. Regardless of whether the initial household head was male or female, Harrison and Rein found that if the head held a bad job (which they saw as exogenous to the characteristics of the individual), this fact increased the relative dependence on future welfare for their households by 16–20%. For households initially headed by females, those in counties with high unemployment became relatively more dependent on welfare over time than those living initially in counties with low unemployment. As mentioned earlier, the former were 2% more likely to go on welfare eventually. Furthermore, women in

---

7. Human capital was measured by years of schooling and by labor force eligibility.

unionized jobs with relatively high wages during the first study year were 12% less likely to go on welfare over the next 5 years than women in nonunion jobs whose wages were relatively low compared to national averages.

Other researchers have also indicated the importance on work and welfare status of local labor market conditions (among other labor market factors). Venti's study (1975; see also Sumrall, 1976) argues that aggregate unemployment rates do not reflect the experience of this population, which is generally employed in jobs that are not covered. Conventional unemployment data are based on unemployment in covered industries. Venti also observed that aggregate unemployment data may not reflect conditions of the local labor market that are relevant to a potential welfare population. In his study (limited to Massachusetts) Venti attempted to identify the sources of growth of the state's caseload. He stressed the relation between changes in labor market structure and changes in AFDC caseload growth. Venti rejects several prevalent theories of what makes caseloads grow, such as those stressing individual choice and human capital. His results support a theory that emphasizes the structure of the labor force as a key factor in determining the size of the welfare caseload and the numbers of unemployed.

He explains the observed patterns of unemployment and the growth of the welfare caseload as functions of (a) changes in the traditional structure of jobs (the move from a manufacturing to a service economy); (b) the structural barriers separating workers from the areas experiencing growth; and (c) the mismatch between skills and types of jobs in the growing sector. His findings support the view that characteristics of the new jobs themselves affect the caseload size. New jobs in the service and retail trade are affected by high turnover and seasonality, and they are likely to be characterized by instability—a shorter duration of steady work per employee than jobs in industry provide. He concludes that changes in the economy of Massachusetts have caused the shift in employment, two separate effects causing the caseload to grow: "the structural employment caused by steady decline of the traditional nondurable goods manufacturing sector, and the inadequacy of jobs that are available—low wage, high turnover, seasonal jobs—to support families categorically eligible for AFDC [p. 23]."

In his final regression equation, Venti is able to explain an incredible 99.8% of the variance in the monthly AFDC caseload with a combination of variables measuring employment structure, population growth, the supply of welfare "slots" (a function of the WIN program and the state takeover of the administration of the welfare caseload), and business cycles and aggregate labor-market conditions (including the unemployment rate). Other equations which considered changes in welfare benefit levels and/or wage levels failed to explain caseload growth. These conclusions offer strong evidence of the importance of labor market variables exogenous to the individual (including unemployment rates) at a disaggregated level in explaining changes in the rate of welfare participation. Venti's data suggest that a high percentage of all welfare mothers are on the rolls as a result of the absence of alternative possibilities. He rejects the view that they are exercising individual choice.

The importance of the local economy was further suggested by a recent Rand Corporation study in California (Abrahamse *et al.*, 1977). This research sought to determine whether participation in some occupations is more likely to result in welfare receipt than participation in others. The authors' analysis concluded that occupational category is not a significant predictor of welfare receipt when skill levels are held constant.

This would tend to contradict some of the previous reported findings. However, when the hypothesis was tested for whether conditions in certain industrial sectors seemed to affect the size or changes in the caseload more than conditions in other sectors, the finding was that they did. The study distinguished between sectors where workers move more to and from welfare because of the skill mix, pay level, or other aspects of the work, and the sectors where chain reactions are induced that ultimately result in changes in the caseload. The most direct impact (though the conclusions are very conservative) was found in services, trade, agriculture, and manufacturing. Those found to have more of a chain reaction, or bellwether effect, were government, transport, utilities, real estate and insurance, mineral extraction, and the manufacturing subcategories. In general, then, the conclusions tend to support the influence of labor market factors in California (with special attention to some industries) on the size of the caseload.

Many factors, including demand for low-skilled labor and discrimination by race and sex, determine the industries where potential welfare recipients will crowd (Miller & Ferman, 1972; Venti, 1975). As some researchers have contended (e.g., Miller & Ferman, 1972), even when these markets provide stable employment and full-time wages these two factors prove insufficient to lift a family, especially a large family, out of poverty.

Using data on poverty families from the PSID, Levy (1976) demonstrates that even if poor male family heads had jobs which provided normal hours of work, their poverty would be reduced only slightly.[8]

---

8. Normal hours are the mean hours worked by all family heads for each race and sex grouping [p. 45].

For women, normal hours would leave their poverty status unchanged. Large families and low wages inhibit the poverty-reducing impact that stable work can provide, and families often teeter on the edge of dependency. If illness occurs or unanticipated expenses arise, they turn to welfare.

The market itself has an independent impact on the size of the caseload. Much research has found evidence that segmentation in the labor market locks large groups of low-wage workers into low-skilled industries where chances are limited for significant upward mobility in occupational categories or wage rates. What researchers have not generally agreed upon is the relative weight of individual characteristics, labor market factors and (as the next section will explore) the welfare programs themselves in affecting the size of the caseload or the work and welfare patterns of low-income families. Research has only recently begun to place emphasis on the importance of labor market variables in explaining observed patterns of poverty and dependency. These results challenge earlier predominant explanations based on personal resources and human capital.

IMPACT OF THE WELFARE SYSTEM

A theory of growing importance and interest holds that the very design of the current welfare system encourages dependency by providing substantial work disincentives. One contention, tied to labor market factors, is that if the guarantee of a welfare grant at zero income is equal to or greater than the expected income from work, rational economic choice would lead an individual to choose leisure over work. The theory of individual choice, therefore, posits an economic decision which would result in higher AFDC participation rates in states where the guarantee is equal to or near the expected wages of low-income workers. Figure 2.1 demonstrates the way in which this decision could be made. The horizontal axis demonstrates the distribution of occupations of AFDC mothers. The vertical axis represents the wages these occupations are expected to yield. The expected wages of many mothers would leave them at or below the poverty line. If family size is large and the welfare guarantee above or close to the wages expected from employment, a family has an implicit incentive to choose welfare rather than employment.

As early as 1967, Hausman found that in view of their employment and occupational characteristics, 70% of the AFDC mothers and 40% of AFDC-UF fathers could not expect to receive wages as high as their welfare entitlements. Other researchers (e.g., Durbin, 1969; Greenberg,

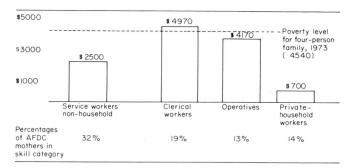

FIGURE 2.1. *Percentages of AFDC mothers with selected skills producing incomes below the poverty level.* [*From* Work and Welfare in the 1970s, *prepared by S. Levitan for Welfare Policy Project, Duke University Institute of Policy Science and Public Affairs and Ford Foundation, New York, 1977. p. 23.*]

1971) have supported this hypothesis, as has research on the existing incentives provided by welfare program design features.

Benefit Levels. Though the incentive for maximization of income clearly exists, the more important research question is to what degree welfare guarantees (benefit levels) effect the labor supply (employment) of low-wage workers. Saks's (1975) study on New York City's AFDC caseload found that a 1% increase in the grant level would result in a .9% decrease in the labor supply (Hausman (1970) found a .37% decrease). Though Saks was able to distinguish cases of different characteristics, a strong negative relationship between grant level and labor supply held for all.

A study using national data confirmed this relationship when Williams (1975) regressed the expected wage, the age of dependent children, the ethnic group, health, and grant level on labor force participation (measured three ways by cross-sectional data) for active, closed, and denied cases in 10 states. He found that for every 10% increase in grant level, there was an associated 11% decrease in the labor supply of female heads of households.

Garfinkel and Orr (1972), studying the effects of the AFDC program on the labor supply of mothers, found that employment rates decreased by 4.5% as the annual guarantee increased by $1000.[9] These authors found that a $1000 increase had an even stronger effect if the initial guarantee was smaller. For example, if the guarantee were to increase

9. Additional findings for AFDC mothers (Garfinkel & Orr, 1974) revealed that a 10% change in the guarantee resulted in a 7% change in the employment rate.

from $500 to $1500, the corresponding decrease in employment would be 14%. Hausman (1970) found an even stronger reduction in the employment of AFDC mothers when he compared their employment rates in three southern states with different guarantee levels. His estimates suggest that a $1000 increase in the guarantee is associated with a 40% decrease in employment rates for this group.

Estimates of the labor supply response of prime-age males to changes in guarantees come from Garfinkel's (1974) analyses of several of the negative income tax (NIT) experiments. There is considerably less agreement on the precise nature of the potential impact in such cases than there is in the case of female heads of families. According to Garfinkel evidence for men and women indicates that increased income transfer levels result in decreased labor supply, which is consistent with economic theory. However, most of the NIT findings indicate that the labor supply of prime-age males decreases far less than that of female heads of households. Indeed, Garfinkel concludes that the most reliable studies on the labor response of men indicate that income transfers lead only to small reductions in their work effort.

Though most studies find a significant relationship of welfare guarantees and wages to rates of welfare participation and employment, Lyon (1977) points out the importance of exercising caution in the interpretation of the findings:

> Two major conclusions can be drawn from efforts to trace the welfare decision as a choice between earnings from work or income from a welfare check. First, researchers have found the welfare decision difficult to trace (or model) and they have been appropriately cautious in stating their conclusions. The main reason is simply that there is not enough data to account for all the economic and administrative factors that enter into the welfare decision. Movement on and off the rolls is as much a function of the changing supply of welfare (eligibility rule changes, work test and administrative stringency) as it is of the demand for welfare [p. 17].

Lyon posits that different models may actually be required for labor supply estimates in different jurisdictions. Nevertheless, whatever weaknesses exist in the estimation models, most of them do conclude that increases in the size of welfare grants decrease the employment rates of low-income workers (see Table 2.4).

In Table 2.4 the results of several studies are compared for the labor supply effects of AFDC mothers resulting from changes in welfare program parameters. Although they differ, they all demonstrate the significant impact of the "cost of work" upon labor supply. However, caution must be exercised in comparing the results of these studies.

TABLE 2.4

Estimated Marginal Changes in Employment of AFDC Mothers for 1% Change in Guarantee and Tax Rate

Study	Sample	If guarantee increased by 1%, employment rate will decrease by:	If tax rate is reduced by 1%, employment rate will increase by:
Hausman (1970)	Findings from the 1967 AFDC study, state data, Alabama, Kentucky, & Mississippi	.37%	.4%
Garfinkel & Orr (1974)	Findings from the 1967 AFDC study, state data	.7%	.7%
Saks (1975)	New York City AFDC files, 1961–1967	.9%	—
Williams (1975)	National AFDC survey, 1968	1.1%	1%

Typically, researchers present an average change in the dependent variable associated with an average change in an independent variable. The absolute value of independent variables differs among samples. Elasticities will vary, depending upon the absolute values of the independent variables. For example, Garfinkel and Orr (1972) found that a $1000 increase in the guarantee would result in an employment decrease of 4.5%; however, if the initial guarantee was increased from $500 to $1500, the employment rate would decrease by 14% (Garfinkel, 1974).

Benefit Reduction Rates. The welfare system implicitly reduces the attractiveness of work, not only through its benefit levels but also through its benefit reduction rates, which reduce benefits as recipients begin to earn employment income. The benefit reduction rate, or tax rate, is the rate at which benefits are reduced for each dollar of earned income. The reduction of a recipient's benefits by 60 cents for each dollar of earned income would be a 60% tax rate. The tax rate can be viewed as the cost of work for recipient families. The best review of literature of transfer programs and work effort is Garfinkel's work, which describes the tax rate in an income transfer program as a mechanism that reduces the reward for working.

Indeed, if the guarantee in an income transfer program enhances the beneficiary's ability to afford not to work, it leads to reductions in labor supply. Conversely, the tax rate can alter the evaluation of the benefit–loss relationship by altering the cost of not working. The larger the guarantee, the smaller the cost of not working; the smaller the tax rate, the greater the cost of not working. Though economic theory and empirical study have revealed the influence of guarantees and tax rates on labor supply, researchers differ considerably in estimating the magnitude of the effects. Indications are that different groups exhibit different labor supply responses to the same program parameters, and the degree of responsiveness to changes in these parameters clearly must be a function of more factors than the guarantee and the tax rate alone. As noted in an earlier section, attributing part of the variation to differing work attitudes and ambitions is unfounded. It is likely that the important factors in explaining work response are demographic and labor market characteristics.

Substantial research has been done on these issues, much of it sparked by criticism of putative low levels of work effort among current welfare recipients. In addition, many national interests encourage the design of a new system with more reasonable work incentives. Garfinkel's paper (1974), which reviewed most of the important work in this area, was part of a series of research papers, entitled *Studies in Public Welfare*, published by the Subcommittee on Fiscal Policy of the Joint Economic Committee of the U.S. Congress. Garfinkel based much of his research review on cross-sectional data for the 1960s. Estimates were based on the effect a negative income tax on married males of prime ages had on the labor supply (annual hours worked or annual hours in the labor force). Estimates of the effect of change in the guarantee or in the tax rate showed a startling range. Eight studies recorded estimates of labor responses for each $1000 increase in the guarantee; they ranged from a .6% decrease (Garfinkel & Masters, 1978) to a 14% decrease (Hill, 1973). The impact of a 10% increase in the tax rate ranged from labor responses that were 5% positive to 5% negative. Garfinkel attributes these broad variations largely to alternative methods of measuring nonemployment income, selecting an appropriate sample, and increasing wage rates. He doubts the accuracy of all the estimates, and particularly the highest one. Findings from the New Jersey income maintenance experiment suggest that the cumulative impact of a benefit guarantee of $2500 and a tax rate of 50% of recipients' earned incomes would result in a small but significant reduction in the number of employed male heads.

Admittedly, studies of the effects of tax rates on current AFDC recipients suffer from many problems. Conclusions on the precise size of the estimates vary; but analysts agree that increased tax rates on earnings tend to decrease employment and that decreased rates increase employment.

A fine example is provided by the 1972 Appel study. The 1967 amendments to the Social Security Act reduced the nominal tax rate on AFDC recipients' earned incomes from 100% (the loss of $1 of benefits for each $1 of earned income) to 67%. Appel thus had a natural laboratory to evaluate the change in labor supply of AFDC mothers after the tax rate was reduced. He limited his study to the effect of lowered AFDC benefit reduction rates in Michigan on work incentives. After isolating such factors as changes in labor market conditions and increased grant sizes, he concluded that the rate of employment increased substantially despite a falling demand for labor. Since most recipients were not aware of the work incentive provisions, "the measured effect of the incentive is quite likely to be an understatement of the potential effect [p. 79]."

Garfinkel and Orr (1974) used 1967 national data to estimate the change in employment rates resulting from changes in tax rates. They concluded that a 10% decrease in the tax rate would result in a 7% increase in employment among AFDC mothers. Hausman (1970) examined the effect of guarantee levels and tax rates on AFDC mothers in three southern states and concluded that a 10% increase in the tax rate would lead to a 4% decrease in employment rates.

These studies clearly show that tax rates and guarantees have a measurable impact on the supply of labor provided by welfare mothers. Many other studies of the working poor (including findings from NIT) tend to confirm that the poor will act in their own economic interests. However, several qualifications are necessary. The nominal tax rate may differ from the effective (actual) tax rate. As Barr and Hall (1975) caution, delays in reporting income by recipients and discretion and flexibility in defining deductible expenses (such as child care and other work expenses) may make the effective tax rate far lower than the nominal rate.

Garfinkel's (1974) critique of Hausman's (1970) findings was that if the guarantee was serving as a proxy for how much administrative pressure states exert on AFDC mothers to work, the estimate could be too high. "In the absence of a measure of variations in administrative compulsion to work, the guarantee level will reflect not only the negative effects of higher guarantees on labor supply, but also the negative effect of less administrative compulsion to work [p. 26]." Unmeasured administrative practices may affect labor supply responses of welfare families in ways which obscure the true magnitude of the effect of the guarantee and tax rate.

Certain differences found in the nature and size of the labor supply effects of tax rates and guarantees tend to lend credence to some of the conclusions stated earlier in this chapter. Results from the New Jersey negative income tax (NIT) experiment, (and similar studies reviewed by Garfinkel, 1974) indicate significant variations in work responses for groups with different demographic characteristics. For example, women were more likely to withdraw their labor supply with increasing guarantees and higher tax rates than were men, and white and Puerto Rican recipients were more likely than blacks to do so. The personal characteristics of recipients clearly affect work and welfare patterns.

Though stronger work incentives (lower guarantees and tax rates) tend to result in increased work effort among welfare family heads, it may not be concluded that they also result in more case closings or reduced program costs. Clearly, greater work incentives increase the amount of income a recipient can receive before losing eligibility for benefits. Low tax rates tend to move the break-even point (at which benefits fall to zero) farther out on the income scale. This means that families who would have earned their way off welfare under a given tax rate might still be eligible under a reduced rate; they would presumably remain open cases for a longer time. In terms of program costs, under low tax rates benefits continue to be paid, both to families that under a higher tax rate would have become ineligible and to those that already work (see Aaron, 1975). There are indications that administrative costs would increase as a result of changed structures of work incentives (Appel, 1972; Garfinkel & Orr, 1974).

Multiple Benefits. The existence of other income-conditioned welfare benefits (e.g., medicaid, food stamps, public housing, day care services), is hypothesized to weigh against the work incentive effects of a low tax rate. Several important studies indicate that the potential cumulative marginal tax rates facing recipients of AFDC who also receive benefits from other in-kind programs can reach levels in excess of 100% (Aaron, 1973; Hausman, 1972). For example, as income rises, rent in public housing rises and the value of food stamp bonuses falls; as eligibility for AFDC terminates so does automatic eligibility for medicaid and, perhaps, for day care. Receiving multiple benefits can thus be observed to change the implicit guarantee the eligible families enjoy and the tax rate they face. The cumulative cash value of all benefits alters the work incentives of the guarantee by effectively raising its level.

A recent study of New York City's AFDC program (Lyon *et al.*, 1976) revealed the *average* cash value of AFDC benefits and in-kind programs was $6600 for a family of four. Expected wages from a job paying the minimum wage would be $4200. Indeed, in total, the AFDC grant alone accounted for only 55% of the income available to the average family eligible for welfare. These findings confirmed those of an earlier study on the incidence of multiple benefits in New York City (Bernstein, Shkuda, & Burns, 1973).

Clearly, the cumulative marginal tax rates from multiple benefit receipts and the absolute level of cumulative benefits available to AFDC families diminish work incentives. Some analysts suggest that automatic medicaid eligibility for AFDC program recipients may influence dependency. It is possible that some families, facing increased needs for health care, reduce their labor supply to become eligible for medicaid.

Though precise estimates are lacking on the cumulative marginal tax rates facing families receiving multiple benefits, economic theory suggests that such benefits decrease labor supply; so also would the total cash value of benefits available to eligible families.

Accounting Period. Several researchers have posited that the nature of the AFDC accounting period provides further disincentives for stable work effort. Monthly income accounting allows for quick adjustment of benefits to changes in earned income. Thus, workers have an incentive to bunch earnings in periods when they are not on AFDC, since earnings accrued prior to application for AFDC eligibility are not counted for purposes of calculating benefits (unless available as savings or assets above eligibility limits). Thus, the method of calculating AFDC benefits favors unstable employment (by providing incentives to bunch earnings and to work irregularly) (Allen, 1973). However, there are no empirical estimates that document the extent of this behavior among current welfare families.

Program Administration. The Rydell *et al.* study (discussed in Chapter 1) showed administrative closings to be a most significant determinant in case closings and openings. It has also been shown that stringency in enforcing work requirements and discretion in defining allowable deductions from income in determining the taxable base for the benefit reduction rate can alter a recipient's implicit calculations of the cost of work. The importance of administrative factors in the work and welfare decisions of families suggests that findings from different states need to be evaluated separately since identical program parameters are likely to result in different work and welfare patterns, according to different state policies and practices. However, these differences are likely to be important only in the short run since a far broader and more consistent range of factors can explain the nature and length of dependency over a longer period.

CONCLUSION

This chapter has investigated the usefulness of three paradigms hypothesized to explain welfare dependency: models based on personal resources and human capital; the labor market; and economic rationality. Early research stressed the importance of the personal and labor market characteristics of the recipients themselves in explaining dependency. This research produced consistent findings that welfare recipients often exhibit characteristics that present obstacles to employment. Many of the studies reviewed found limited educational attainment, family composition factors, health and family problems, age and race to be important employment disadvantages characterizing welfare family heads. Lack of solid work experience and employment training poses additional hardships. Nevertheless, these factors alone have not been able to explain all the variations in work and welfare patterns.

More recent concerns have produced research indicating that the perverse economic incentives of the welfare system itself have some impact on an individual's work decisions. In particular, research on the relationship between welfare benefit levels and employment rates among heads of welfare families have concluded that welfare decisions are influenced by a comparison of existing benefit levels with prevailing wages. Since wages are not conditioned by family size, while benefit levels are, it is not surprising to find that larger families are more likely to choose welfare, and once on welfare, will find it more difficult to find employment where wages are competitive with welfare benefit levels.

Most currently, however, there is strong and convincing evidence that when these factors are taken alone, they fail to reveal an important dimension of welfare dependency. Specifically, the availability and types of jobs for low-income workers in a local labor market appear to have a significant and independent effect on the probability and length of welfare dependency, even after human capital and other factors are controlled for (Harrison & Rein, 1976). In explaining dependency by a consideration of local labor market structures, new research has identified a critical and previously undervalued determinant of welfare dependency.

A reanalysis of earlier theories regarding personal characteristics as an important factor in the length and nature of the dependency of welfare recipients argues for dismissing emphasis on the lack of motivation to work. Though there is some reason to be concerned about the adverse influence of the welfare system on incentives to work, empirical analysis suggests that the impact is probably not as great as it was earlier assumed to be.

The size of the population that risks economic dependency is far greater than was previously assumed. Research does not support the view of a static population receiving welfare in the absence of work or motivation to work for generation after generation. The causes of welfare dependency are demonstrably far more complex than they were previously acknowledged to be.

Although, different research approaches have suggested the appropriateness of different models for explaining the determinants of work and welfare patterns, it is impossible to conclude with any certainty which provides the greatest explanatory power. The welfare decision has been seen to be complex. Data bases have not generally been available for testing the relative explanatory power of more than one model. More often than not, models are adapted to a specific data base without prior consideration of testing alternative hypotheses in a rigorous way. Therefore, the implications of the research for policy are not clear and simple.

The solutions to poverty and welfare dependency are at least as complicated as the causes. Though the focus has been on aggregate populations, there is a considerable degree of heterogeneity in the low-income population. What the findings do suggest is that welfare reform based on strategies involving income and services alone may not alter work and welfare patterns very much. Though such strategies are clearly indicated, failure to recognize deficiencies in the labor market as independently significant in aggravating and intensifying the economic dependency of the low-income worker may result in considerable disappointment with even heroic welfare reform policies.

3

Family Composition

When a woman with children becomes a family head, her chances of becoming poor and going on welfare greatly increase.[1] Once on welfare, she faces a decreased probability that she will become employed or return quickly to economic independence. Previous chapters have indicated the significance of family stability variables in determining the probabilities of going on welfare, the length and nature of welfare experiences, and the probability of finding and maintaining employment suitable for self-support.

Changes in family composition provided consistent explanations of changes in economic well-being of American families throughout all the years PSID data were collected. Findings showed that individuals' chances of falling into or climbing out of poverty were closely related to changes in the composition of their families.[2] (Duncan & Morgan,

---

1. Even after adjusting for demographic and environmental variables, female-headed families with children were shown to be 2.5 times more likely to be persistently poor than similar families headed by married couples (Morgan, et al., 1974).

2. Duncan and Morgan report that by the seventh year of the study, fewer than 33% of the original families had the same composition as in the first year, and more than 33% were headed by someone not head of the same family in 1968 (Duncan & Morgan, 1976a).

51

TABLE 3.1

Major Changes in Family Composition and Poverty Status

1968 family status and change	All sample individuals (%)	Group (%)	Poor in 1967 who were nonpoor in 1973	Nonpoor in 1967 who were poor in 1973
Wives of household heads:[a]	22.3		.42	.08
Married throughout		84.8	.45	.06
Divorced & remarried		2.3	.56[b]	.07
Widowed		6.8	.33	.24
Divorced		5.7	.26	.33
Unmarried female household heads:	6.2		.36	.17
Remaining unmarried		80.6	.37	.18
Married		14.9	.88	.08

Source: Adapted from *Five Thousand American families: Patterns of Economic Progress,* Vol. IV, Ed. G. J. Duncan and J. N. Morgan, University of Michigan, Institute for Social Research, 1976, Table 1.1, p. 5.

[a] More former wives were left in the panel than former husbands because of different mortality and other losses.

[b] Estimate based on fewer than 25 observations.

1976a). Table 3.1 shows this close relationship between family status and economic well-being. Of the women already married when the PSID began in 1968 who remained married throughout, 45% of those who were poor at the beginning of the study became nonpoor. Women who were already married when the study began but who became divorced or widowed and did not remarry subsequently fared far worse.

Fewer than one-third of the women in these two groups who began in poverty managed to climb out. More dramatic, was the fact that 24% and 33%, respectively, of those women who became widowed or divorced and who began above the poverty line[3] eventually fell below it. These percentages were four times as great as those for women who remained stably married [Duncan & Morgan, 1976, p. 7].

The most striking characteristic of the welfare population is that the dominant family type is one headed by a female. The growth in the welfare rolls nationally has been accompanied by a growth in the proportion of such households. Though the percentage and number of this family type have grown even more rapidly throughout the population at

3. Poverty was defined as being in the bottom fifth of the income needs distribution. Families were ranked by the ratio of their income to an estimate of their needs based on family size and composition.

large, the situation is received with greater alarm within the poverty population.[4] Indeed, between 1960 and 1974, the percentage of female-headed families with children increased by 67%, from 9% to 15%; of the 4 million families in 1974, 45% were living in poverty (Sawhill, Peabody, Jones, & Caldwell, 1975). The apparent economic and social consequences of becoming a female household head are of such seriousness as to warrant particular attention.

Changes in family composition and marital stability are clearly important in any analysis of welfare patterns. Data for 1973 showed about 50% of all families in the nation headed by females to be receiving welfare benefits—an increase of 20% since 1967 (Sawhill *et al.*, 1975). Recent data on the AFDC program indicate that more than 94% of those eligible are receiving benefits (Boland, 1973). Families headed by females, whether on welfare or not, clearly represent a high-risk population.

A fundamental research question emerges: Does the economic vulnerability of female-headed families result in their disproportionate presence among the welfare poor, or does the system itself provide economic incentives for otherwise intact families to break up? Either answer to this question raises important policy issues. If, in fact, the breakup of families occurs independently of possible welfare benefits, but ultimately results in welfare dependency for large numbers of these families, the independent causes of family instability still must be investigated. Perhaps a national family policy designed to discourage family instability and develop supportive services, such as employment and child care, should be promoted. But if marital instability can be attributed to effects of the welfare system, proposals for welfare reform might emphasize features likely to promote marital stability (or at least be neutral to family type) to diminish the induced incidence of families headed by females. It is thus necessary to review the evidence of the behavior the welfare system induces in order to identify areas suitable for policy reform.

Other factors in family composition, principally illegitimacy rates and fertility patterns, influence economic status; an illegitimate birth may make a single mother eligible for welfare benefits. Our review of the reasons for case openings indicated that pregnancies out of wedlock often precipitated financial instability and subsequent receipt of welfare. Many analysts have hypothesized that eligibility requirements for AFDC that discriminate against single individuals and intact families

4. Bradbury (1977) points out that between 1960 and 1974 the number of female family heads with children generally increased 2½ times (from 1 to 2.6 million), whereas the number among the poor increased by ⅓ (from 1.5 to 2 million).

provide incentives for new family formation; and that eligibility requirements inhibit the marriage or remarriage of unwed mothers because an absent father may be required if they are to remain eligible for welfare benefits. A review of the research findings may in part resolve whether it is the economic vulnerability of unwed mothers that most often explains their presence on welfare or whether welfare itself influences the choice and timing of illegitimate births and the later marriage or remarriage of the single parent.

It is clear that the total number of children has important economic consequences for a family. Any measure of family economic well-being must be based on the relationship of income to family size; a given income cannot support 10 children as easily as two. Existing data demonstrate that the number of children in a family strongly influences the probabilities of going on welfare, the length and nature of the welfare experience and, in addition, the probabilities of gaining employment sufficient for self-support. Many critics of the welfare system have argued that the current AFDC benefit structure (increased monthly benefits as family size increases) encourages welfare mothers to have more children. An analysis of recent literature (see page 75) will in part resolve the different points of view.

Family stability and family composition are sensitive and controversial issues at the personal level. Though much of the research deals with aggregate trends, individual attitudes and practices in family decision-making should be considered when the data permit. This is essential if fundamental questions about differences in values and behavior among the poor are to be answered.

DETERMINANTS OF MARITAL INSTABILITY

Psychologists, sociologists, and economists have done considerable research on the causes of marital instability. Fundamental to research on family stability must be the question of whether low income is the cause of marital disruption or its result. Much current work has addressed the variables determining an individual's choice of whether to remain married or not. Our interest here will be directed toward understanding the more generalized trends. Since a primary reason for AFDC case openings is marital breakup, and since divorce (or desertion) is becoming a far more prevalent fact of life nationally, the discussion will analyze what is known about the aggregate determinants of marital dissolution.[5]

---

5. Podell's findings on welfare mothers in New York City (1969) differed from those of other studies reviewed on this point.

The discussion will not consider the changing norms and cultural sanctions which have clearly influenced aggregate changes in rates of marital disruption. Though these factors are no doubt important to the population as a whole, it is not clear that they have any special impact on the low-income population considered here.

Though the growth of the welfare rolls is most often attributed to the increase in the number of female-headed families, this growth is probably more a function of the increase in participation rates and liberalization of administrative practices than a function of the absolute increase in the number of such families. However, any further increases in the AFDC rolls may reflect the increased number of such families since their current participation rates are already about 94% of those eligible (Boland, 1973).

Research by Sawhill *et al.* (1975) and a monograph by Ross and Sawhill (1975) contain two of the most useful reviews of analyses of the socioeconomic variables affecting marital stability. This section of this text depends strongly on them. Several previous studies concluded that income is the most significant factor influencing rates of marital dissolution (Carter & Glick, 1970; Cutright, 1971; Goode, 1965, 1971). In measuring the relationship between social status and marital stability, Cutright separated out the joint effects of education, income, and occupation. When education and occupation were held constant, he found that income alone explained the variation.

Sawhill *et al.*, however, cautioned against the definitiveness of these conclusions, claiming that several considerations make these consistent findings suggestive rather than conclusive. Most of the studies used cross-sectional data. Though these studies investigated different aspects of divorce, few of them were able to examine the actual divorce process. When looking at divorced men at one point in time, divorce is dependent not only on the divorce rate but the remarriage rate with which income is also correlated. "Since remarriage rates are positively associated with income (Sweet, 1973), we cannot unambiguously attribute the variation in the percentage of divorced males with income to a variation in the divorce rate with income (Sawhill *et al.*, 1975) [p. 14]."

In all these studies, income data were provided for men only and generally included income only after the divorce. Such data do not provide a comprehensive picture of the family's economic circumstances prior to divorce; the wife's employment and earnings, though usually secondary to those of the husband, may significantly alter the income determinants of divorce. Since age relates to income, and marital stability varies both with age at the time of marriage and duration of the marriage, the inclusion of a control based on age is critical. Yet several of the previous studies failed to consider the age factor.

New longitudinal data bases have provided opportunities to over-come these earlier limitations. An early attempt to use data provided by the PSID was made by Hampton (1975). In his preliminary analysis, he substituted a 6-year average of total family income for the less adequate measures of male income at a point in time (usually following the di-vorce) found in other studies. In order to take into account the effect of female earnings for couples who had separated, Hampton averaged the total family income before separation but only earnings afterward. From his predictive equation of marital disruption he found: (a) income as the strongest single predictor (inversely related to separation); (b) the im-portance of the time of the first birth (the earlier the birth, the greater the likelihood of separation); and (c) the importance of the husband's age (the younger the husband, the greater the likelihood of separation). Contrary to expectation, blacks were less likely to separate than whites. Predictors for black families were different from those for white families and included income, husband's age, size of family, and size of city of residence; families from large cities were more likely to separate than families from small cities. A possible bias associated with the artificial reduction of income may be present, however, owing to the exclusion after separation of female earnings from average family income. It is argued that a bias is created by the automatic reduction of the income of separated couples; this may contribute to the resulting inverse relation-ship (Sawhill et al., 1975).

Analyses of data from NIT experiments in various sites throughout the country have provided considerable insight into the dynamics of marital instability. All the experiments provided longitudinal data files, generally recorded quarterly, on experimental and control families. Though interest centered around evaluations of the effect on labor sup-ply of various tax rates and guarantees, other impacts were also explored. Analyses of the stability of the experimental families were done in several sites. The New Jersey–Pennsylvania experiment focused on urban families; the North Carolina–Iowa experiment on rural ones. Other sites included Gary, Indiana, and Seattle–Denver.

It has been hypothesized that a transfer program which did not discriminate by family type would have a neutral or stabilizing effect on recipient families. However, both the urban and rural experiments pro-duced findings contrary to this expectation: The marital dissolution rate was higher for families receiving income-transfer payments than for families in the control groups. Analysis of the Seattle–Denver data (Hannan, Tuma, & Groeneveld, 1977) conclusively demonstrated that women receiving income maintenance had higher rates of marital disso-lution than comparable controls. Though each experiment found differences in the breakup rate among different experimental and ethnic groups (receiving different guarantees and tax rates), the control groups consistently exhibited lower dissolution rates than did the experimental groups. Sawhill *et al.*, seeking to explain these seemingly confounding results, suggested (along with other researchers) that the stabilizing effect on marriage of more income may be offset by the destabilizing effect of the greater financial independence of women.

Some research has addressed the impact of the financial independence of women on marital stability. Though most studies suffer from the limitations of cross-sectional data, their findings nevertheless tend to be consistent with Sawhill's hypothesis. Two studies using 1960 census data indicated that the percentage of divorced women rises as their incomes increase and as they advance in their occupational status (Carter & Glick, 1970; Havens, 1973). Several other studies have demonstrated a positive relationship between the divorce rate and both the proportion of married women in the labor force and the ratio of female earnings across states (Frieden, 1974; Santos, 1975).

A recent unpublished study (Levinger, 1974), cited by Ross and Sawhill, showed that the income of the wife was the determining factor in whether divorce would actually take place among couples who had filed for it. Johnson (1976) demonstrated that the frequency of divorce among married women aged 30–44 was related to their current wage or salary income after total family income, the length of the marriage, and other variables were controlled for.

Duncan and Morgan, in their analysis of the determinants of family instability for the PSID (1976) also focus on the economic aspects of changes in family living arrangements. While they concede a weakness in explanatory power due to a lack of sociological and psychological variables, their general findings support the research just reviewed. They found that divorce or separation among married couples became more likely if the wife was in the labor force. This effect was most notable if her work hours were extensive. They caution, however, that the perceived relationship may not be causal. For example, wives may be working to escape an unsatisfactory marriage or in anticipation of divorce.

THEORETICAL FRAMEWORK

While a variety of theories exist to explain the observed relationships between economic variables and family behavior, most of the available research has not been founded in any particular theoretical mode. Ross and Sawhill (1975) hypothesize the dimensions of marriage

and the family as an economic institution which, first, transfers resources from those who work (more often, men) to those who do not
and, secondly, establishes the socioeconomic status of its individual
members within the social structure.

> One hypothesis is that these intrafamily transfers affect stability
> because they make women financially dependent upon the marriage
> relationship. As women acquire direct access to economic resources as
> workers or welfare recipients, rather than indirect access as wives, it
> reduces the gains from the traditional specialization of labor within
> marriage and lowers the cost of marital dissolution [Sawhill et al., p.
> 22].

Though these economic relationships continue to be demonstrated
in the literature, research has failed to isolate any one of a variety of
possible explanations. Sawhill and others summarized several possible
theories to explain the observed relationships. The "role performance
hypothesis" stresses the importance of the relative success of the male as
a breadwinner on the mutual affect between husband and wife (Cutright, 1971). The "assets constraint" hypothesis posits the accumulation
of assets in upper-income families as increasing the costs of marital
dissolution (Bradbury, 1977). A more individual psychological approach, the "personal adjustment hypothesis" suggests that there are
factors which simultaneously predispose an individual to success on the
job and success in marriage. In addition, a pure income effect might be
operating based on the fact that more economic resources simply al-
leviate a large number of factors that contribute to interpersonal ten-
sions, such as poor living conditions, overcrowding, and economic in-
security. The "independence effect," which has been hypothesized to
offset the "income effect," posits that resources available to the wife may
offset the constraints which accompany higher income since resources
(or ability to acquire them) change the woman's economic dependence
on the relationship and the cost of dissolution.

Sawhill and her colleagues sought to test a theoretical model to
explain the previously observed empirical relationships. Their work is
most impressive in its attempts to consider a wide range of determinants while at the same time retaining a theoretical justification for their
inclusion. They have overcome the limitations of earlier work by means
of a comprehensive and longitudinal data source provided by the PSID.
The panel data recorded 1894 observations, including those made of
husband–wife families that were intact at the beginning of the first
study year (1968). The findings of the multivariate analysis help to ex-

plain in some depth the factors associated with the high levels of marital instability among the poor and, more specifically, among the welfare poor. The multivariate analysis tested four vectors of independent variables on marital dissolution: the duration and timing of the marriage, an independence effect, an income effect, and the effect of the cultural environment on marital dissolution. The results help to clarify the findings of earlier studies.

The research of Sawhill and her colleagues reinforced the importance of the timing and duration of marriage. As the duration of marriages increased, separation rates declined markedly. This supports the authors' views that each spouse makes certain investments over the course of the marriage and that with increasing age, the supply of alternative partners decreases. Over time, the population of intact couples is reduced by the breakup of the least successful marriages in the initial cohort. An additional 10 years of marriage reduces the separation rate by 3%.

Most important to analysis of the welfare population is the finding of significantly higher separation rates for those who marry young. Ross and Sawhill suggest that there is probably the least value congruence initially among these couples; value divergence increases over time. Their findings indicate that a 5-year delay in the age of marriage reduces the separation rate by 2%. As shown hereafter, early marriage is often associated with premarital pregnancy; for the potential welfare population this correlation is particularly significant.[6]

To test the hypothesis (the independence effect) that wives who are less dependent upon marriage for its economic benefits are more likely to perceive fewer costs associated with marital dissolution (and are therefore more likely to dissolve their marriages), three variables were considered: the wife's annual earnings, the potential welfare benefit available in the state of residence, and the presence of children under 18. Findings revealed that if all other factors are held constant, a $1000 increase in female earnings was associated with a 1% increase in marital separation rates.

The availability of welfare benefits and the presence of children appeared to have no significant effect. (These issues will be considered in more detail in a later section.) Regarding the small but significantly perceivable effect of female-earnings on marital stability, Ross and

6. This finding, related to the instability of teenage marriages, is supported by numerous studies; for example Moore and Waite, 1977; Glick and Norton, 1977; Bumpass and Sweet, 1972.

Sawhill, along with Duncan and Morgan (1976), caution against immediate interpretation:

> It may be, for example, that wives seek employment in anticipation of
> divorce . . . alternatively, it may be that husbands think their working
> wives are performing their homemaker and maternal roles less ade-
> quately creating marital strains, or that time pressures in two-earner
> families undermine the marital relationship [Ross & Sawhill, 1975, pps.
> 57–58].

Stronger evidence supporting the significance of the female independence effect has come from recent analysis of longitudinal data from
the Seattle–Denver Income Maintenance Experiment. A woman's actual
or predicted wage rate had a large effect on marital dissolution rates of
sample families. A $1 increase in a wife's hourly wage resulted in in-
creases in the dissolution rate of more than one-third for whites, one-
half for blacks, and almost three-quarters for Chicanos. Eligibility criteria restricted the sample to families whose income did not exceed
$11,000 if there were two wage earners and $9000 if there was one wage
earner. The results therefore lend particular strength to the significance
of an independence effect for a lower income population (Hannan *et al.*,
1977).

Feldman and Feldman's study (1972) of welfare and nonwelfare
low-income working women attempted to assess (among other things)
the impact of working women on their families and their marital relationships. Wives who worked reported less marital satisfaction and less
adequacy in their homemaker roles than reported by women who were
not working.

More research which considers the *expected* as well as the actual
earnings of the wife would be necessary to test more precisely the independence effect since a woman's potential earnings may be just as important as current earnings in her assessment of her economic dependence from the marital relationship. It would also be desirable to test
how the wife's working and earnings, and both partners' sex-role attitudes, effect marital stability. Though several studies have investigated these issues for a welfare population (Feldman & Feldman, 1972),
no attempt has been made to follow couples over time to evaluate the
impact of these factors on marital stability.

In testing the importance of an income effect, Ross and Sawhill
considered a large range of measures. The most important single variable among those in the vector measuring the income effect proved to be
the husband's employment history; Ross and Sawhill see this as a good
indicator of his ability to provide for his family. Findings revealed that
separation rates were twice as high among families in which the hus-

band had experienced serious unemployment over a 3-year period prior to the start of the survey. What is most startling, given the previous literature, was that the absolute level of earnings had no effect on separation rates and that there was no indication of a pure income effect. The results are interpreted to reflect a "role performance rather than an income effect." Indeed, the importance of the measure of unemployment history suggests that the *stability* rather than the precise *level* of income may be critical in explaining marital dissolution rates.

Though Ross and Sawhill's analysis provided no evidence that the presence of children had any measurable effect on rates of separation and divorce, a more recent analysis using PSID data found the reverse. Hoffman and Holmes (1976) considered a variety of economic and demographic variables to explain the separation and divorce rates of a sample of husbands and wives married at the beginning of the study (1968). Having followed these families over 7 years, Hoffman and Holmes found that the presence of very young children did indeed have a measurable and significant impact for the sample families in deterring either spouse from seeking divorce or separation. However, this proved to be significant only when children under 2 years old were present.

A variety of economic factors seem to explain differences in marital stability. Studies using longitudinal data files generally provide the most convincing evidence. Much of the research confirms the significant effects on marital dissolution rates of the instability of a husband's employment and the income or potential income from a wife's employment. Socioeconomic and demographic variables—region of residence, age, age at marriage, and duration of the marriage—are also important. Many of these predictors seem particularly germane to the current and potential welfare population, a population that exhibits to a disproportionate degree characteristics such as unstable employment for the male and early age of marriage.

EFFECTS OF THE WELFARE SYSTEM ON MARITAL INSTABILITY

Controversial and frequent criticisms of the current AFDC program are that its design provides work disincentives and encourages family dissolution. While there is concern about large increases in the size of the welfare population, a variety of additional factors have influenced the growth of the welfare rolls, including changing eligibility criteria, administrative discretion in determining countable income, and liberalization in agency administrative policy. These serve to encourage or discourage clients' petitions for assistance.

The basis for program eligibility, in addition to objective financial need, is the nature of the family unit. Current eligibility criteria for AFDC cash assistance require the presence of children deprived of parental support. This includes needy children whose parents are incapacitated. Twenty-six states have exercised the option provided by the federal government in 1962 to provide benefits to intact families in which the father is unemployed. Nevertheless, participants in these AFDC-UF programs represent only about 4% of the total AFDC caseload. Therefore, the de facto requirement for acceptance into the AFDC program is to be a female head of a family with few or no earnings.

Many analysts have argued that this de facto limitation of eligibility serves as an inducement for family breakup or nonformation. Two fundamental reasons support this behavior. One is that for the unhappy marriage, the welfare option for the mother provides an opportunity to escape. In many intact families with a low income, the household head, even working full time, cannot provide family support greater than AFDC payments and in-kind benefits (food stamps, medicaid, public housing, etc.). Thus, for the unhappily married woman in such families, the economic costs of separation can be small. The welfare option can be hypothesized to serve as a facilitative function. This concept is closely related to the independence effect discussed above. Similarly, many researchers hypothesize that the welfare option also serves, temporarily or permanently, to facilitate the postponement of marriage of the unwed mother and remarriage of an already divorced female household head.

The second reason for family breakup or nonformation is that the availability of welfare income may provide the option for income maximization, which therefore acts as a precipitating factor in abandonment (feigned or real) and subsequent welfare receipt. For the low-wage worker even full-time employment may not ensure sufficient income. When both cash assistance and in-kind benefits are considered, the standard of living provided by AFDC may be far more attractive than that provided by full-time low-wage employment. It has also been hypothesized that rational economic choice, based on an assessment of the alternatives, may encourage male heads of households to feign desertion, and in so doing provide for their families the critical criterion for AFDC eligibility.

In general, research on the importance of welfare as a precipitant of marital dissolution has provided rather inconsistent and varying results. Clearly, certain methodological problems reduce the importance and validity of some of the findings. Dependence on aggregate point-in-time data prohibits the consideration of other factors that influence individuals toward or away from divorce. The lack of consistent predictors

from study to study implies that the factors which predict marital instability are varied, complicated, and not easily revealed through economic
and socioeconomic models alone. Considerably more knowledge and
data related to the sociological and psychological preconditions of divorce would be necessary to produce more consistent and stronger predictive models. Nevertheless, recent evidence on the importance of the
independence effect has contributed a great deal to current understanding of the options that are open to women and that affect the stability of
marriage. The fact that individual variables seem to be extremely sensitive to the precise specification of the model need not dilute the strong
suggestions from a variety of studies that alternative options for women
do indeed tend to influence rates of marital dissolution.

Evidence from Cross-Sectional Analyses. In a study made for the Joint
Economic Committee, U.S. Congress, Cutright and Scanzoni (1973) attempted to assess the effect of welfare on family stability by comparing
the marital status of women in states with higher and lower AFDC
benefits. Using an aggregate and admittedly gross measure, they tested
for the effects of AFDC benefit levels on rates of entry into marriage by
younger women. They used data from 1950, 1960, 1970 to estimate the
effects. They concluded that welfare benefits do not contribute to family
breakups. However, confidence in their conclusions is weakened because of their dependence on aggregate data and their inability to isolate
specifically the effects of welfare itself.

In the same volume, Honig (1973) presented the results of her study
to determine the impact of the level of welfare payments on family
stability. She examined the impact of differences in AFDC payment
levels in 44 metropolitan areas in 1960 and 1970, including consideration
of other significant variables thought to influence relative differences in
marital status, such as wage levels, unemployment rates, nonwelfare
income of females, and restrictions on eligibility for welfare programs.
After controlling for these variables, she concluded that AFDC benefits
indeed have an impact on marital status and that the magnitude of the
impact is considerable. The 1960 figures indicate that a 10% rise in the
AFDC caseload is associated with a 3% or 4% rise in the proportion of
female-headed families. She also concluded that a 10% increase in the
level of benefits raises the percentage of female welfare recipients by 20%
for whites and 14% for nonwhites. Findings for the 1970 sample indicated the same direction of the impact but at a lower magnitude.

The dependence on cross-sectional data for both studies limits the
importance of the findings. The problem is similar to that found in
studies conducted earlier on the determinants of family instability gen-

erally; the results indicate something about the relationship between the level of welfare benefits and family status, but they do not necessarily indicate anything about welfare and marital dissolution. Data were lacking that are necessary for evaluating the process by which the levels of welfare benefits may or may not influence family structure. For example, the current proportion of women who are separated is affected by both separation rates and remarriage rates; Honig, and Cutright and Scanzoni, fail to distinguish between these two factors. Lerman (1973) cautions that the level of AFDC benefits may induce female headship by discouraging stable marriages and by helping mothers in disrupted marriages to head their own households. Honig fails to distinguish these two separate effects. Other methodological shortcomings include the failure to consider family size when using measures of average welfare benefits; the failure to consider additional factors that distinguish between states offering AFDC-UF and those offering only AFDC (Bradbury, 1977). These problems require that the results be interpreted with caution.

One recent study on the impact of welfare on marital dissolution was conducted by Bernstein and Meezan (1975) on a sample of 451 welfare mothers in New York City. Though this small, sample from a single site somewhat limits the ability to generalize, the study is useful as an initial exploration into the variety of conditions contributing to marital dissolution among this population. Though the authors were able to find consistent responses indicating that the availability of welfare influenced a full 14% of the women in their decision to break up their marriage, an overwhelming majority, 86%, said their decision was *not* influenced by welfare. However, since these women were still on welfare at the time of the interviews, the authors suggest that they may not have been fully candid in their responses. The responses of an additional 14% of the mothers that they still loved their husbands (or boyfriends) and saw them at least once a week seemed to suggest that these mothers had separated in order to maximize their income; but this was only a suspicion. Even taken at face value these findings indicate that a small but significant number of mothers who separated from their husbands were influenced by the availability of welfare.

A question more clearly resolved by the study was the degree to which welfare was seen as an option to escape from unsatisfactory marriages. The degree and number of destructive circumstances which plagued the relationships of many of these women (such as the husband's drug addiction, alcoholism, or resort to physical abuse) appeared to be the most significant factors leading to their exercise of the welfare option. The proportion of those who were merely opting for income maximization remained considerably less clear.

Ross and Sawhill provide further evidence from an analysis of data from the 1970 Census of Population and Housing. Using data from 41 cities, the authors sought in their analysis to explain the variation in the proportion of women (16–54 years old) who are female household heads with children. The authors hypothesized that greater income opportunities for women outside the home explain the variation. Thus, the average welfare benefit available in the county, including the value of the average food stamp bonus, was included as a predictor. This figure was then divided by the average full-time earnings of men in each city's low-income area. This ratio is able to account for the relative attractiveness of welfare, given the limited support a working male could provide. Among additional variables included in the equation were the prevalence of welfare in the area, the existence of the AFDC-UF program in the state, female-earnings, median family income, male unemployment, and the measure of population mobility. Separate regressions were run for blacks and whites.

For the white women, none of the welfare variables was found to be significantly related to the proportion of female headed families. In contrast, the variable measuring females' earnings proved to be very important. The findings revealed that a 10% increase in female earnings increased the proportion of such families by 11.5%. In addition, it was found that male unemployment had a destabilizing effect, while median income had a stabilizing effect. The control variable of the proportion of the population in the low-income area that was made up of children was significant and positive, also representing a destabilizing effect.

In contrast, the equation for blacks revealed the welfare benefit variable to be both significant and positive in explaining the proportion of black families headed by females. No other welfare variables were important, nor was that of women's earnings in comparison with men's. The authors conclude that for black women the welfare benefit seems to play the same role as women's relative earnings play for whites, if not as strongly. A 10% increase in the welfare benefit seems to result in only a 2.1% increase in the proportion of women who are female heads. For blacks, median family income proved to be quite important. A 10% increase in intact family income leads to a 6.7% decrease in female headship for whites and a 7.2% decrease for nonwhites.

The authors contend, therefore, that the findings generally support their original hypothesis: for both whites and nonwhites in low-income metropolitan areas, economic factors have an important impact on family behavior. The differences between the impact of welfare benefits for nonwhites and earnings of females for whites can be explained. For black women, the possibility of earning an income is greatly constrained by discrimination and a disproportionate unemployment burden. Additionally, nonwhites tend to have larger families than whites, and the average available welfare benefit is higher. These differences could be explained by cultural factors. A higher percentage of eligible nonwhite families receive welfare benefits than is the case for white families. Nonwhites also tend to stay on welfare longer than do their white counterparts when age, education, and family size are controlled. This observed difference between the impact of welfare on white and nonwhites was not found in the Bernstein and Meezan study reviewed earlier.

A study by Bogue (1975) analyzed survey data provided by the University of Chicago's Community and Family Study Center on the marital tension and dissolution among low-income families. A random sample of 315 black AFDC mothers was selected. The mothers were interviewed to discover the circumstances that preceded and accompanied the dissolution of their marriages. Reformulating current hypotheses that explain the high rate of dissolution among black couples, Bogue abandons the earlier hypothesis that primary reasons are black culture, family disorganization, and economic forces in favor of one that explains the marital instability of welfare mothers as a function of premarital and extramarital pregnancies, especially unwanted pregnancies.

His findings revealed that 65% of the mothers in the sample had become pregnant outside marriage. Almost 25% did not have a union sufficiently stable to lead to marriage, and as a result they bore their children out of wedlock. Of these out-of-wedlock mothers, 87.5% responded that they were a little unhappy or very unhappy about their pregnancies. Of those who were pregnant at the time of their marriage, about 50% said that they were very unhappy and that their pregnancies were thus unwanted. In total, 45% of all first pregnancies of the AFDC mothers were both extramarital and unwanted.

In response to questions about their pregnancies and subsequent marriages, 31.7% of these mothers said they did not expect at the time they married that the marriage would last. When asked how boyfriends (or husbands) had reacted to the pregnancy, 36% said the father had either argued for an abortion or did not want to take any responsibility. These responses were even higher for the 40.1% in the group who were premaritally pregnant and unhappy about it. When the mothers were asked if they would have married the man if they had not been pregnant, 50.5% of the entire sample stated that pregnancy was the main reason for the marriage; and of those who had been premaritally pregnant and unhappy about it, 74.4% stated that pregnancy was the main reason for the marriage. Consistent with the reported importance of age at marriage in the probability of marital stability (Sawhill *et al.*, 1975), 40.9% of the women in this sample married when 20 or younger.

The author concludes, therefore, that in marriages brought about by unwanted pregnancies, these pregnancies are the cause of subsequent marital dissolutions. Such unions are not founded on stable conditions; they are, as the author concludes, inherently unstable. Based on unwanted pregnancies rather than on romance, they are entered into in the expectation that after a brief time they will be dissolved. Further, and more strongly, he argues that this is a valid explanation for the dissolution of 40% of all AFDC marriages in Chicago.[7]

Evidence from Longitudinal Analyses. In the study of marital stability reviewed earlier, Ross and Sawhill (1975) used a number of variables to test for the presence of an independence effect. One variable measured the welfare benefits the state made available to 'a wife. As was mentioned earlier, the analysis of this variable proved it to have no impact on the separation rates of all the sample families in the PSID that had been followed over a 6-year period. Clearly, this finding is limited in significance to the low-income end of the larger sample of families. Yet, even when these families were analyzed as a subset, increased levels of benefits could not be found to have an impact on separation rates.[8]

Ross and Sawhill explain the lack of perceived impact in two ways. First, they argue that welfare benefits are a contextual variable rather than a family attribute; thus, existing variations in state benefit levels must be relied upon to test this hypothesis. They claim that in a mobile society such distinctions may be blurred and that the more general availability of welfare may be just as important in affecting behavior as differences in state benefit levels. They also argue that the availability of federally financed in-kind benefits (e.g., food stamps) has narrowed the differences in the value of total benefits and in the differences of states' incentives for marital dissolution. However eloquently they argue, they provide no empirical evidence that these arguments explain the lack of a perceived relationship between welfare benefit-levels and the patterns of family instability that they have evaluated.

More recently, Hoffman and Holmes (1976) used a slightly different

7. A similar study of 1213 couples over 5 years in Detroit revealed that of the 59 couples who had been separated over the study period, 41% of the women had been premaritally pregnant (Coombs & Zumeta, 1970).

8. Cherlin (1976) also found no effect of AFDC on marital disruption among 2696 white women aged 30–44 using the national longitudinal survey of labor market experience as his data base.

model of the determinants of family instability than Ross and Sawhill with the first 7 years' data from the PSID. Contrary to the findings of Ross and Sawhill, those of Hoffman and Holmes showed a significant and positive impact of welfare benefit levels on the divorce and separation rates of mothers in the sample. In attempting to measure an independence effect, which they call the "attractiveness of alternatives," the authors considered both the potential wages of wives and the AFDC benefits available in their states of residence. Among poor families, the presence of high welfare benefits in a state appeared to decrease marital stability by 12%.[9] The relationship appeared to be quite strong (Hoffman & Holmes, 1976, p. 59).

While a variety of the research reviewed revealed welfare benefits as a good predictor of marital dissolution rates (Honig, 1973; Bernstein & Meezan, 1975; Hoffman & Holmes, 1976), other research has found no support for such claims. It cannot be concluded, however, that the impact is of profound magnitude, even when it has been found; nor is it free from the influence of a great many other considerations. What is clear is that a variety of profound disadvantages (including early marriage, severe economic instability, unemployment, and premarital pregnancy), often combined with incentives resulting from the welfare program, seem to explain the large degree of marital instability among the low-income population. Resort to welfare is one of the options many low-income women can adopt if they dissolve their marriages.

Assuming that the hypothesis based on the welfare option and income maximization was appropriate, even if factored into the full, a great deal of variation in separation rates remains unexplained. Thus, to concentrate efforts on this small though significant determinant would probably not prove to be a wise policy. Indeed, findings from the NIT experiments have failed to reveal that changes in the eligibility requirements of welfare programs can decrease the instability of these marriages.

EFFECTS OF THE WELFARE SYSTEM ON REMARRIAGE

Some researchers have hypothesized that the availability of the welfare option not only affects marital dissolution, but also the speed at which single women marry or remarry. In their work on the determin-

9. Poverty is defined here by a low ratio of income to needs based on family size and composition.

ants of family instability, Sawhill *et al.* (1975), having analyzed PSID data, found no evidence that welfare benefits promote marital dissolution. Nevertheless, they contend that the proportion of women who are divorced at any given time is a function of both the divorce rate and the remarriage rate. Another hypothesis may be, therefore, that although welfare does not precipitate separation, it may well affect the rate at which female family heads remarrry. As suggested earlier, welfare may act to inhibit or postpone remarriage for separated women and marriage for mothers with illegitimate children. This may be largely a matter of the timing of marriage or remarriage decisions since previous data (recorded by tracking women over time) showed that eventually most divorced women remarry (Sawhill *et al.*, 1975). However, age and number of children also appear to affect remarriage rates (U.S. Bureau of the Census, 1971).

A survey in 1967 of a cohort of women born in 1920–1924 revealed that of the 96% who had been married, 17% subsequently terminated their first marriage, and 11% had been widowed. Of interest was the finding that 66% of the divorced women later remarried, while only 33% of the widows did so (U.S. Bureau of the Census, 1972).

Not very much research has been done on the determinants of remarriage. One of the critical variables in remarriage rates is the woman's age at the time when her prior marriage terminated. Some of the differences observed between the remarriage rates of divorcees and widows can be explained by this fact. Remarriages seem to occur 4½ times as often for women whose prior marriage ended before they were 40 as compared with marriages ended after 40 (Sweet, 1973).

Studies using data from the Survey of Economic Opportunity also revealed that remarriage rates are affected by many other variables, including the time period since disruption of the previous marriage, the wife's age when the previous marriage was terminated, and the duration of the previous marriage. These variables appear to be negatively related to the probability of remarriage. Further, both race and the presence of children appear to be important factors in remarriage probabilities. Blacks are less likely to remarry than whites, and women with children are more likely to remarry than those without children. Additional multivariate studies have tended to reinforce these findings. Sawhill *et al.*, (1975) however, point out that previous studies have failed to ascertain the importance of the presence of children in remarriage probabilities.

Though no definitive work has been done on the relationship between remarriage probabilities and economic opportunities for women, Sawhill *et al.* report on the preliminary results of some forthcoming studies. Bane (1975) suggests that remarriage rates are inversely related to welfare benefits and women's potential earnings. Caldwell's work at the Urban Institute (Washington, D.C.) indicates that receiving welfare does indeed decrease the probability of marriage (Caldwell, 1975).

Using a model similar to the one they developed and tested to explain separation rates, Sawhill et al. used the PSID data to explain variations in remarriage rates. The premise of the model is that the choice to remarry is based on the relative attractiveness of the available options. A variety of variables are thus expected to influence a woman's preferences and remarriage probabilities, including her age, number of children, the time elapsed since her last marriage, etc. Additionally, age is likely to influence the availability of eligible men; a variety of economic factors may influence the range of options. The findings of Sawhill and her colleagues add significantly to our understanding of the welfare impact.

The most important result reported is that being on welfare makes women very much less likely to remarry. After controlling for variables such as age, race, income, assets, duration of previous marriage, and presence of children, women not on welfare were three times as likely to remarry within the 5 years of the PSID as those on welfare. In addition, though the sample is small, there were no significant differences in remarriage probabilities between those receiving different levels of welfare. The only significant difference was between those receiving welfare and those not.

When the effect of welfare recipiency as an inhibiting influence on remarriage was analyzed more closely, data showed that it lessened the probability of remarriage more strongly in the years immediately after termination of the prior marriage. Though strong, this negative effect declines somewhat as the years pass. The authors argue that welfare operates to relieve the economic pressures to remarry right away. Other important variables explaining remarriage rates include income (positive); assets (strong and negative); and age, being nonwhite, and the duration of the previous marriage (all negative). The authors have suggested a possible flaw in their research. They claim that they have not adequately controlled for the personal characteristics of their sample; these may in fact be related to welfare dependency and opportunities for remarriage.

Though in their analysis of data from the first 6 years of the PSID Sawhill and her colleagues found that marital breakup was not affected by a family's welfare status, they found that AFDC recipients were less likely to remarry than were nonrecipients. A more recent study, however, using the first 7 years of the PSID data found the case to be precisely the opposite. Duncan (1976) developed an economic model thought to explain the marriage or remarriage rates of female heads of households unmarried at the beginning of the 7-year study period but married during it. He specified variables thought to influence the "demand" for marriage among these women. He hypothesized that the higher the welfare income, the less the likelihood for marriage (i.e., need for a spouse or an alternative income source was limited). The likelihood was affected by the additional variables of size of the city, number of children and their ages, and the woman's age, physical appearance, race, and marital status. The level of welfare benefits was found to have no effect on the marriage rates of women with dependent children; but no analyses were reported of differences in marriage rates for those who were and were not receiving welfare. The comparisons merely attempted to distinguish between levels of transfer income rather than between recipient and nonrecipient status. This study is not, therefore, directly comparable to the results of Sawhill *et al.* (1975).

A variety of studies have shown that marriage to acquire a male head of the family is the most effective means to move from poverty to nonpoverty status. Data from the first 7 years of the PSID (see beginning of this chapter) demonstrate the significant change in poverty status for those women who married during those first 7 years. Thus, the potential inhibiting effect which welfare may have on marriage or remarriage has significant implications for the future economic well-being of single recipients who are family heads. While the amount of welfare income does not appear to influence the rates of remarriage and marriage, Sawhill's analysis suggests that recipient status has an important inhibiting effect. The real issue with regard to various welfare reform proposals which include eligibility for intact families is whether the delay or postponement of marriage, observed as a result of the present system, will remain. No research evidence on this issue is yet available.

EFFECTS OF THE WELFARE SYSTEM ON ILLEGITIMACY

Data from the 1973 AFDC study (U.S. DHEW, 1974) indicate that 45.6% of all AFDC families contain at least one illegitimate child. The comparable figure for the population as a whole is about 20% (Bogue, 1975). Cutright (1973a) reports that 80% of nonwhite and 60% of white illegitimate births occur in women whose incomes are lower than 125% of the poverty level. Indeed, the illegitimacy rate of poor women is eight times as high as that of the nonpoor.

Bogue (whose study on family breakup was cited in the previous section) considers premarital pregnancy and illegitimacy as independent variables that explain a considerable amount of later marital instability among AFDC families. In this section, we are viewing illegitimacy as a dependent variable. Most research efforts to date have concentrated on the degree to which the welfare option explains high rates of illegitimacy among poor women. Few researchers, however, have been able to convincingly demonstrate the importance of welfare in explaining variations in illegitimacy rates.

Many methodological and conceptual difficulties occur in any attempt to study the determinants of illegitimacy or its relationship to a family's welfare status. However attempts to develop a model which explains illegitimacy have been inadequate because of the difficulty in capturing all the complicated steps in a woman's decision-making process of whether or not to bear a child out of wedlock. The process begins with the decision to engage in pre- or extra-marital sex; from there, the risk of pregnancy is a function of the decision to use or not to use contraception and the particular contraceptive selected. The health of the woman determines the probability of a live birth. Decisions about continuing or aborting the pregnancy and marrying before the birth of the child and forming a new family unit have an impact on the number of illegitimate births which result in welfare receipt.[10]

Sorting out the range and levels of determinants of illegitimacy is a difficult research problem. No researchers to date have been successful in identifying and testing empirically the myriad individual factors. Nevertheless, a few modest attempts have been made to explain the factors associated with illegitimacy and welfare receipt. In his study for the Joint Economic Committee, Cutright (1973a) hypothesized a positive relationship between increased in state AFDC benefit levels nationally between 1940 and 1960 and increases in the rates of illegitimate births. He also hypothesized that state illegitimacy rates were related to the level of state AFDC benefits. Having tested against 1960 data, he concluded that increased welfare benefit levels did not lead to higher rates of illegitimate births. He found that an analysis of 1970 data produced the same findings. Although Cutright admits that illegitimate births

---

10. Indeed, Furstenberg, Gordis, and Markowitz (1969) argue that the illegitimacy figures generally underestimate the actual incidence of premarital pregnancy. Many births terminate in abortion, and many more result in unplanned and generally undesired marriages, which Bogue (1975) concluded result in a great many of the family breakups that subsequently lead to welfare receipt.

have become an increasingly significant source of growth in the AFDC caseload, he is unwilling to conclude that the welfare system per se has led to the births. His results suffer from the limitations of aggregate data. Problems similar to those evident in separating welfare as a contextual issue in a model of family stability serve to weaken confidence in these findings as well. Lacking evidence to the contrary, the existence of the welfare system itself, rather than the level of benefits, is more likely to be the important factor.

Another attempt to measure the impact of welfare on illegitimacy included controls for a variety of other predictors thought to influence the illegitimacy rate. Fechter and Greenfield (1973) developed a model using cross-sectional data for both 1960 and 1970, for blacks and whites separately.[11] The study again used the variations in the level of AFDC benefits as an independent variable. In addition, however, education, the unemployment rate, women's earnings, the income of males, the total income of intact families, and region of residence were included among the independent variables. Among all the variables in the model, welfare benefit levels did not assume any significance; rather, the most important single predictor was education, and this was followed by region of residence (which appears to account for the different cultural orientations).[12]

Most researchers have concluded that welfare benefits are not precipitating factors in illegitimacy. What welfare has been shown to influence, however, are certain other decisions subsequent to an illegitimate birth. Included among these is the tendency toward new household formation. The availability of welfare has enabled young married mothers to set up their own households apart from their nuclear or extended families. This trend appears to be one of continuing importance even among the general population. A growing propensity to form a separate household has been documented by Cutright and Scanzoni (1973) and is, for example of equal importance in explaining the apparent growth in female-headed families for whites and blacks.

Most researchers conclude that most illegitimate pregnancies are unwelcome, unplanned (Zelnick & Kantner, 1974), and not a result of a conscious decision based on the knowledge of eligibility for subsequent

11. Zelnik and Kantner (1973) concluded that racial differences account for the largest and most persistent differences in the proportion of women who have had sexual experiences prior to marriage even when socioeconomic differences are controlled for.

12. Moore and Caldwell (1976), using a longitudinal data file of 4611 adolescent women (ages 15–19) found that neither the level nor the variability of AFDC appeared to effect the childbearing decisions of the adolescents studied.

welfare receipt.[13] Poverty and welfare are thus seen as results of unwanted and unanticipated pregnancies rather than the cause.

A study by Janowitz (1976) sought to evaluate empirically the impact on illegitimate birth rates of AFDC payments along with a variety
of other socioeconomic predictors. She argues that theory suggests AFDC
would affect illegitimate birth rates in several ways. First, the higher the
grant, the lower the economic sanctions against childbearing. Second,
the size of the grant might simply influence a pregnant woman's decision of whether to remain single or to marry and thus legitimize her
child. In her model, Janowitz also considers the impact of AFDC administrative arrangements likely to influence either decision. Clearly,
the existence of an AFDC-UF program in the state may affect the degree
of economic pressure to form or maintain a female-headed family.

The factors that determine the decision that can result in the conception and birth of an illegitimate child (mentioned earlier) were grouped
into two categories by Janowitz: variables which affect premarital conceptions, and variables which affect the legitimacy of births. Regressions were run separately for white and nonwhite mothers and will be
presented here separately. In addition, results were presented separately by age of the subjects.

The findings for white mothers clarified very few causative factors;
only the wages of the males proved to be at all significant, and then only
at the 5% level. For the nonwhite group, however, considerably more of
the variation in illegitimacy rates was explained. This was particularly
true for the youngest age groups (15–19 and 20–24). Findings revealed
that the level of the welfare payment had a positive impact on illegitimacy. The coefficient increased with the age group up to ages 25–29 and
then declined, becoming insignificant. The existence of the AFDC-UF
program in the state appears to be significant for the youngest age
group, but not for others. It is in fact negative for the older group aged
30–34. Several of the findings are thus unclear. At least it is certain that
for younger black women, welfare payments seem to have an impact on
the illegitimacy rates. This conclusion is strengthened by the significant
and negative impact that income appears to have for this group. The
author concluded that the high illegitimacy rate in this group is related
to the failure of the welfare system to include poor households headed

13. Furstenberg, Gordis, and Markowitz (1969) point out, however, that there is still
disagreement on this point. Young, in the *Unwed Mother*, concluded from a study of a
sample of 100 unwed mothers: "All of these girls, unhappy and driven by unconscious
needs, had blindly sought a way out of their emotional dilemma by having a child out of
wedlock [1966, p. 93]."

by males. The importance of the educational attainment variable among nonwhite women suggests that knowledge about contraception may be explained by educational level.

As in the case of studies of marital instability, this analysis fails to capture the process of decision making for this group. Neither does the nature of aggregate data permit inferences about this process. Furthermore, the findings are diminished in importance because the sample is small in light of the number of independent variables considered. The results offer only preliminary support for the argument that welfare has some impact on illegitimacy rates nationally for young women.

Illegitimacy, as Bogue (1975) demonstrated in his study (reviewed earlier), is intimately related to issues of marital stability and welfare dependency. Earlier chapters have noted the set of circumstances with which applications for welfare are strongly correlated. The birth of an illegitimate child often begins a process of dependency which becomes complicated with loss of employment, unstable marriages and long-term welfare tenure. It is for these reasons that illegitimacy must be seen as a condition compatible with preexisting multiple handicaps.

EFFECTS OF THE WELFARE SYSTEM ON FERTILITY

Many researchers have hypothesized that successful family planning is the single most significant factor in deterring the growth of the welfare rolls. Attitudes and behavior about family planning among welfare mothers will therefore be an important consideration in the following section. Clearly, welfare is relevant to the determinants of illegitimacy rates as well. It seems reasonable to assume, on the basis of the previous analysis, that welfare does not promote illegitimate births. However, it may provide options for the formation of new families and the postponement of marriage. It cannot be concluded, however, that the exercise of this option is patently undesirable, since marriages based exclusively on the desire to legitimate a birth have been shown to result in high rates of dissolution.

As a review of the literature shows, hypotheses about the nature of fertility patterns of the welfare poor and the effects of welfare on those patterns are similar to hypotheses addressed to illegitimacy. Two fundamental notions have directed the research. One is that the behavior patterns of the welfare poor differ from those of the rest of the population in regard to sexual activity, the desire to become pregnant, fertility, and use or desire for contraception. The second notion is that such choices may be influenced by the "pronatalist" approach of the welfare system, which provides higher benefits as family size increases.

Research to date on the behavior and attitudes of welfare mothers toward pregnancy and contraception has not supported the notion that they have any greater sexual activity or desire to become pregnant than do nonwelfare mothers. Placek and Hendershot (1974) have made an important contribution to the study of these questions. Their investigation tests what is commonly known as the "brood sow" myth, which states that "welfare mothers define welfare economic status favorably, are extremely active sexually, refrain from using contraceptives, want to become pregnant and become pregnant [Placek & Hendershot, 1974, p. 658]." Their study of 300 welfare mothers analyzed data to test this explanation of welfare fertility. This study provided an in-depth survey including information about the circumstances and events surrounding each woman's pregnancy intervals. It also included data about respondents' activities regarding welfare and family planning.

Results based on a comparison of welfare and nonwelfare women indicated the following: The great majority of AFDC recipients did not go on welfare at the birth of their first child and did not stay on welfare continuously during the remainder of their subsequent childbearing. This supports a much earlier finding by Burgess and Price (1963) in their national study. They found that of all children receiving AFDC in 1960, 81.5% were born in wedlock while their mothers were not on welfare. Of the 18.5% of births that were illegitimate, only 5.6% occurred while the mother was on welfare. Placek and Hendershot reported similar findings ("Myths about welfare are refuted," 1972).

Additional findings indicate that welfare women were no more likely than nonwelfare women to see their financial condition as relatively good when not pregnant. Women on welfare were no more likely to report having any more uninterrupted periods of intercourse than were others. Contrary to the "brood sow" myth, women on welfare were substantially less likely to stop using contraception than women not on welfare (38% versus 58%). Indeed, with rising pregnancy order, the number of welfare mothers using contraception increased regularly and substantially, indicating that the increased payments with rising family size were not an important motivating factor in becoming pregnant. An important and significant difference between the welfare mothers and nonwelfare mothers was in the proportion who viewed their pregnancies as wanted. Welfare mothers were considerably less likely to want pregnancies than nonwelfare mothers (33% versus 50%). Of the total sample of 300 welfare mothers, 23% said that none of their pregnancies had been wanted; 67% said at least one of their pregnancies had been unwanted. Further, of the 18 mothers who were pregnant at the time of the interview, 12 stated that the pregnancy was unwanted. The overall conclusions drawn from the data indicate that participation in the AFDC program probably does not motivate women to bear more children than they would have otherwise borne. On the contrary, participation in the AFDC program is probably related to "family planning"; that is, practicing contraception and successfully preventing pregnancy.

Studies on family size preferences have consistently indicated that throughout the population, desired family size is between two and four children. In addition, it has been found that preferences are fairly good predictors of fertility behavior. Researchers have hypothesized, however, that this may not be the case for poor, black, lower-class women (Haney, Michielutte, Vincent, & Cochrane, 1973). Indeed, research continues to show that a substantial proportion of lower-class women have more children than they want. The emerging hypothesis, known as "value stretch," states that among this population segment, the degree of commitment to stated size preference is not sufficient for effective contraceptive practice. The value stretch hypothesis posits that for this group the range of values is wider and the commitment to them weaker. Data on family-size preferences and reproductive behavior of 990 black females were examined to test the hypothesis that lower-class women have stretched middle-class values to encompass their behavior, that is, higher fertility. The group interviewed was limited to black women below the poverty line ($3800 for a family of four), and those characterized as lower-middle class.

Findings indicated that the lower-class value stretch of acceptable family size was a relevant concept if restricted to a small part of the population. This included black females who were older and had at some time been married. The authors argue that these attitudes are particularly relevant to a family whose chances for upward mobility become increasingly doubtful. They are reinforced by family size: the more children a woman has, the less her chance for increased education, a better job, and attracting a male of higher economic class. The critical variable, they conclude, may be a women's perception of her chances for improving her life, since it is those who perceive of themselves as "locked into" the lower-class society who may incorporate the value stretch as a means of adaptation.

A study by Beaver and Chapek (1975) has tested to some degree the relationship between fertility and income, including a measure for perceived lifestyle expectations. Measures were expected income of the husband, based on age, occupation, education, etc., as well as such socioeconomic variables as earnings, religiosity, number of children already in the family, and background. The one notable finding in support for the hypothesis of Haney *et al.* was the importance of the measure of lifestyle expectation, that is, the husband's predicted future income, in explaining actual fertility behavior.

Winegarden's 1974 analysis on the fertility of AFDC mothers uses an econometric model that accounts for a variety of effects including welfare-system measures: total grant; welfare availability (as the percentage on welfare of all poor female-headed families with children); and marginal grant for each additional child. He cautions that there are inherent limitations in the data (aggregate and cross-sectional) and in the analytic approach. Nevertheless, within these limits, his study provides the best source of information yet available on the relationship of welfare to fertility patterns.

The results he reported indicate that the size of the welfare grant does not affect the childbearing of AFDC women. Nor does the incremental payment associated with an additional child seem to have any explanatory power. The greater availability of welfare seems to have a small but perceivable effect on the childbearing of welfare women. The elasticity of current fertility with respect to the availability of welfare was estimated to be .23%. This means that a 10% increase in the availability of welfare could result in a 2.3% increase in fertility.

The results suggest, contrary to the expectations of economic theory, that larger payments to welfare families might induce changes in taste away from having children and toward other goals; and that the propensity to have children may in fact be related to the certainty with which welfare assistance can be anticipated rather than the level of that assistance.

> This does not mean that children are conceived as a conscious process of qualifying for welfare payments, but it does suggest that greater accessibility to the AFDC rolls may affect fertility by moderating the expected economic penalties of childbearing under conditions of severe poverty [Winegarden, 1974, p. 165].

Presser and Salsberg (1975) studied 408 women (some receiving and some not receiving welfare) in an attempt to evaluate whether welfare and nonwelfare poor differed in their behavior and attitudes toward family planning and fertility. Of these women, 38% were black and 62% were white; 30% of the total first births were illegitimate. One question was designed to elicit the behavior and attitudes of these women after the birth of their first child. The responses revealed very little support for the contention that the availability of welfare influenced the decisions of those on welfare. Indeed, serious family planning was found to be significantly lacking for both groups. In terms of family size, at the first interview, mothers on welfare indicated that they desired significantly fewer children than did nonwelfare mothers. A second round of interviews, however, revealed that mothers on welfare were more likely to alter their preferences than were the nonrecipients, though the former group still maintained a net desire for fewer children. Data on a subsample of black unmarried mothers, when compared with those for white mothers, revealed no significant differences in the family size desires of mothers on or not on welfare.

Both the groups, welfare recipients and nonrecipients, indicated a remarkable lack of family planning. As many as 25% of nonrecipients and 52% of recipients stated that their first birth had been unplanned. For the subsample of black unmarried mothers, the situation appeared to be far more extreme: 74% of recipients and 93% of nonrecipients reported that their first births had been unplanned. In addition to low motivation for family planning in this subsample, the authors report that lack of knowledge about the subject was also evident.

The authors conclude that welfare is not a critical distinguishing factor in these behaviors. They suggest that poverty itself rather than recipient status may be the key element in fertility patterns. Presser and Salsberg (1975) state: "Early motherhood may be the result of indifference to timing rather than a reflection of a strong commitment to that role. Accordingly, welfare may be viewed as the consequence of an untimely birth rather than a stimulus for that birth [p. 239]."

One of the most profound methodological shortcomings of much of this research is the definition of the populations, both experimental and control. (The tremendous difficulty in defining the welfare population was noted in Chapter 1.) Recent research has clearly shown that the population at risk is far larger than had ever been anticipated. Over a given time frame, there is a great deal of turnover in the rolls, and considerable mobility. Thus, it may not be relevant to talk about the differences between the welfare population and the nonwelfare population at a point in time since the status of many persons may be reversed over some longer time frame. Presser and Salsberg concede this limitation and even document the shifts in their two populations over the two points in the survey (a 1-year interval).

Analysis of the data from the income maintenance experiments in New Jersey provides further evidence. Cain (1974) evaluated the effect of the experiment on the fertility of participating mothers and compared them to a control group over the first 2½ years of the experiment. Find-

ings revealed no apparent differences between the two groups or between families receiving payments of different levels. Educational levels
and wage rates of the women were negatively related to fertility. However, there was no evidence that for poor intact families more generous
benefits led to increased fertility. Cain warns, though, that fertility decisions are generally subject to long-range planning and that data for only
a 2½-year period may not necessarily reflect the impact of transfers on
fertility over a longer period.

The argument about whether welfare or nonwelfare poor women
are more conscientious in carrying out family-planning decisions has
not yet been adequately resolved; and since the daily lives of both
populations exhibit many of the same characteristics, the distinction
may not be meaningful. In any case, a variety of surveys has produced
information on the family planning experiences and attitudes of this
population.

Podell's study, which surveyed welfare mothers in 1969, asked a
detailed series of questions on contraception regarding knowledge, attitudes, and use. His data, however, are not fully representative of the
national populations: a far higher percentage of his sample have more
children then the national average for welfare mothers (U.S. DHEW,
1977). Of his sample, 40% had five or more children. National statistics
indicate that only 10% of all AFDC families have five or more children.
Nevertheless, responses of these mothers to questions about contraceptive knowledge and practices are at least suggestive.

From questions of birth control practices it was discovered that 12%
of the welfare mothers had been surgically sterilized; 5% were pregnant
at the time of the interview; 12% were not having sexual relations; 15%
were aged 45 or older. Of the sample, 28% were not using any form of
contraception, 27% were. Excluding those for whom contraception was
not relevant (older women, sterilized women, and pregnant women),
two noteworthy findings were that education was not found to be related to the practice of birth control and that the younger a woman was,
the more likely she was to practice birth control. Those with more children, especially preschool children, and whose husbands were at home
were far more likely to use birth control. Those who were more likely to
consult other people about their problems, who were more exposed to
the information media (newspapers, magazines, and television), and
who felt bothered by being on welfare, were more likely to use birth
control.

Unlike several other researchers, Podell did not find a generalized
lack of information about family planning among his sample. He found
that 66% of his sample (for whom birth control was applicable) knew

about birth control pills; of those in their teens or twenties, 85% know about the pill. About 70% of the sample knew where they could obtain advice about birth control.

What is most striking about the survey, given the relatively high degree of knowledge and information possessed by the group, was that almost 60 percent of the women responded that if they could plan their child bearing now they would want only two or fewer children. Though black families actually had more children on the average than white families, their preferences tended to be for smaller families than whites. Unmarried mothers tended to want fewer children than other groups. Since most of the welfare mothers in the sample, as well as nationally, have their first child in their teens, it is of considerable value to review briefly some of the information available on the knowledge and birth-control practices of unmarried adolescents.

Furstenberg *et al.* (1969) surveyed 169 unmarried pregnant adolescent girls who had come to a clinic for prenatal care. Over 85% were black and most came from broken, low-income homes. Though there is no information about their welfare status or that of their parents, it is clear from demographic descriptions that they resemble the young welfare mother in many important ways. About 66% of the interviewed girls said they were shocked and upset when they discovered they were pregnant. Only 16% indicated positive feelings toward the pregnancy. The findings support the conclusion, stated earlier in this chapter, that unmarried mothers neither wanted nor anticipated their pregnancies.

Contrary to Podell's findings, in this study it was found that most girls had not attempted to prevent the pregnancies from occurring. Over 25% said they had not thought much about the possibility of becoming pregnant. While 41% reported using some form of birth control, only 22% had ever used a female birth control method, and, in most cases these were confined to the nonprescription forms. Among the girls who used birth control, only 30% used it regularly. Most girls were found to have some knowledge of birth control, and only 7% were unable to define it or mention some type. Few were found to have detailed knowledge however. Many felt birth control was ineffective or inefficient and some mentioned that the pill was unsafe. Most acknowledged the inadequacy of their information and were eager to learn more.

A study by Furstenberg (1971), using a survey of 337 pregnant unmarried black teenagers, supports the picture of inadequate and inaccurate birth-control information. His findings support the contention that the pregnancy, far from being specifically motivated, was the unanticipated result of sexual activity. He concluded that the unwanted pregnancies among teenagers in his sample resulted from their failure to gain adequate information from their mothers. Ignorance was the major reason for nonuse of birth control. Others avoided birth control because of fear that it would harm them. "Despite the strong relationship between attitudes and behavior, it is not clear from the data at hand whether aversion to birth control was a source or consequence of inexperience [p. 196]."

CONCLUSION

Few issues are as significant to economic well-being as that of marital status and family composition. The evidence reviewed in this chapter provided a considerable amount of insight into the dynamics of the recursive nature of family instability and poverty. The family which starts out marginally with respect to income and its correlates is more likely to exhibit the characteristics found to be reliable predictors of family breakups. The employment instability of males is a most important characteristic. Findings from 8 years of PSID data have revealed that changes in the numbers of hours worked are a primary determinant of economic well-being. The instability of employment for low-income workers (underemployment or continual periods of unemployment) proved to be a major predictor of marital instability. Indeed, stability rather than level of income has been found to affect marital instability. Large segments of the low-income population face unstable employment; 20% of the employed heads of households interviewed in the PSID were unable to work as much as they would have liked to.

Age at the time of marriage was also found to be a predictor of family instability. Surveys of welfare mothers show that most married young, often as the result of an unwanted and unanticipated pregnancy. Failure to adopt contraceptive measures may be a major factor in a whole series of events which often result in welfare dependency. This failure not only results in the increased probability of illegitimate pregnancies, but also in increased family size. Earlier chapters have illustrated the profound impact that increased family size has on the probability of remaining poor and going on welfare and on the risk of long-term dependency. Recent studies have also suggested the inhibiting nature of a large family on a mother's probabilities of marriage or remarriage. Fertility of the population at risk may therefore be a critical variable in the dynamic process of economic mobility or its absence for the poor or marginally poor family. The studies reviewed here have indicated a lack of meaningful attitudinal differences among this population as compared with middle-class mothers with respect to family size preferences. The important difference appears to be the amount of information on family planning and its successful use. This appears to be especially critical for the teenage girl. An unwanted pregnancy before she has established the educational background and job history necessary for later economic independence can confer irreversible disadvantages.[14]

The view that welfare itself induces marital instability has had some support from research. Several studies have demonstrated that welfare payments have a small but significant effect on the rate of marital dissolution (e.g., Bernstein & Meezan, 1975; Hoffman & Holmes, 1976). Others have found no such effect. (Cherlin, 1976; Cutright & Scanzoni, 1973; Sawhill et al., 1975).

An emerging theory receiving considerable support is that welfare effects marital stability by reducing a woman's economic dependence on marriage. Research findings have provided support for the hypothesis of a female independence effect; that is, the income or earnings of females (or the availability of welfare benefits) facilitates a woman's exodus from an unsatisfactory relationship by reducing her economic dependence on marriage (Bradbury 1977; Hannan et al., 1977; Hoffman & Holmes 1976; Ross & Sawhill 1975). Welfare in this view provides an option to remaining in an unhappy marriage. Less support has been found for the hypothesis that welfare payments induce the husband of an intact family to desert for reasons of income maximization.

Findings from the Seattle–Denver Income Maintenance experiment support this view. When income maximization incentives were removed through a universal program, marital dissolution rates failed to decline. Indeed, families in the experimental group experienced higher rates of dissolution than comparable controls. Though a variety of explanations exist, one that has gained the most widespread support is the dominance of the female independence effect over the income effect, particularly at lower levels of support.[15]

It appears likely that welfare may act to reduce a woman's economic

14. In a recent study by Moore (1978), findings revealed the mother's age at first birth to be a significant factor in welfare recipiency. In a sample of 50,000 households from the 1976 Current Population Survey, she reported that first births occurred at age 19 or younger for 61% of the welfare mothers as compared with 35% among women living in nonwelfare families.

15. However, these results have confounded most researchers. The expectation of a universal program with benefits comparable to those AFDC was that it would have no impact on dissolution rates if the independence effect dominated, and would reduce dissolution rates if income maximization explained dissolution rates in AFDC. A variety of hypotheses exist to explain the higher rates among the experimental group (see Hannan, Tuma, & Groeneveld, 1977 and MacDonald & Sawhill, 1978.)

dependence on marriage in the same way that a woman's wages do. As a matter of public policy, considerably more research would be necessary to conclude that these separations are negative results; these are marriages of unknown quality. What data do exist (e.g., Bernstein & Meezan, 1975) suggest that providing women with options may result in a more desirable outcome rather than a less desirable one.

Welfare has also been shown to effect the remarriage rates of previously married women and the marriage rates of unmarried women with children. By reducing the economic necessity for marriage, welfare has been shown to result in delay or postponement of marriage for many women. However, this finding is by no means supported by all researchers.

Finally, no definitive evidence is available to support the hypothesis that welfare induces women to bear illegitimate children. Illegitimacy has been found to be the result of unplanned and unanticipated pregnancies, and welfare receipt is more often the result than the cause.

Many of the personal and human capital variables which inhibit economic well-being may be unchangeable for a population at a given point in time. However, some family variables that have an important economic impact on this population may be subject to change at any point in time under policies which affect the distribution and accessibility of family planning services. Government policy that would allocate resources sufficient to prevent unwanted pregnancies would of itself go a long way in intervening in an inevitable progression to poverty, instability, and dependency.[16]

16. Moore (1978) estimates that there are 1.6 million sexually active teenage women who are not currently receiving family planning services.

4

Health

The importance of health factors in the actual and potential dependency of the population at risk has been shown in Chapters 1 and 2. Most studies that assess the employability of the welfare population have considered the presence and degree of physical limitations as a factor related to an individual's probability of seeking and obtaining employment. What has been most disturbing about the research has been its failure to sort out the relative significance of ill health as a causal factor in poverty. Clearly, inability to sustain adequate employment because of health limitations has a good deal to do with welfare dependency and poverty. Nevertheless, there is considerable support for the opposite argument that the correlates of poverty themselves provide a causal link to illness.

Much of the data on the incidence of health conditions that limit employment among persons on welfare come from surveys made of welfare recipients. In fact, knowledge about the seriousness of health problems among the welfare poor is generally dependent upon their self-assessments. There has been considerable scepticism about the accuracy of these data because there is reason to believe that recipients may see illness as a justification or rationalization of their unemployed status rather than as the objective cause. Some researchers have argued that there may be a considerable unconscious need among welfare recipients to define their unemployment as health determined because society views illness and disability more sympathetically and sees it as more legitimate than failure to work (Roe & Eickwort, 1974).

Sources of knowledge and appropriate interpretive techniques on "objective" health indicators are still very limited. Nevertheless, the issues related to the health status of the welfare poor appear to be so important in understanding their dependency that review and analysis of the best indicators and explanations are necessary. Whether ill health is a cause of continued and persistent dependency or its result, its incidence has a great deal to do with the work and welfare patterns of the population at risk. The provision and use of health care services will in part indicate the present and future employment patterns of AFDC families (Lowenthal, 1971). To be sure, the use of such services has considerable impact on the future health status of the heads of recipient families and, more importantly, of their children. Medical problems are very frequently cited as the reason for the opening of welfare cases (Rydell et al., 1974). Recent research has also been able to identify convincing links between health and achievement in school. Clearly, educational success has important implications for the employment status and later level of economic well-being of families. Health may best be seen as one critical intervening variable of the many that relate to work and welfare.

Statistical information on the objective incidence and the severity of illness among the poverty population is generally developed using indicators from national health surveys. Far fewer data have been available for the welfare population exclusively. Nevertheless, since health problems may be precipitants to welfare status and may also be reinforced by the circumstances of poverty, a consideration of data on poverty groups in general permits useful generalizations for welfare families as well. Research on inadequate nutrition reveals that the poor are at far greater risk than higher-income groups. The consequences of poor nutrition among poverty groups are often severe and often complicate and induce significant chronic health disabilities. Nutrition therefore becomes a topic of importance in understanding the health status of the poor.

The percentage of low-income people who experience chronic and nonchronic disease is higher than the percentage in other groups.[1] Ill-

1. The 1975 Health Survey (U.S. DHEW, 1976) indicated that for people between the ages of 45 and 65, the prevalence of chronic conditions (e.g., arthritis, diabetes, hearing and visual impairment, heart condition and hypertension) remains two to three times higher for low-income people than for others.

ness is generally more severe for the poor than for other groups. Proper medical care at the appropriate time can in many cases alter the probability of long-run disabling conditions for low-income families. A study cited by Davis and Schoen (1978) found that among low-income 18-year-olds who were rejected by the Selective Service, 33% of the health conditions identified could have been prevented or corrected had they been treated before the age of 9. As many as 62% could have been prevented if they had been treated before the age of 15 [p. 83]. The health care system has the potential to reverse or at least minimize the fundamental health disadvantages with which poor families start out. Poor families, many researchers agree, underuse or misuse available health services. Their decisions about the timing, frequency, and nature of their contacts with the health care system are thought to be different from those of middle-class families. A thorough examination of the factors that lead poor people to use health care facilities may substantially improve understanding of the present and future health status of the poor.

Researchers generally use two interrelated models to explain variations in the use of health services among different groups. The first stresses the importance of the social and economic characteristics of the population of the potential user. Use of health services is the last step in a decision making process begun when an individual identifies an existing condition as illness, decides that it requires professional care, and then selects a health agent of a particular sort—private doctor, specialist, clinic, emergency room. Socioeconomic and cultural factors are thought to influence decisions at several distinct points. The second model strongly emphasizes variables related to the structure of the delivery system: cost, organization, access, availability. Because of external factors, the poor are seen to use health services less than the middle class. Clearly, the appropriateness of either model implies the use of very different options for intervention. Socioeconomic and cultural variables are not easily altered; they remain fixed in the population over a period of time. Characteristics of the system, however, can be altered through public policy.

This chapter will first examine the current health of the poverty population, paying particular attention (where the data permit) to the special health problems of the welfare population. Second, an attempt will be made to assess the success of the socioeconomic and cultural model in explaining the nature and the degree to which health care services are used by the poor. Finally, the delivery system model will be introduced; an attempt will be made to assess its importance in explaining present patterns of use and possible alterations for the future.

HEALTH DEFINITIONS

Good health remains a multidimensional concept, sensitive to many cultural variations. Conceptual difficulties arise in any attempt to develop a criterion of good health from which specific deviations among the poverty population can be measured. Health status is not only variable by income but by initial health, environment, and the individual's position in the life cycle. Some phases of life are more apt to be free from health problems than others (Boaz, 1977). The poor health of low-income populations is generally inferred from a variety of indicators. Research has shown that assessments of health are often socially defined and vary according to the specific social and/or professional setting. This must be remembered in attempts to evaluate the reliability of client health surveys; cultural and social differences in defining health remain important in predicting variations among different populations regarding decisions to seek care.

The clinical definition of health, to which most practicing physicians subscribe, apparently differs greatly from lay definitions. Some conditions defined as illness in some settings are accepted as "natural" in other settings (Kosa & Zola, 1975). Inconsistencies between self-reported incidence figures and those based on clinical examinations appear to be quite profound, even for specific conditions which would appear to provide little room for confusion (Birch & Gussow, 1972). Extreme conditions, such as a temperature of 105 degrees, and a broken leg, and loss of sight, are obviously identified as serious by all groups. However, only about 5% of the general population ever experience such significant symptoms (Kosa & Zola, 1975). Many experience a variety of nondisabling illnesses and symptomatic episodes. Survey data on the incidence of these illnesses and symptoms are often at odds with data from other measures of objective health status.

MEASURING HEALTH STATUS

Clients' self-assessments are difficult to interpret because of the role social and cultural factors play in identification of illness. Standard objective measures provide other sorts of conceptual difficulties for interpretation. Data provided by findings of clinical examinations on the variations of health status among the general population suffer from a variety of sampling problems. Since the poor and middle class seldom use the same types of health service, few sites provide the opportunity to select a random sample for clinical examination. Comparisons of data from different populations using the same site rarely exist. Problems of this sort have made most analysts dependent on secondary data provided by national surveys.

Rates of use of health services often provide a basis for measuring the variation of illness among different population groups. For example, data from the 1973 Health Interview Survey (U.S. DHEW, 1973a) reveal important differences in hospital utilization rates by income group. Children in low-income groups were reported to have had twice as many hospital days as those in upper-income groups. Adults in low-income groups have 2½ more hospital days than those in upper-income groups. Though these data suggest that the poor are twice as sick as the well-off, this conclusion cannot be so easily made. The data provide no information about objective needs among the two groups. Are members of both groups experiencing the same sorts of conditions in the same severity when entering the hospital? Do other factors prompt lower-income people to use hospitals for conditions that other groups handle through ambulatory care? These issues become more important when utilization rates for private physicians are used as indices for health status. Do high utilization rates reflect greater objective need, greater illness? or do low utilitization rates reflect deteriorating health through nontreatment and lack of preventive care?

Davis and Reynolds (1977) recognize the limitations of utilization rates as valid measures of need. Using data from the 1969 Health Interview Survey, these researchers made a crude adjustment of private physician utilization rates, controlled for the greater level of need that poor people have. The adjustment for health status results in a striking change in patterns of utilization rates between income classes. The findings show that when initial health status is controlled for, utilization rates increase uniformly with income. Welfare families eligible for medicaid use physician services about as often as middle-income families with comparable health problems. However, poor persons lag substantially behind other poor and middle-income persons in the use of services.

There is an absence of any knowledge of patient need when evaluating the usefulness of a measure based on hospital or physician visits. Perhaps no generally accepted measure of need exists. Nevertheless, several researchers have attempted to develop better measures of health status than utilization rates. Aday (1975) suggests that disability days are more useful than medical utilization rates to measure health variations. After consideration of many other measures (e.g., health level and symptoms), some analysts argue that a measure of disability days is most related to service use, as compared with all other measures of need; incapacity and pain are the layperson's most obvious indicators that medical care is needed. Nevertheless, using diability days as a measure of illness is not without limitations. This measure does not capture qualitative distinctions in the condition limiting a person's normal activities, though the total number of days may reflect the severity of the condition.[2] Disability days caused by cancer differ qualitatively from those caused by a common cold. Allen (1974) points to the variation in the health status of the poor as compared with that of the general population. Data from a 1971 survey indicated that the general population averaged 6.1 "bed disability days";[3] those with incomes of less than $3000 a year averaged 12.6 days a year.

The incidence of chronic or nonchronic illness is commonly used to distinguish how various subsets of the population fare. The 1973 National Health Survey defined chronic disabling conditions as those which prevent individuals from performing their major occupation (e.g., employment, housework). On the basis of survey data, it was found that of all American adults (ages 45–64), 4% had chronic medical problems; of those below the poverty line, 16%—four times as many— had chronic medical problems.

The incidence of chronic disease among the poverty population is particularly important; it virtually excludes the possibility of employment sufficient for self-support. However, available cross-sectional data do not clarify whether the incidence of chronic illness can explain the poverty of those who experience it, or whether poverty itself produces the preconditions for chronic disease. It seems likely that both effects are present.

Perhaps the most objective measure of a populations's health status is the mortality rate. Mortality rates measure the proportion of individuals in a specific population who died from particular diseases. Table 4.1 reveals that the death rates from a wide range of causes are higher for the poor, especially the nonwhite poor, than for other populations. Comparative mortality rates are of great value; other data on the variation of the incidence of disease are subject to unreliability—errors of diagnosis, classification, and misreporting. However, death rates are not subject to individual judgment. They provide the best objective source of data for the discovery of variations in the greatest health risks to which population subsets are subject (Birch & Gussow, 1972).

Many health researchers claim that infant mortality is the best indi-

2. This may be especially true if an individual is willing to lose a day's wages. For those jobs not having sick pay, one can assume that the individual perceives the condition as serious enough to require attention.

3. Days per year in which a person is confined to bed by illness or injury.

TABLE 4.1

Vital Statistics Measures for the United States by Poverty Status of Residence and Color for 19 Selected Cities, 1969-1971[a]

Vital statistics	United States, 1969–1971	Total all cities			Poverty areas[b]			Nonpoverty areas		
		Total	White	All other	Total	White	All other	Total	White	All other
Mortality:										
Crude death rate (per 1000 population)[c]	9.5	10.9	11.8	8.9	12.0	14.6	10.5	10.6	11.3	6.7
Births:										
Crude birth rate (per 1000 population)	17.9	17.9	15.6	23.9	23.5	21.6	24.6	16.1	14.7	23.1
Infant mortality rate (per 1000 live births)	20.0	23.2	18.6	30.7	30.2	24.2	33.4	19.7	17.4	27.0
Low birth weight (2500 gms. or less; per 100 live births)	7.9	9.9	7.4	13.9	13.1	9.3	15.1	8.3	7.0	12.4
Lack of prenatal care (live births to mothers with no care; per 100 live births)	1.7	2.8	1.9	4.2	5.0	4.2	5.3	1.8	1.5	2.8
Death rate for T.B. (per 100,000 population)	2.5	4.7	3.5	7.5	9.5	8.7	10.0	3.0	2.8	4.3

Source: U.S. Department of Health, Education and Welfare, Selected vital and health statistics in poverty and nonpoverty areas of 19 large cities; National Center for Health Statistics, Rockville, Md., November 1975, p. 6.

[a] Cities: Atlanta, Baltimore, Buffalo, Chicago, Cincinnati, Cleveland, Dallas, Denver, Indianapolis, Los Angeles, Memphis, Minneapolis, New York, Philadelphia, Pittsburgh, San Diego, San Francisco, Seattle, and Washington, D.C.

[b] Areas of residence were classified as poverty or nonpoverty on the basis of U.S. Bureau of Census definitions.

[c] In recent years there have been divergences between the crude death rate and the age-adjusted death rate. As birth rate declines, the average age of the population rises. With old people accounting for a larger share of the population, the proportion of deaths automatically rises. Therefore, in comparing populations of markedly different age distributions, it is preferable to look at age-adjusted death rates or life expectancy rates (David & Schoen, 1977). These, however, were not available for comparative purposes here.

cator of health status. It is argued that the rate at which infants die in a population is an indicator of the health hazards to which all are exposed.

So strong is this association between a people's health status and the rate of survival of its infants, that the infant mortality rate of any population and the direction and speed of its change are generally acknowledged to be among the most highly sensitive indicators of the present and future well-being of that group [Birch & Gussow, 1972, p. 13].

Table 4.1 summarizes a considerable amount of statistical data and provides some evidence on the health correlates of poverty. For all health indicators, residents in poverty areas exhibit a consistently higher incidence of conditions threatening to life. The infant mortality rate is 30% higher in poverty areas than in comparable nonpoor areas; the proportion is even higher for nonwhite residents of poverty areas.

Infants with low birth weights are born 30% more often to residents of poverty areas than to residents of nonpoverty areas. Nonwhite residents of poverty areas have more than twice as many children with low birth weights as compared with white residents of nonpoverty areas. On all objective health indicators presented, residents of poverty areas fare poorly, Nonwhite poverty-area residents fare the worst.

Health status can be measured or at least indicated in a variety of ways. In virtually every case, the data provide dramatic evidence of the health condition of the poverty population. In general, the poor experience greater severity of illness for longer periods of time than do comparable groups in the general population; they die younger; and they appear to receive less medical care in terms of their objective needs.

NUTRITION: A CAUSAL FACTOR

The conditions typical of poverty (crowded, dilapidated, unsanitary housing, inadequate diet, etc.) appear not only to exacerbate illnesses generally distributed throughout the population, but to produce additional pathologies, such as lead poisoning, infection from vermin, and rodent bites, that are all largely restricted to the poor. Reviews of the literature on the health status of the poor reveal much evidence linking nutritional deficiencies with a variety of serious and often irreparable physical and mental deficiencies. Many of the behavioral manifestations attributed to poor children and traditionally thought of to be of cultural origin are currently being rediagnosed as organic conditions induced by poor nutrition.

Though sound evidence appears to link other medical problems directly to the conditions of poverty, this discussion will consider only the incidence and consequences of conditions induced by poor nutrition. There are four reasons for this decision: first, nutrition problems are subject to policy intervention; second, data are generally available and interpretable; third, the consequences of inadequate nutrition appear to explain other problems associated with the poor (failure in school, mental retardation, high incidence of chronic medical conditions, etc.); and finally, public welfare policies already extend to subsidizing the diets of poor families. Even within the poverty population, the extent and degree of dietary inadequacy varies. Though income is important in explaining the incidence of malnourishment, education has proven to be a strong predictor also.

NUTRITIONAL STATUS

Few Americans have access to any direct means of measuring their nutritonal status. However, the media have heightened public awareness of the health consequences of poor nutrition. Though many know the consequences of poor nutrition, few are able to identify a medical condition as caused or exacerbated by inadequate diet. Professionals are seldom able to help. Those making medical examinations rarely inquire into patients' nutritional status, even though poor diet may have been a causal factor in the symptoms the individual came to have treated.

Extensive research on both animal and patient populations is providing valuable findings that result in more uniform standards of dietary adequacy. Based on these standards, the 1974 HANES Report (U.S. DHEW, 1974) found the poverty population to be at a greater "nutritional risk" than other groups.[4] (Table 4.2 presents some key findings.) The HANES Report (1971–1972 data) found great deficiencies of vitamin and mineral intake in the diet of Americans. Though biochemical measurement showed that deficiencies in nutrition were often high in groups above the poverty level, the report concluded that the poverty population was much "worse off."

In 1968, the United States Department of Agriculture published *Dietary Levels of Households in the U.S.* This report showed a high prevalence of poor diets in families living on incomes under $3000 a year. It

4. Nutritional risk was defined as insufficient dietary intake of vitamins A, C, and B-6, thiamine, riboflavin, iron, and/or calcium. The *Preliminary Findings of the First Health and Nutritional Examination Survey* . . . (U.S. DHEW, 1974) clearly shows that the greater percentage of persons with intakes less than the standard in groups with incomes below the poverty level constitutes a nutritional risk.

TABLE 4.2

Comparison of Percentage of Persons with Nutrient Values Less Than Standard, and Mean Nutrient Intake as a Percentage of Standard, by Race, Age, and Sex for Income Levels

| | Percentage of persons with intakes less than standard | | | |
| | Whites | | Blacks | |
Age, sex, and dietary element	Above poverty level	Below poverty level	Above poverty level	Below poverty level
1–5 years, both sexes:				
Vitamin A	37	52	51	46
Calcium	12	14	25	35
Iron	95	94	95	94
18–44 years, female:				
Vitamin A	65	74	67	64
Calcium	56	56	72	75
Iron	92	94	95	95

Source: U.S. Department of Health, Education and Welfare, Public Health Service, *Preliminary findings of the First Health and Nutrition Examination Survey, United States, 1971–1972* dietary intake and biochemical Findings, Rockville, Md: National Center for Health Statistics, 1974, Table B, p. 19.

concluded that the adequacy of a family diet was directly related to income level as shown in Figure 4.1. The Senate Select Committee, citing the same publication, reported that household surveys conducted in the spring of 1965 found that only 9% of the families with annual incomes of $10,000 had "poor diets."[5] The proportion of poor diets increased regularly with each reduction in income level: 10% of the families in the income range of $5000 to $6999; 36% of families earning under $3000.

Poor people consistently exhibit higher levels of health deficiencies related to poor nutrition. A 1966 study of the Headstart Program (a program for culturally disadvantaged preschoolers) reported that 80% of the participating children had high levels of iron-deficiency anemia (Mermann, 1966); there were similar findings in surveys by the Child Development Group of Mississippi in 1967, and in a study of poor children in a Los Angeles County pediatric emergency room (Wingert, Friedman, & Larson, 1968). Studies of six elementary schools (on the Lower East Side in New York City and in Boston's Roxbury section) led to similar conclusions.

5. Poor diets are those containing less than 66% of the recommended allowance of one or more essential nutrient.

Good diets   Poor diets

	Good diets		Poor diets
under $3000	37%	27%	36%
$3000–$4999	43%	33%	24%
$5000–$6999	53%	29%	18%
$7000–$9999	56%	32%	12%
$10,000 and over	63%	28%	9%

FIGURE 4.1. *Income and quality of diets. Good diets are those which met recommended dietary allowances for seven nutrients. Poor diets had less than two-thirds of the allowances for from one to seven nutrients.* [*From* Poverty, Malnutrition, and Federal Food Assistance Programs: A Statistical Summary, *U.S. Senate, Select Committee on Nutrition and Human Needs, September 1969, p. 5, in* Food Stamps and Nutrition *by K. Clarkson, Washington, D.C.: American Enterprise Institute for Public Policy Research, 1975, Figure D-1, p. 76.*]

The New York City study examined the clinical and dietary status of 642 poor school children aged 10–13. The diets of 71% of the children participating were evaluated as "poor"; the diets of only 7% percent were evaluated as "excellent." Parental permission was required in order for children to participate, and as a result, only 45% of the total population was sampled. Considerable suspicion exists that those most likely to show the most extreme nutritional deficiencies were not adequately represented in the sample (Christakis, Miridjanian, Nath, Khurana, Cowell, Archer, Frank, Ziffer, Baker, & James 1968). Although only 19% of the sample were children from welfare families, results nevertheless indicated that the probability of nutritional deficiency was higher for the children in welfare families than for the rest of the children.

The Harvard University School of Public Health studied children in the Roxbury section of Boston to evaluate the adequacy of their diets and their nutritional status (Myers, O'Brien, Mabel, & Stare, 1968). The sample included 332 fourth, fifth, and sixth graders, of whom about 66% were black. Researchers provided ratings for the nutritional soundness of the children's meals over a 4-day period. For breakfast, 54% of the children failed to get satisfactory ratings; similarly, 60% had unsatisfactory lunches, and 42% had unsatisfactory dinners. The younger the child, the less likely he or she was to have satisfactory ratings. Blacks were less likely to have satisfactory ratings than whites.

Studies revealing the dietary inadequacy of children abound (Filer

& Martinez, 1964; *Hunger, USA,* 1968; U.S. Senate, 1969, and 1973a). There is good reason to believe that existing surveys underrepresent the nutritionally "worse off." Because poor families generally underuse service agencies from which many of these studies select their samples, they have a far lower probability of being sampled. Very poor children are less likely to see doctors, and nonreponse and unreliable data are far more likely to be a problem in studies of the very poor. Thus, current findings on the incidence and severity of malnourishment for the welfare population and other very deprived groups may grossly underestimate the seriousness of the problem. Though surveys do not indicate the precise degree and extent of nutritional inadequacy among groups with the lowest income, recent research continues to note the significant incidence of infant mortailty caused by this inadequacy, and of the inhibited physical and mental growth and development among poverty groups. Available documentation is reviewed in the next section.

SOME CONSEQUENCES OF POOR NUTRITION

Most researchers on nutrition agree that malnutrition is linked with poverty and that it has a synergistic relationship with disease. Among serious and often irreparable conditions which malnutrition causes among the poor are low birth weight, infant mortality, mental retardation, intellectual malfunction, and many varieties of deficiencies in development and growth. In most cases, these conditions, largely traceable to nutritional inadequacies, are exhibited in far higher proportions by poor people. The time at which malnutrition occurs in the life cycle affects the physical and mental consequences, the seriousness, and the reversibility or nonreversibility of the resulting condition. Malnutrition during fetal formation and infant development has the most dramatic consequences. If the mother lacks a proper diet prior to and during pregnancy, the fetus will be denied essential nutrition and an unhealthy infant will be born. Many such infants die in the early weeks or months after birth; those that survive are often permanently damaged through stunted body size and retarded brain development. Although our present concern is what happens to the children of poorly nourished mothers, note should be made of the dangers to the lives of women in their childbearing years.

A variety of factors contribute to the probability of producing normal, healthy offspring. Clearly, predisposing genetic factors are very important. However, for a great many environmental reasons, poor women have far higher incidences of birth complications and resulting biological risks than other groups. Over three times as many poor and nonwhite mothers die from pregnancy complications. The poor often live in conditions hostile to life, where risk of disease is greater. Two ciritical factors that public policy can address affect the probability of a woman producing a healthy child: preconceptual and prenatal medical care, and good nutrition. Medical care during and prior to pregnancy can often correct or prevent diseases and conditions hazardous to both infant and mother. (Barriers to proper health care for the low-income population will be discussed in a later section). The vital statistics in Table 4.1 provide strong evidence for the differences in the use of pre-natal care between women in poverty and nonpoverty areas. When women are poor, lack of adequate medical care severely worsens their disadvantaged status.

In its report *To Save the Children . . .* , the Senate Select Committee (U.S. Senate, 1974) stated:

> At the lowest income level (under $3000) 10% of all infants born weighed 2500 grams or less—the level considered premature—compared to 8% or less at higher income levels. Infants of normal birth weight or above (3000 grams +) constitute only 69% of all infants born in families with income under $3,000–$4,999; 75% of those with $5,000–$6,999; 76% of those with $7,000–$9,999; and 79% of those with $10,000 and over incomes (p. 8).

The proportion of births of normal weight or above rises directly with income, and low birth weight is a primary factor in infant mortality.

The timing and nature of medical care for expectant mothers, as mentioned earlier, have important effects on the probable health status of mothers and infants; these factors have a crucial relationship to the incidence of children with low birth weights as well. The National Center for Health Statistics (cited in Kehrer & Wolin, 1976) estimated that of 4 million women who gave birth in 1963, only 21% had seen a physician or had gone to a medical facility during the 3 months before conception. The percentage of women receiving medical attention prior to the beginning of the second trimester of pregnancy increases with income. Of the women with incomes of less than $3000 who had babies in 1963, only 4.25% had visited a physician or medical facility by their second trimester, as compared with 76.3% for women with incomes of $10,000 and over. Conditions appear to be improving, and more recent data indicates increasing use of prenatal care by low income women. Data from 1971 shows that although poor women are still 20% less likely to have seen a physician early in their pregnancy, as many as 71% sought prenatal care early in their pregnancies in 1971 (U.S. DHEW, 1972).

Low Birth Weight and Related Illnesses. Many health problems are associated with low birth weight. During the first year of life, the risk of death is 30 times greater for such babies than for babies weighing a normal 5.5 pounds; and when they do survive, they are twice as likely to have birth defects (U.S. Senate, 1974). In addition, the effects seem to persist far beyond infancy, appearing as long-term physical or intellectual disabilities. The evidence shows that such children suffer more physical and neurological handicaps, including mental retardation, and that the incidence of blindness is two to three times higher. Schaefer, director of DHEW-funded nutrition survey, found that 70—80% of the children suffering from mental retardation come from economically disadvantaged homes (U.S. Senate 1974). The great majority of researchers consider poor maternal nutrition and low birth weight to be central causal factors for this. Following children over time who had been malnourished at various ages, Graham concluded that those malnourished in their youngest years had the poorest prognosis for full physical and mental recovery and growth (Graham, 1966).

The mental development of malnourished children is marked by irritability, unresponsiveness, and apathy (Birch & Gussow, 1972). During periods of chronic malnutrition, children have a reduced ability to respond appropriately to significant stiumuli in their environment; and continued malnutrition is accompanied by progressive behavioral regression. The nation's school breakfast and lunch programs were legislated partly in recognition of these relationships. Of most concern is the widespread observation that *children who are stunted or who have been exposed to the risk of malnutrition are overrepresented among groups who experience failure in school.*

In their longitudinal study of children with low birth weights, Rubin, Rosenblatt, and Balow (1973) found that such children scored significantly lower in the areas of intelligence, language development, and academic achievement. Having found low birth weight to be associated with impaired school progress, the authors concluded that weight was a major correlate of neurological, psychological, and educational impairment and that male and female children with low birth weights constituted a high risk population in terms of eventual impairment in their functioning in school.

Read (of the National Institute of Child Health and Human Development) reported (1969) that in cases of acute malnutrition, personality changes occur that result in depressed levels of intellectual functioning. Studies maintain that after normal or adequate nutrition is restored to malnourished children, scores for language improve more slowly than do scores for adaptive behavior. Studies of Chilean children have shown that when severely malnourished infants are rehabilitated, they have I.Q. scores lower than adequately nourished children. Interpretation of these findings is limited, however, by the inability to assess the relative importance of early childhood malnutrition and genetic factors in explaining I.Q. The degree to which early growth traumas can be reversed is not clear. Many contend that probability of successful reversal is dependent upon the age at which the severe malnourishment occurred. It appears unlikely that the physical and mental consequences of nutritional deprivation in the first 18 months of life can be reversed (Winick & Cooobs, 1972).

It is generally accepted that somewhat over 70% of the children suffering from mental retardation come from economically disadvantaged families; and there is a great deal of evidence that the poor nutrition of both mother and infant can explain these mental deficiencies. Researchers have not been able to control for a variety of environmental, cultural, and social factors that may also affect the mental and behavioral functioning of poor children. Since statistical associations for human subjects are subject to difficulties in interpretation, researchers have depended on the results of animal studies, where strict scientific conditions can be met so that more evidence can be provided on the developmental consequences of inadequate nutrition during the critical periods of growth.

A variety of controlled experiments with rats provided evidence regarding brain damage. A study by Winick and Coombs (1972) on the mental development of rats showed that early malnutrition curtailed both protein and DNA synthesis, resulting in permanently underdeveloped brains, with fewer cells of normal size. In a study of malnourished rats, they found certain reflexes and physical movements to be impaired. Other animal studies have provided additional support for the assumed relationship evident in human subjects. Restricted nutritional intake during the period of maximum brain growth results in a decrease in the rate of development, in neuromotor abilities, and in learning capacity. Genetic changes that suggest the intergenerational consequences of nutritional deprivation have also been found (Cowley & Griesel, 1966, Dickerson & McCance, 1960; Platt, Heard, & Steward 1964). In general, studies using animals further reinforce the significant consequences of poor nutrition for growth and development; the most dramatic include low birth weight, retardation of both mental and physical functioning, and, in severe cases, the tendency for these organic changes to have intergenerational consequences. Other less permanent and less irreparable damage can also be observed in poverty populations.

Anemia. A national nutrition survey directed by Shaefer and con- ducted by the Public Health Service of DHEW reported on all indices of malnutrition (U.S., Senate, 1974). In an analysis of preliminary data, Shaefer found "an alarming prevalence of characteristics associated with undernourished groups [p. 2]." Findings revealed, more specifically, that 15% of those studied were anemic, having homoglobin levels so low as to require medical attention; the figure for children under 6 was 33% of the 12,000 individuals surveyed: 80% had family incomes below $5000.

Although it has been argued that anemia in children has an irrever- sible effect on I.Q., Edwards, a DHEW official (1974), testifying before the Senate Select Committee on Nutrition and Human Needs, described the relationship as only marginal on the basis of a variety of research efforts on malnourished children. The more immediate consequences, however, are a variety of behavioral manifestations and the predisposi- tion of anemic children to illness and even death. Whether or not anemia impairs intellectual functioning, considerable evidence suggests that it interferes with learning. Edwards argued that DHEW's 10-state nutritional survey revealed iron-deficiency anemia to be the most fre- quently encountered nutrition problem among infants and young chil- dren. He further described the behavioral consequences of anemia on children: "Anemic preschool children exhibit apathetic and irritable behaviors. They also differ from nonanemic preschool children in atten- tiveness, distractability and attention span [U.S. Senate, 1973a, p. 125]."

Impressive findings were published on the potential impact of fed- eral food assistance plans to offset or reverse many of the most prevalent effects of inadequate nutrition on poor children. Kafatos and Zee (1977) conducted two surveys among a sample of 4000 black preschool children from low-income families in Memphis; the initial survey was in 1969, the followup in 1972. The original sample was selected for participation in a Department of Agriculture supplementary food program betweeen 1969 and 1972, and 250 children who had been interviewed and exam- ined in 1969 were reexamined in 1972 for the purpose of evaluating the impact of improved nourishment on their health. The findings were dramatic for two reasons. First, they demonstrated strongly the relation- ship between poor nutrition and many physical and mental conditions among poverty children; second, simple and direct forms of interven- tion, such as food assistance programs were shown to have impressive positive effects on the health status of poor children.

Kafatos and Zee compared the sample children before and after participation in the food assistance programs to see the degree to which they deviated from normal distributions in weight, height, hemoglobin and hematocrit scores, and frequencies of low blood levels of vitamins A and C. After controlling for changes in community conditions (median income and family size), they found definite nutritional improvement in the study group. The high incidence of retarded height and weight first noted in 1969 was significantly lowered in 1972. In fact, the 1972 distribution closely resembled a normal distribution for healthy white children. Anemia, found in 25% of the sample children in 1969, was found in only 11% in 1972. The authors recognize the limitations of their findings: they were unable to monitor the actual daily food intake of each child. However, they assert their confidence that the observed nutritional improvements are the result of food and nutrition intervention programs.[6]

Strong conclusions can be drawn that the inadequate diet and nutrition of poor families have profound temporary and permanent effects on their chances for economic self-sufficiency. Indeed, the consequences of poor health and inadequate nutrition reinforce one another and have significant consequences for success in school and employment thereafter. The data have not demonstrated that these conditions alone determine welfare receipt; nevertheless, the severe disabilities which these conditions place on their victims doubtless explain a good portion of the progressive and multiple disadvantages of many welfare families.

Increased income and specific government food programs have been directly linked to improved health indicators. However, the availability and the level of government resources have not been sufficient to ensure poor families of freedom from health disabilities associated with nutritional inadequacy. Many of these problems may be subject to prevention and control through proper medical attention; however, many of the data on the use of medical services indicate that poor families receive far less care than their conditions objectively require. Explanations of this lack of use of medical services are a prerequisite in defining appropriate policy intervention. The following section, therefore, explores the evidence on the use of health services and assesses current models available to explain variations in such use among the poor.

UTILIZATION OF HEALTH CARE SERVICES AMONG THE POOR

The previous sections have demonstrated that the poor fare far worse than other population groups on most measures of health status.

6. A recent study of poor families indicated that participants in the Food Stamp Program had higher levels of nutritional adequacy than nonparticipants (Lane, 1975). However, other studies contradict these findings (see Clarkson, 1975).

Data collected at regular intervals by the National Center for Health Statistics continue to reinforce the common perceptions that the poor have a higher incidence of all kinds of health problems. They consistently exhibit higher rates in the incidence of heart problems, emphysema, visual impairments, and chronic and disabling diseases. Although data gathered over the last decade, since the passage of legislation for medicaid benefits, confirm great progress in the increased use of health services by the assisted-poor, the objective rate of the incidence of disease among the poor remains much higher. Services are therefore still comparatively underused. The Federal Government has greatly increased medicaid expenditures, but the benefits have been unevenly enjoyed by the poor. Many of the conditions related to poverty and their consequences (described in the previous section) have long-range and permanent effects; in addition, the poor are less likely to seek and receive care for many medical conditions to which all people are prone, regardless of income status.

Much evidence exists to support the assumption that receiving appropriate treatment from a suitable provider at the proper time has a great deal to do with the objective health status of any population group. It is even more important for a group in which the incidence of poor health is great.

SOCIOECONOMIC DETERMINANTS OF HEALTH CARE
UTILIZATION

A number of models in the literature of medical sociology explain the variations in utilization of health care services on the basis of socioeconomic and cultural variables (Mechanic, 1975a; McKinlay, 1972; Suchman, 1965a,b). Unfortunately, considerably more is known about those who seek care than about those who do not. Nevertheless, many surveys have been done of groups known to be chronic underusers. Analyses of survey findings reveal a variety of critical determinants of health care behavior. In general, research findings demonstrate that demand and supply factors combine to explain decisions about health care.

Much of the literature emphasizes the direct relationship between specific types of help-seeking behavior and socioeconomic, demographic, and environmental variables. (Nelson, 1976). Nelson posits a model of general help-seeking behavior that stresses the existence of a variety of stages in the decision making process that may result in seeking help (see Figure 4.2). Most researchers who identify such a temporal process introduce and test general lists of requirements which

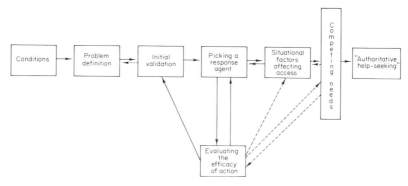

FIGURE 4.2. *A minimal "model" of the help-seeking process.* [From B. Nelson, On Becoming a Client: Authoritative Help-Seeking as Dependent Participation, *paper prepared for World Congress of International Political Science Association, Edinburgh, Scotland, 1976, p. 10.*]

must be met before an individual moves through the process and seeks help. Research findings suggest that these socioeconomic and environmental variables are critical in explaining the likelihood, the timing, and the nature of an individual's use of health care services.

For organizational convenience, this discussion separates explanations of demand and supply factors and is limited to an assessment of the usefulness of variables pertaining to demand in explaining utilization patterns; but it should be clear that they alone are not sufficient. Socioeconomic, cultural, and institutional variables are often mutually reinforcing, and in reality factors of supply and demand are highly interrelated. For example, an individual's attitudes and perceptions about the value of a physician's care and the probability that the individual will seek such care may be explained by education and the norms of the cultural environment; but prior experiences, such as unresponsive or impersonal treatment and long traveling time, may serve to reinforce a cultural predisposition toward nonuse. It will be demonstrated that by themselves determinants related to the system and to individuals are not sufficient to explain existing patterns. Present configurations of socioeconomic factors and characteristics of the delivery system interact together so as to produce the resulting use of health care services by the poor.

Education. For the poor, utilization of the medical system can have a variety of meanings—from talking to the local pharmacist to being admitted to a hospital. For the purposes of this discussion, we will be concerned with the utilization of conventional medical care services.

Most of the research has shown that an individual's educational level has a significant relation to attitudes about and perceptions of conventional medical care. Education has been found to be an important factor in determining the time at which an individual will enter the medical system and the type of care sought. A classic study by Suchman (1965b), for example, revealed that the less educated, blue-collar, low-income population is less informed about disease, holds more unfavorable attitudes toward professional medicine, and is more dependent upon lay support during illness. Education appeared to be the variable most highly related to willingness to seek medical care.

The median level of educational attainment among welfare family heads is substantially lower than that of the general working population. Table 2.1 in Chapter 2 confirmed that welfare mothers were twice as likely to have had less than an eighth-grade education as compared with all females in the labor force. Welfare fathers were three times as likely to have had less than an eighth-grade education as compared with males in the general labor force.

In a study of the health status of welfare mothers, Roe and Eickwort (1974) found the education of the sample women to be a major determinant of their health status and their health care patterns. All women were or had been on welfare in the recent past. Those with the lowest educational levels were consistently found among the most medically neglected and needy. Those with less than an eighth-grade education reported more nervous symptoms and were generally in need of attention. A substantial portion required glasses and dental work but had not received them.

The authors found that the more education a woman had, the better able she was to handle her own health problems. Women who were better educated reported more satisfaction with their lives and a higher state of overall happiness than less educated women. In conclusion, the study found a profound degree of medical neglect, poor health, underutilization of available medical facilities, and a general lack of preventive care among mothers presently and formerly on welfare. The health status of the sample population was found to be influenced by sociocultural factors, among which education proved to be extremely important.

A considerable amount of research has concluded that when illness is perceived as serious, use of services does not differ very dramatically by educational level or socio-economic status. However, regarding preventive care, differences in utilization patterns for low- and middle-income people are significant. Many researchers argue that education explains these differences (Davis & Reynolds, 1977). Many of the studies reviewed conclude that the traditional messages of health education regarding preventive care are not effective with low-income populations and that low-income people wait until a condition becomes serious before they seek care.

Coburn and Pope (1974) found that educational level directly affected the degree of use of preventive care. This was concluded from noting the incidence of polio vaccinations and dental checkups for different socioeconomic groups within a sample of 2180 people. When the separate effects of education, occupation, and income were examined, education was the most significant determinant of the incidence of vaccinations; for dental checkups the effects of education and income were about equal.

National surveys have documented that use of medical services is more strongly related to education than it is to income level. The 1963–1964 National Health Service survey found that in almost all instances, persons in families where the head had some college education were at least twice as likely to have used medical care services as persons in families where the head had less than 8 years of education; this was the case regardless of income.

Pomeroy's study of the use of health services by welfare families in New York (1969) was not able to support the hypothesis that education has an important influence in utilization levels. Initial relationships proved insignificant when the effects of ethnicity and reported health status were held constant. Education proved important in the Roe and Eickwort (1974) study, in which the population was largely white; Pomeroy's sample was mainly black and Puerto Rican. There is some indication, therefore, that the impact of educational attainment may differ by ethnic group. Pomeroy found that for black welfare recipients, education appeared to be inversely related to the use of health care services, regardless of their reported health status.

Pope, Yoshioka, and Greenlick (1971) concluded that educational attainment was important in the ability of patients to work their way through the medical system. His study revealed that those with higher education, occupation, and income were more likely to use the telephone for reporting symptoms to a physician and less likely to be dependent on face-to-face neighborhood contacts. Education appears to influence both the timing involved in seeking help and the choice among health-care providers. The low-income population tends to rely more heavily on nonprescription drugs, podiatrists, chiropractors, and paraprofessional advice than on more conventional types of health care.

Berkanovic (1974) suggests that the best use will be made of the health-care system only when patients can navigate the labyrinth of facilities and clearly understand their pattern. Frequent use, which serves as an educational process, leads to a better understanding of the system. The literature indicates that the poor are reluctant to seek medical care when ill. Their basic attitudes reflect considerable fear and ignorance of the care system. In studies by Podell (1969) and Pomeroy (1969), a substantial portion of the heads of households in their sample welfare population (66% or 2179) stated that at times they did not go to a doctor even when feeling ill. In Roe and Eickwort's study (1974), almost 50% (230) of the women said they could care for themselves and did not seek the services of a physician. The women interviewed also indicated that their past experience with the medical system had been minimal. Of the women sampled, 62.7% (294) stated they never went to the doctor as children or only went when very sick.

Techniques for medical education that do not include actual experience seem to have minimal success in encouraging the poor to seek health care when it is needed. Feldman's study (1966) suggests that the better educated the people are, the better they are able to learn from health manuals made available through the mass media. In his survey sample of 367 households, he found that a lower level of education or intelligence often prevented people from understanding a message even when they read it. Rosenstock's (1966) survey of 2493 adults revealed that low-income and poorly educated groups tend to obtain health information from face-to-face contact with neighbors and friends. Samora, Saunders, and Larson (1961) cite reasons why low-income persons often misunderstand health information to which they may be exposed. He cited the inhibiting effects of a limited vocabulary and education and of memberships in ethnic groups which cling to foreign languages.

Education also plays an important role in health care and maintenance in the home through its effect on the purchase and use of health care items. The 1969 Podell study of AFDC women in New York City found that nearly 60% of welfare households did not have a clinical thermometer; 20% did not have a medicine cabinet, and over 80% lacked a bathroom scale. White families were most likely to have these, and Puerto Rican families least likely. The number of households without such articles is a significant indicator of the degree to which AFDC homes lack even the basic means to preserve family health. Roe and Eickwort's study (1974) confirms the low level of education of AFDC mothers and their resulting misinformation about basic medical care. The evidence indicated that the women were unaware of health services available to them or had erroneous information about such services. For example, 50% of the sample (235 women) had annual gynecological checkups. However, 90% percent of the sample had never sought advice from a family planning service. The forgoing findings confirm the view that when dealing with welfare families, providers and lay people cannot assume that the client possesses basic health information.

Attitudes and Perceptions. Basic attitudes toward the medical system are formed in a variety of ways. Some studies argue that for most of the poor, attitudes seem to be developed from cultural backgrounds, ethnicity, religion, and past experiences with the health care system. Through an intermingling of the variables, the behavior and attitudes of the poor toward the use of such services differ from those of the rest of the population. Rainwater (1968) and others suggest that whether a person's income is low, middle, or high, the desire for good health may differ little. The crucial distinction between groups is how desires translate into utilization patterns.

In studies conducted by Monteiro in 1967, 1968, 1969, and 1971, a representative sample of Rhode Island residents did not display differences in their willingness to visit a physician based on income level. When the 1100 respondents were presented with a list of illnesses, those with a lower income did not show less of a tendency to judge the illness as something requiring a physician's attention.

These data seem to reveal that for illnesses that are serious or perceived as serious, action is taken regardless of other socioeconomic factors. However, if there is no perceived threat, low-income people may delay action or not act at all. The result, is that minor conditions are not cared for until they become serious. For this reason, when poor people enter the health care system, their conditions are likely to be more acute.

Davis (1977b) found that low-income families are more likely to seek care for a specific illness than for general preventive reasons. Her study reported that of all physician visits by families with low incomes (less than $5000), only 10% were for preventive reasons; in families with incomes over $15,000, 15% were for such reasons. Other data confirm this pattern. Between 1971 and 1973, 34% of high income women and 57% of low-income women did not have Pap smears; 45% of adults with low incomes and 31% of those with high incomes had not had a physical examination in the previous 2 years (U.S. DHEW, 1976, cited in Davis & Schoen, 1978).

The literature suggests variables which considerably influence an individual's perceptions and attitudes regarding health care. Suchman found that the more ethnocentric and socially cohesive a group is, the more likely they are to be ignorant regarding the medical profession.

Nelson argues that the family plays an important role in the decision to use services. Family, close friends, and peers provide necessary support for the initial validation of a health problem. They often assist a person in finding adequate health care and may also legitimize having a problem. "Family and friends can, if they are supportive, provide legitimation for not meeting regular obligations while dependent [Nelson, 1976, p. 13]." However, since reliable information is seldom available from the friends and neighbors of welfare recipients and other persons assisted by government programs (e.g., Supplementary Security Income [SSI]), their inability to determine which specific agency to contact is the point at which the help-seeking process will break down (Nelson, 1976).

As noted earlier, welfare recipients often have a negative orientation toward the health care system; because of bad past experiences with other social agencies, they may feel that the payoff for entering the system is limited. Bullough (1972) cautioned that this may not be the case for blacks. In her study of Los Angeles, she noted the differences in the levels of utilization by blacks and Mexican Americans. Bullough attributed the blacks' higher utilization rates to their longer history in coping with the inequalities of the American health and social service systems. She implied that, in this case, racial inequality was a contributing factor in better use of available services.

A study by Alpert, Kosa, and Haggerty (1967) attempted to correlate the attitudes and behavior of mothers regarding medical care. From 489 interviews with low-income families in Boston, mothers were found to be the primary agent in the family for defining and organizing the response to illness and for determining the type of action to be taken and the type of medical help to be sought for various symptoms of illness. Support for this view is provided by many other researchers. In addition, the way a mother evaluates her own health seems to be related to the manner in which she evaluates her children's health. Pomeroy (1969) found that 61% (1320) of his sample of welfare mothers regarded their own health as poor or fair; over 35% reported their children's health as fair or poor. This is substantially larger than the national sample, which records only 8% of all women reporting fair or poor health for their children. Pomeroy found that when reported health was considered to be poor or fair, the mean number of physician visits tended to be higher as compared with visits reported by mothers who said their health was good or excellent. Thus, there is reason to believe that mothers' perceptions of poor health for themselves and their children result in higher levels of utilization.

Becker, Drachman, and Kirscht (1974) found that the amount of confidence a woman has in the medical care she receives determines whether she will seek care for her children. Mothers who evaluated their own health as poor tended to be dissatisfied with the health care provided, and by and large they did not comply with physicians' follow-up instructions. Mothers who complied with prescribed regimes were more concerned about the present illness and relatively more interested in their children's health. These women perceived illness as a threat, but they displayed confidence in the physician's ability. Those who followed instructions appeared to have a more satisfactory interaction with the health care service.

Dodge, West, Holloway, Bridgforth, and Trovis (1970) interviewed 1464 mothers of children in the first through third grade in the public schools of Galveston County, Texas, in order to assess the mothers' desires regarding health care for their children. Results were analyzed by race, income, and education. In general, mothers did not differ significantly in assessing the importance of specific preventive care for their children. Further, no significant differences were found among mothers of different educational levels in their stated preferences for sources of these preventive health measures. Significant differences were found, however, among the mothers in their actual sources of care for their children in the past. Lower-income mothers were more likely to have used public sources of health care in the past, and upper-income mothers, private sources. Though maternal desire for children's health care was not found to differ demographically in this sample, no information was available to help assess the relation of stated desire and preferences to actual performance.

The literature reviewed above places considerable value on socioeconomic factors as an explanation of different levels in the use of health care services. Though income historically has played the critical role in rationing health care, the availability of medicaid has dramatically reduced the importance of available resources in explaining the use of health care services. This is most significant for the welfare population.

Additional Constraints. Considering the needs of the poor, government assumption of medical costs has not resulted in optimal use of services. Socioeconomic factors may explain some of this, but additional considerations are likely to be involved. Low-income families, especially welfare families, may meet additional barriers in seeking care, even when the predisposition and desire to obtain it exist. Families headed by females in particular, have special problems. The demands on single parents for managing child rearing, housekeeping, and sometimes employment often preclude their having adequate time and resources to care properly for family health. Family heads with limited resources often neglect health problems in taking care of more immediate and pressing needs. Practical barriers, such as employment demands and lack of child care facilities and transportation, may make it impossible to use even free medical services.

Podell and Pomeroy reported on the basis of their interviews with welfare mothers that for these women child care problems presented a major barrier to seeking health care for themselves and their children. Some 59.2% of AFDC mothers have at least one preschool child. Roe and Eickwort (1974) report that in their sample, mothers with preschool children were unlikely to use preventive health services for themselves. These same mothers were found to wait a longer period of time before seeking medical attention when they were ill or had symptoms. Many researchers have argued that though the direct costs of medical care for the welfare poor have been largely removed, the indirect costs are often substantial. Child care is only one among several heavy unreimbursed costs that act as disincentives to welfare families that consider using appropriate health care services.

The location of the health facility has proved to be important among the organizational and institutional factors critical to our understanding of patterns of usage among poor families. Transportation to appropriate providers may be costly and inconvenient for welfare families. In addition, transportation costs represent nonreimbursable out-of-pocket expenses. The cost and time involved in reaching health providers have been consistently cited throughout the literature as significant barriers for both preventive and crisis care (Stewart & Crafton, 1975). Employment responsibilities also often prevent the poor from establishing desirable health care patterns. Welfare and low-income workers seldom hold jobs where sick leave is provided. The indirect costs associated with foregoing a day's wages or risking the loss of the job because of absenteeism may be substantial for low-wage workers.

In summary, many situational constraints, and conditions of competing needs for limited resources, may intervene even among groups favorably predisposed toward conventional medical care. These practical barriers can often be assigned a dollar cost. Evidence has been presented for the appropriateness of the socioeconomic and cultural models that seek to explain the use of health care services. However, considerable disagreement exists throughout the literature on the usefulness of this approach. Many researchers believe that the variables employed in testing the models are far too collinear and that the results are of questionable validity. Often the interactive effects of background variables can inflate their importance.

Those who stress institutional factors argue that since the availability and delivery of health services often vary along socioeconomic lines, it is not surprising that these variable appear to explain utilization patterns. These critics view the observed utilization patterns as a function of the medical system's failure to provide services properly. It is not surprising, they argue, that poor families do not use fragmented services far from their homes. The poor have different health care needs from those of the nonpoor, and current delivery patterns are not suited to their requirements. Stewart and Crafton (1975) distinguish between these two views—one view sees the poor as apathetic and unmotivated, and the other sees the system as ill suited and unresponsive to the needs of the poor. The next section will review the literature which evaluates the approach based on institutional factors. An attempt will be made to analyze the importance of the structure and delivery of health services in explaining the utilization patterns of the poor.

ORGANIZATIONAL DETERMINANTS OF
HEALTH CARE UTILIZATION

The inception of the medicaid program in 1965 removed what had previously been assumed to be the major obstacle to utilization of medical care services by the very poor—lack of financial resources. Data on the impact of the medicaid program on the health status of the poor are limited. Nevertheless, some studies on the impact of medicaid on utilization patterns are available. Several of those reviewed below begin to reveal that after financial and socioeconomic factors are held constant, the poor still face a variety of institutional constraints on their use of services, constraints ranging from unsupportive personnel to unavailable facilities. Such institutional factors, exogenous to the individual, have been revealed to account for a substantial degree of underutilization.

Availability and Accessibility of Service Providers. After reviewing much of the literature on the determinants of utilization rates, Brook and Williams (1975) concluded that a different pattern of utilization exists among the poor for preventive versus curative care but that for chronic and serious conditions, the poor are likely to seek and use medical services relative to need as are higher-income groups. Brook and Williams also conclude that variations in behavior among members of different socioeconomic and ethnic groups may be more a function of the availability and accessibility of facilities than of a lack of motivation. Brook and Williams review a study on the different uses of physicians' services among poor and nonpoor patients in a prepaid group practice:

> Many aspects of care are similar when evaluated in a system where poverty groups have effective access to care, without financial and other

barriers. . . . [Many] of the reported differences in the behavior of poverty populations [relate] to differential access to medical care [Greenlick, Freeborn, Colombo, & Prussin, 1972].

Utilization rates for different types of delivery systems seem to reflect which services are most accessible and available to the poor. Although utilization rates fail to account for objective need, the changes in these rates when specific barriers are removed do permit analyses of the determinants of or impediments to utilization.

A 1000-family interview survey of the utilization of private doctors (Olendzki, Grann, & Goodrich, 1972) found that the proportion of persons who considered a private doctor their main deliverer of medical care rose from 1% before medicaid to 10% after. However, the large majority of medicaid recipients continued to use clinics. A total of 729 respondents were surveyed in five waves of interviews, three before medicaid and two after. The final report noted that some who preferred private care were unable to take advantage of it because of practical barriers. Before medicaid was implemented in 1963–1964, poor persons seldom had a private doctor as the main source of medical delivery; only 7 respondents (1%) gave such an answer. By 1968–1969, 10 times as many said that a private doctor was their main source of medical care. The findings of Olendzki et al. suggest that an overwhelming reason why more people did not choose a private doctor under medicaid was their assessment that private care did not suit their needs.

In 1961–1962, 42% of the respondents preferred a clinic to private care. In 1969–1970, the figure rose to 57.6%. For those who preferred a private physician, 127 persons (12% of the sample), while continuing to use clinic service, stated the reasons for doing so as follows: special facilities or treatment was needed, 34.6%; clinic or emergency room was more accessible, 26.8%; could not find a good doctor, 20.5% doctor refused medicaid, 18%; recommended to clinic, 11%. Other data suggest that people do differ in their responses to a widening choice of resources for medical care. Some will switch to their preferred source of care whatever the practical difficulties are; but many others, a majority of the welfare population surveyed, do not change their aspirations or their behavior patterns when the financial barriers to private care are removed (Olendzki et al., 1972).

Davis (1977b) found that the percentage of low-income patients who saw a physician during a given year rose from 56% in 1963 to 65% in 1970, after the start of the medicaid program. Increases were also found in the use of prenatal care; 58% of the mothers used services for prenatal care in 1963; 71% used them in 1970. Although medicaid has been instrumental in improving access to medical care for the poor, Davis concludes:

> [They] still do not participate in mainstream medicine in comparable quality, convenience, and style received by more fortunate persons. Poor persons continue to receive care in crowded, dreary clinics with long waits and few amenities. Care is frequently episodic, fragmented, and impersonal, with patients seeing a different physician upon each visit and for each type of ailment [p. 205].

Any given level of health care, Davis argues, may be less effective in meeting the needs of the poor than the needs of people with higher incomes. This finding suggests that other factors, such as the special needs of the poor and practical barriers in service delivery, in part determine patterns of utilization of medical services. Bernstein's study (1968) of the participation of private physicians in New York City's medicaid program concluded that medicaid *failed to direct a significant* number of general practitioners (G.P.s) in private practice into the service of the poor. Only 26% of the city's qualified G.P.s served any medicaid patients in the study period (August 1967–September 1968).

Studies have indicated that a major factor determining the use of private physicians by medicaid eligibles is simply the number of private physicians within their neighborhoods. For example, almost 18% of all physicians in New York City are G.P.s in private practice. Applying this proportion to the total numbers of physicians in each health district indicates that areas such as Mott Haven, Central Harlem, Williamsburg, Greenpoint, Bushwick, and Brownsville each have less than 13 private G.P.s per 100,000 residents. In these areas even 100% participation would represent insignificant availability. In higher-income neighborhoods the ratio of private G.P.s is usually larger. This suggests that physicians still prefer to practice in upper-income neighborhoods, regardless of the excessively large unserved population in poverty areas. Where physicians choose to set up their offices reflects their professsional expectations; most see middle-class patients and expect middle-class behavior and attitudes. Elesh and Schollaert (1972) examined doctors' preferences for locations in which their practices were to be established and found that they desired to practice in a community that reflected the income level to which they aspired. This preference and the resulting distribution of physicians would seem to preclude the use of physicians' services by a significant portion of the population.

Though medicaid has clearly increased access to medical care for substantial numbers of poor families, the benefits have not been equally enjoyed by all those who are eligible. Davis and Schoen (1978) reported that even when individual and family characteristics are accounted for, black medicaid recipients in all areas receive less ambulatory care than other groups. Black recipients in the South have lower hospitalization rates as well. Since background factors, such as education, family size, working status, and availability of medical resources, were held constant, Davis and Schoen suggested that racial discrimination (either overt or institutional) by service providers may account for the lower usage rates. This finding appears to support the literature on physicians' preferences regarding location of office and type of practice.

The National Health Survey statistics of 1973 showed that 10% of the visits of white children to health facilities take place at hospital clinics and emergency rooms as compared with nearly 30% for minority children. Some 61% of the families with incomes below $5000 used emergency rooms in 1973 as compared with 37.4% for families with incomes over $15,000. Thus, the emergency room would appear to function as a comprehensive source of medical services for all types of illnesses among the poor; the private physician may play a secondary role.

The Lejeune study (1968) of 2170 welfare mothers in New York City showed that mothers preferred to use emergency room clinics for medical care. During the 12-month study period, the welfare women cited 1.2 office and home visits to private physicians and 3.9 contacts with medical personnel through clinics and emergency rooms. Medical contacts for children in the family were even more heavily dependent on the emergency room and clinics with 5.9 contacts taking place there as compared to 1.9 contacts with a private physician. Of the total sample population, 39% (847 women) listed the emergency room as their "usual" source of care, and another 37% listed the clinics. Whites were more likely to give a "doctor" as their usual source of care (39%) than blacks (23%) or Puerto Ricans (15%).

Torrens and Yedvab (1970) account for high utilization of the emergency room by suggesting that the indigent population see it as a replacement for the family physician. The emergency room, according to the answers of 1113 patients attending four different hospital emergency rooms in New York City, serves as the place to go for *all* health problems, whether urgent or not: it is the logical entry point to the entire medical system. From the survey, Torrens and Yedvab describe three major roles for hospital emergency rooms: a treatment center for traumas; a substitute for a physician when a private practitioner or outpatient clinic is not available; and a family physician to the poor.

Whether or not more physicians can be attracted to low-income areas through medical insurance programs such as medicaid remains unclear. Nevertheless, whatever the increase by the poor in their use of private physicians, it appears to result from the implementation of the medicaid program. The degree to which the poor still limit their use of private physicians appears to result from additional institutional barriers, some of which are discussed below.

Emergency Room: Guaranteed Accessibility. An examination of the extent to which the poor use the emergency room for all needs shows how availability and accessibility govern their patterns. The tendency to use emergency rooms suggests that they dislike or lack a family physician. Satin and Duhl (1972) support Torrens and Yedvab's theory and state that the large number of applicants found to use emergency rooms suggests that the facilities have been forced to function much as a community physician does. Some researchers surmise that if other forms of care and services were made as accessible and available to the poor, they might begin to replace the emergency room. This is held to be desirable because emergency services seldom match the standards that are set for primary care in appropriate settings. In the meantime, the lack of community physicians or other service providers of primary care at convenient hours leaves the emergency room as the only option for health care for many of the poor.

Davis and Reynolds (1977) substantiate the claim that the poor do not obtain care in the same settings from the same kinds of physicians as do persons with higher incomes. In 1974, almost 27% of U.S. families earning less than $5000 as compared with 15% of those earning $15,000 had no "usual" place for obtaining care. The poor do not receive care with the same ease or convenience as higher-income groups. They are far more likely to receive care from G.P.s rather than from specialists, and in hospitals and outpatient settings rather than in physicians' offices. Some 70% of the care the poor receive comes from the general practitioner rather than the specialist; the comparable percentage for persons with higher incomes ($15,000) is 40%. Few poor children receive care from pediatricians. In 1975, even with medicaid, poor children were 57% less likely to have seen a physician in the 2 previous years than nonpoor children (U.S. DHEW, 1976). Women of childbearing age are twice as likely to receive care from specialists if they have higher rather than low incomes. Although as many as 75% of welfare recipients are now likely to receive health care in private settings, 87% of the people with family incomes of more than $15,000 are likely to do so.

Sparer and Johnson (1971) evaluated the utilization rates of neighborhood health centers funded by the Office of Economic Opportunity. The results indicated that compared to major medical centers, private physicians, and other health care providers, neighborhood health centers were found to be the most successful in meeting the needs of their population. They provided diverse medical specialists under one roof, and clearly, offered the type of care low-income populations are often forced to seek in hospital outpatient clinics or emergency rooms. Were neighborhood health centers more widely available, the utilization rates of emergency rooms would probably decrease because fewer poor people would use them for primary care. Similar findings came from Bellin and Geiger's (1972) study of a neighborhood health center in Dorchester, Massachusetts. The center had a significant impact on the area's target poverty population. High levels of utilization were achieved, and increased numbers of neighborhood residents cited the community health center as their regular source of health care.

Organization of Medical Services. Although medicaid has given welfare recipients a nominal choice in the type of medical services they may receive, their effective choice is limited. (Hester & Sussman, 1974) The sheer complexity of bureaucratic barriers may explain why the poor are reluctant to use available services. Many medical procedures serve the convenience of the professionals rather than the clients. Clinic hours, the types and number of services provided, the location of the facility, and the acceptance of medicaid are for the most part determined by the professional providing the service rather than by the needs of the recipient population.

Since the poor use emergency rooms more often than other groups, it would be of value to examine how this unit is organized and why the poor consider it the most desirable facility. Emergency rooms operate 24 hours a day, 7 days a week. For the indigent person with problems such as child care and the difficulty of losing a day's pay, the 24-hour service may prove to be most convenient. Private physicians or clinics do not provide such extended hours. In the emergency room, medicaid is honored as payment in full. Therefore, the poor know there will be no additional expense and the hospital will definitely accept the card as payment.

However, a private physician has the option of whether or not to accept and treat medicaid patients. As suggested earlier, even if every private physician in poor neighborhoods did accept medicaid, the number of physicians would still be grossly inadequate. A New York City medicaid report (Kavaler, 1968) stated that the majority of the offices that accepted medicaid patients were in marginal or depressed areas of the city. However, these practices were huge, with 30% of the offices catering exclusively to medicaid patients. For the most part, care was episodic, with patients receiving primary attention and little or no screening or preventive techniques. On the whole, these patients did not receive necessary consultations with physicians, a service made available to patients in better neighborhoods.

Davis and Reynolds' (1977) study of the impact of medicaid on the health care of low-income people supports the view that the poor experience much inconvenience in using health services:

> The poor spend 50% more time traveling and waiting to see a physician than do higher-income persons. Combined waiting time and traveling time is also higher for the poor on welfare, a total of 81 minutes per visit compared with 66 minutes for other poor persons (and 43 minutes for those with family incomes above $15,000 [p. 399].

Although the emergency room may not provide care in the best long-term interest of the patient, poor people know they will be treated for whatever conditions and illnesses afflict them. In many clinics and private physicians' offices, the poor patient cannot receive care for all conditions. Though a clinic normally provides some variety of specialists, the patient requires extensive knowledge to navigate the maze of regulations and registrations for each specialist; in addition, enormous amounts of time are lost.

The modern private practice is highly specialized. Private physicians who provide primary care may not be equipped to treat in one setting the range and severity of the health care needs of the poor; a variety of specialists and settings may be required. Given that modern medical care is highly fragmented, it is difficult for the patient to understand how to obtain needed services. Even when understood, access remains a problem. In addition, practical considerations, such as having carfare, may prevent the patient from making the journeys necessary for specialized care. The poor also face substantial nonmonetary burdens that strain the resources of their households when they seek medical care (Davis & Reynolds, 1977).

Moore, Bernstein, and Bonnano (1972) tested the theory that the emergency room acted as a community physician. The researchers found that the proportion of the indigent population participating in a local community health center were more likely to use the emergency room only *after* being referred by a physician. The community health center participants had a regular source of primary care and tended to use the emergency room only as a backup source of care. The study found that a high proportion of persons who lacked another source of primary care utilized emergency room facilities heavily. In addition, the presence of a local community health care center reduced the number of visits to the emergency room during the hours the health center was open. From the data provided, it can be assumed that the poor use the services best adapted to their specific problems and needs. As shown, emergency room services often provide the greatest convenience and adaptability to the distinct problems a poverty family faces when more appropriate conventional primary services are lacking.

An abundance of studies on attempts at new delivery mechanisms, such as community health centers, have demonstrated that when factors such as convenient location and hours of operation, outreach, and follow-up were designed into the system, the poor were far more likely to use health services (Stewart and Crafton, 1975).

A study of the Tufts-Columbia Point Health Center in Massachusetts (Maloney, 1967) found that eliminating the barriers of time and inconvenience by locating in the target neighborhood and remaining open 24 hours every day resulted in a high degree of motivation among neighborhood residents to seek care. Care became accessible and comprehensive, thereby fulfilling the target population's primary health care needs. Similarly, a clinic for migrants, run by medical students in a rural setting in Oregon (Duncan, Lord, Curtis, Rasor, Nicola, & Viken, 1971), was organized to operate 24 hours a day, 5 days a week. Findings indicated that highest usage occurred during the evening hours, both for appointments and walk-in cases. The flexibility in hours enabled the project to meet the needs of the target population successfully. Snyder, Nana, & Smith (1968) made a study of a medical facility in California with accessible location, no eligibility requirements, and evening hours for the migrant population. The results indicated that the migrant population received significantly more medical care as a result of this flexibility.

Additional studies have found that the manner in which services are delivered also has an important effect on the utilization rates. Innovative health settings that have congenial surroundings, personalized care, and community involvement in the planning and operation of the facility have been extremely successful in attracting increased numbers of low-income users (Haber, 1969; Salber, Feldman, Offenbacher, & Williams, 1970; Stewart & Hood, 1970; Yedvab & Schmidt, 1973).

Though the research on the organizational and institutional determinants of health care utilization has been extremely suggestive in indicating the importance of issues regarding service delivery, much controversy has arisen over the methodological shortcomings of much of the research. Most studies have been retrospective evaluations of "innovative" projects. Lack of specific measurable data that can be compared to a control situation with a similar population have created problems in interpreting and generalizing the findings. The number of possible variations in these projects is often very large. It is difficult, therefore, to isolate the independent effects, for example, the effect of extending clinic hours from that of involving neighborhood residents. It is impossible to conclude with any confidence what the relative importance of any one system change is in explaining increased levels of utilization.

Though there may be important effects that cannot be measured individually, institutional factors remain very necessary in attempts to understand the health care patterns of the poor. Any consideration of the factors influencing health choices that does not evaluate the nature of the choices themselves is severely limited in its usefulness. Clearly, when researchers evaluate the sociocultural models of health care utilization they are asking what factors explain the low or inappropriate utilization of available health care among the poor. However, the availability of health care must be more specifically defined. Are services "available" if facilities are not open at hours when poor people can come (e.g., evenings, weekends)? Are services that are located far from poor neighborhoods or that require long hours of waiting "available"? Unfortunately, there is a high correlation between poverty groups and the incidence of "unavailable" service delivery. Therefore, correlates of poverty tend to appear related to utilization.

Though this review of the interaction has failed to demonstrate without question the superiority of institutional factors as an explanation of the inadequate levels of health care received by low-income populations, it has demonstrated the weaknesses of the approach based on sociocultural factors. Research regarding the impact of alternative delivery mechanisms provides a far more promising answer to improving health care patterns. The variables of delivery are readily alterable through public policy; current research strongly suggests the necessity of addressing these factors in correcting unsatisfactory health care arrangements for the poor.

CONCLUSION

The health status of the poor, and particularly the welfare poor, is far worse than that of other population groups. This has been documented by innumerable studies and surveys using a multitude of indicators. Most dramatic is the evidence of mortality rates and low birth weights among children in poverty groups. Low birth weight has become an important predictor of future health and educational status. It was chosen along with other conditions induced by poor nutrition for special attention in this chapter because its causes are now fairly well known; its incidence is specifically related to poverty populations, and its consequences are dramatic and serious. Low birth weight often explains later incidence of many neurological, physical, and social manifestations; conditions induced by poor nutrition often result in school failure and permanent mental and physical damage. The relevations of this literature have important implications for policy especially since studies show that families participating in the NIT experiments do have a smaller number of children with low birth weights. Direct policy intervention in this area is clearly possible and has been shown to have considerable impact. Evaluations of child nutrition programs demonstrated clear and dramatic health gains for those participating.

Many of the medical conditions that plague the poor and result in disabilities that are permanent or a threat to life can be prevented. Suitable medical care at the appropriate time can dramatically alter the course of health status. Nevertheless, given their level of need, many poor people fail to utilize services appropriately, except in crisis situations. The models usually used to explain this lack of care stress two opposing views. The sociocultural model sees the cultural and class characteristics of individuals as responsible for low or inappropriate levels of utilization. The organizational model sees institutional arrangements as the cause of inadequate medical care. The discussion concluded that though the research on the institutional determinants has a number of important weaknesses, it offers a more promising explanation of observed patterns. The sociocultural model provides no useful policy guides for action.

The relationships between health and education and health and employment require that serious attention be directed toward the health status of the poor. A policy that fails to direct resources toward health care and nutrition is likely to be ineffective in changing the work and welfare patterns of the low-income population.

_____ 5 _____

Education

No single institution in American society has held out more promise as a vehicle for upward mobility than the educational system. As indicated in earlier chapters, the returns from education are neither uniform nor in themselves sufficient to explain completely the variations in the economic well-being of different population groups. But, it operates as a critical resource for upward mobility in a variety of direct and indirect ways. Educational attainment is an important component of employability and has been shown to have a variety of indirect effects on future economic well-being by influencing attitudes and behavior related to health care, nutritional status, and family planning.

Whereas welfare programs are among the most controversial of all government functions, education receives significant and widespread public support and societal commitment. Because the educational system benefits a large cross section of the general population policy intervention appears to be more politically feasible in this area than in many social welfare programs, where benefits accrue exclusively to the poor.

Many of the theories of poverty and dependency have stressed the importance of the human resources that people bring with them to the labor market. The school system has been thought of as the major institution outside the family for imparting societal and cultural values critical to participation in the larger society. It has therefore been charged with the responsibility for acting as a socializing agent for all groups in the society. Education was seen to be the major institution capable of altering patterns of poverty, far more so than the social welfare system, by providing equality of opportunity (Mosteller & Moynihan, 1972).

Data on the educational status of the heads of welfare families demonstrated the degree to which educational deprivation plagued this population (see Chapter 2). Welfare families are faring poorly. The hope has been, however, that with increased educational resources, welfare children will have more opportunities for upward mobility. Available data have for some time identified significant differences in levels of educational achievement when the poor and the welfare poor are compared to other segments of the population. Though evidence of failure to complete high school is striking, the reasons for predictable patterns of such failure among this segment of the population are not so clear. The social science literature on education is abundant. This chapter will therefore restrict itself to a survey of some of the research on the nature and determinants of educational failure among the poor and, where the data permit, among the welfare poor.

A number of theories that explain the rather substantial inequalities in educational achievement among different socioeconomic groups, and three fundamental approaches, are represented in the literature. The first relates the outcomes of education to the socioeconomic characteristics and backgrounds of the students, maintaining that children of disadvantaged backgrounds enter the school system with a plethora of social, intellectual, and behavioral disabilities that prevent them from enjoying the educational benefits received by less disadvantaged groups. These encumbrances of cultural deprivation are believed to be basically immutable, or at least sufficiently predisposing to render school inputs impotent. The variables hypothesized to predict educational achievement according to this model include measures of socioeconomic status, family composition and functioning, and basic physical and social conditions in the home and community environment. Included among the relevant variables are values and attitudes related to the family backgrounds of students and characteristics regarding psychological and physical health that are thought to impede the success of the disadvantaged population.

The prevalent approach of a second group of theories explaining inequality of educational achievement stresses the variations in input factors. Here, the hypothesis maintains that the unequal distribution of educational resources results in unequal outcomes in educational

achievement. Researchers attempt to show that conscious political decisions and economic and racial segregation result in unequal expenditures and inputs in schools and districts with high concentrations of
poor students. Inequality in the number and quality of teachers,
books, and facilities among and within school districts is held to explain
the variation in educational attainment.

A third group of theories stresses the importance within school
systems of institutional constraints on equal educational services and on
the achievement of disadvantaged children. These are seen to be separate from material inputs (such as expenditures and other school-
resources) and are related to the styles, values, and expectations of the
staff, the teachers, and the institutions.

The appropriateness of each approach will be evaluated on the
basis of current research findings. Obviously, each implies a very different set of policy options. Education has been shown to be an important
correlate of employability. It is essential therefore, to explore the extent
of educational deficiency among the children in welfare families and
determine its causes. Indeed, a variety of factors reduce the life chances
of welfare families as compared with other groups. Lack of education
appears to be a persistent problem for the low-income population, often
an impediment in obtaining those types of jobs in industries that are
likely to ensure economic stability. Early failures in school often damage
self-perceptions and later psychological well-being. Education influences other important decisions, such as those regarding the use of
health care services and family planning methods. Though education in
and of itself may be an inadequate predictor of later economic well-
being, its central impact on a variety of factors critical to such well-
being makes it an essential concern for any analysis of the welfare
problem.

SOCIOECONOMIC DETERMINANTS

FAMILY BACKGROUND AND RELATED FACTORS

Family background has been hypothesized to be an important determinant of educational achievement among those who hold that it is
the human resources that children bring to school, rather than the services provided by the school, that most affect educational achievement.
One argument has been that a family's life experiences, opportunities,
limitations, and hardships are shaped partly by factors such as social
class and race. The effects of these conditions are thought to influence
family functioning and to have a direct effect on children's learning.

A common assumption is that the mother has a powerful influence on the family. A variety of studies indicate that the mother's educational level is important because of its effect on child rearing, which has a subsequent impact on a child's educational achievement (Osborn, 1971). However, one report concluded that whether mothers were highly educated or fathers were highly educated, there was no significant difference in the high school achievement of their children (Hood, 1967). Byers (cited in Osborn, 1971) examined the relationship between the educational levels of parents and educational achievement of children. One question was whether the children of mothers who were well educated and fathers who were poorly educated differed in educational achievement, attitudes, aspirations and expectations from children of mothers who were poorly educated and fathers who were well educated. The sample, drawn from among 19,229 high school seniors, separated the students by sex and the parents by sex and educational level. The results revealed that the achievement levels of high school seniors was in keeping with that of the parent of the same sex. No major differences in achievement were found between the group with well-educated mothers and the one with well-educated fathers.

An analysis of the PSID data revealed that for males, the mother's education was found to have a much stronger relationship to the child's achievement level in cognitive skills than the father's education had (Duncan, 1974.) The mother's effect on the level of development of cognitive skills of both boys and girls is related to the view that children acquire some of their cognitive skills at an early age, in the home, and from their mothers. However, the motivation for achievement related more significantly to the father's education than to the mother's. Whereas the total effect of a father's educational level on his daughter's educational attainment was found to be of little importance, the mother's educational level was found to be large and significant. In the case of a fatherless family, the mother is responsible for the motivation for achievement as well as for cognitive development. The educational attainment of an AFDC mother becomes critical when she is the only adult in the household.

In a more recent study using PSID data, Duncan (1977) makes an ambitious attempt to evaluate a variety of factors and their interrelation (direct and indirect) on the paths to economic well-being.[1] He acknowledges the importance of a temporal sequence of events that begins at birth

1. An abundance of research has been done by both sociologists and economists on the returns to education and the relationship between education and future economic well-being. (For other views see Becker, 1974; Bowles & Gintis, 1976; Duncan, Featherman, & Duncan, 1972; Jencks, 1972; Sewell & Hauser, 1975; Taubman, 1975; and Thurow, 1970.)

and leads to learning. Background factors hypothesized to affect educational attainment (which in turn affect jobs and industrial attachment) include the impact of parental educational levels. Those who explain income differentials on the basis of a theory of human capital include parental educational level as proxies for the quantity and quality of time "invested" in children by their parents (Mincer, 1974).

A regression equation, reflecting many independent variables, was designed to predict effects on an individual's earnings. Parental educational attainment was one factor. Two effects were hypothesized: the direct impact on the child's level of educational achievement and the indirect effect on the child's potential as a wage earner. Parental educational attainment operates by helping to form advantageous attitudes and skills during the child's early development.

The results support both expectations of the model. A mother's educational attainment and that of her child, used as independent variables, explained attitudinal variation in the sample and were found to be significant and positive; a father's educational level was not found positive or significant. Each additional year of the father's education was associated with an increase in average earnings of 1.6% for whites and 2.9% for blacks. The mother's educational attainment was associated with a .8% increase for whites and 2.3% increase for blacks. Some of these effects were shown to have operated through the individual's own educational attainment; namely, more highly educated parents of both black and white families resulted in the increased educational achievements of their children. This, in turn, resulted in increased earning. For whites, this indirect effect accounted for 33% of the total impact of the father's educational level and 50% of the mother's educational level (Duncan, 1977).

Thus, the level of parental educational attainment is important to the child's educational achievement in a variety of ways. It's impact, however, appears to be different by race and sex of the parent and race and sex of the child. It operates to influence children's attitudes and values, which in turn affect their educational achievement. The adverse impact of parents who are poorly educated on their children's development is clear. The mother's schooling, or lack of it, may affect her ability to manage the home on limited funds, to be aware of her environment, and to guide her children in making decisions about school and careers (Podell, 1969). As a group, AFDC mothers are poorly educated compared to national averages. A recent study indicated that while most mothers on welfare attended high school, only about 24% were graduated; another 17% never went beyond eighth grade. The AFDC fathers had similar educational histories and in many cases had lower educational attainments. A 1975 AFDC study (U.S. DHEW, 1977) indicated that 33% of the AFDC males had no more than eight years of schooling; only 16% had completed twelfth grade.

It is difficult to determine if low educational levels among parents are significant causal variables of school failure. One study, using data from 1960 and 1970, demonstrated strong correlations for each year. In 1960 the correlation between parents' educational levels and children's educational achievement was .66; in 1975, .73 (Churchman, Shuman, & Kogan, 1975).

FAMILY COMPOSITION

The intact family is regarded as a positive element in child development as well as in educational achievement. The Churchman study revealed that children's achievement in school strongly correlates with living with both parents. For children in the sample, the correlation was .76 in 1960; though this had fallen to .58 in 1975, it was still strong and positive. Broken homes are usually fatherless, and children are likely to have more problems because of the multiple responsibilities placed upon the mother. One study found that children from broken families became high school dropouts more often than children from intact families. However, this finding may occur because broken families are more frequently found in the lower socioeconomic levels and suffer from the adverse variables associated with that status (Kriesberg, 1970). Although pertinent data are scarce, studies of different categories of public assistance (as cited by Kriesberg) were examined to determine if there was a difference between intact and fatherless families that were equally poor. The evidence did suggest that in fatherless AFDC families, the children were slightly less likely to complete at least high school than children of poor families that were intact but dependent upon other categories of public assistance.

In contrast to this, another study indicated that husbandless mothers on welfare exerted more pressure for good school performance, with the likelihood of getting good results, than two-parent poor families. The study also found that children from one-parent homes were likely to perceive their parents as wanting them to go to college (Macaulay, 1975). The key question is the extent to which the absence of the father affects children's educational achievement. Some studies suggest that children from fatherless families have lower I.Q.s and do less well in school (Churchman, 1975; Kriesberg, 1970). Other research has indicated that the father's absence is not by itself a critical factor related to school performance; related factors such as the reason for the absence must be considered before any conclusions can be reached (Sciara & Jantz, 1974).

The findings on the impact of broken homes and female and male heads of families on children's educational achievements are neither consistent nor convincing. Clearly, the connection between the type of family and achievement needs continued scrutiny. It may be that there are other factors which predispose a family toward instability and low achievement. Whatever the family type, however, no studies have demonstrated the singular significance of its impact on educational achievement.

OCCUPATION AND SOCIAL CLASS

The occupation and social class of the head of the household have been found to influence educational achievements and aspirations. Several studies have indicated that some children from the families of low occupational status tend to achieve and aspire less than children with parents of a higher occupational status.

A study conducted in Berkeley, California, used a sample of sixth-grade students from Berkeley Hills, where the fathers of 60% of the students were professionals and/or executives, and from the "flats," where the parents of 80% of the students were working class. Reading and arithmetic scores were used as achievement measures. The analysis revealed that the students from the Hills were superior; virtually all were reading at grade level, using advanced sixth-grade texts or additional enrichment texts. Only 20% of the students from the flats were reading at grade level. Thus, the study concluded that variations in children's educational achievement could be explained by occupational differences among parents (Wilson, 1963).

What served to qualify the conclusions, however, was the comparison within occupational status. Indeed, children with parents of low occupational status who lived in an area of high occupational status were more likely to be reading at grade level than were those living in areas of low occupational status. The authors conclude that a variety of additional factors affect children's educational achievement, not the least of which is the emphasis which parents place upon it. Occupational differences were also found to be a function of the racial and social processes within the school; these serve to reinforce and sustain existing variations in achievement levels (see Bowles & Gintis, 1976).

Additional evidence regarding student achievement comes from a study of welfare recipients and nonrecipients with the same socioeconomic status. The parents were separated by educational level and occupation, using race and sex as control measures. Of the students, 893 had parents who were classified as poorly educated and as blue-collar workers. Of the parents, 106 were receiving AFDC. A total of 40 students had parents who had applied for and had been denied AFDC; 747 had parents who had previously received or applied for AFDC. The dropout rate for the AFDC children was 56.6%; for the children denied AFDC 40.6%; and for nonrecipients 24.6% (Tyler, 1974). The study also concluded that children of parents who had low occupational status tended to have more problems in school and were more likely to drop out.

Even within the same social class, differences have been found between high and low achievement based on parental occupation. Parents of high achievers had a significantly better average occupational level than the parents of low achievers. About 40% of the high achievers, but only 27% of the low achievers, came from homes where the father, mother, or both were employed as skilled or semiskilled workers. While 25% of the high achievers had parents who were unemployed or on welfare, 47% of the low achievers fell into this category (Greenberg & Davidson, 1972). The sample, however, was small (160 students).

The results of the studies indicate that the occupational status of parents has some effect on school achievement; however, the effect of occupation cannot be measured independently or exclusive of other pertinent background factors.

INCOME

A parent's ability to feed and clothe children, to provide appropriate medical care, and to purchase educational materials for them are important and relevant to their education experience. Considerable research has shown that poor children often do not have these basic needs met because the parents lack sufficient income. Because of these factors, family income is a research issue. A study using a sample from New York City welfare rolls included a survey which contained a series of questions pertaining to absenteeism from school; 30% of the welfare mothers reported that they had kept their children home from school at some time because the children did not have the necessary shoes or clothes; another 20% reported that they sometimes kept their children home from school because they were ashamed of the way the children were dressed (Podell, 1969).

A survey of community school districts in New York City indicated that in 1960 the mean family income for districts with the lowest achievements (mean achievement score 4.8) was $4339; for districts with high achievements (mean achievement score 8) the mean family income was $7612. AFDC children accounted for 19.2% of the low achievers and 9.8% of the high achievers. In 1970, for the same districts, the mean family income was $6526 for the district with low achievements (mean achievement score of 5.1) and $14,026 in those with high achievements (mean achievement score 8). The percentage of AFDC children was 4.6 in districts with low achievements and 2.5 in those with high achievements (Churchman, 1975). AFDC children are more often highly represented in districts with low achievements. However, it is not reasonable on the basis of the data to conclude that high percentages of welfare children resulted in the low achievements of the districts. Indeed, it is just as likely that welfare families have no choice but to live in areas where schools are poor.

Several studies have suggested that the income level of a family may be partly responsible for poor achievement in school and dropouts (Masters, 1969; Maynard, 1976; Sexton, 1961; U.S. DHEW, 1966). Some low-income children need to seek part- or full-time employment to help support themselves and/or their families. The need for these children to have employment income is commonly thought to intefere with their educational achievement.

Masters (1969), in an attempt to explore the relationship between dropouts and income, did a study using data from the 1/1000 sample of the 1960 census. He used the data to estimate the probabilities that children from different family backgrounds would fall behind in school or drop out. Those studied were single students living with their families. To ascertain the dropout rate, students 16 and 17 years old were investigated; to ascertain poor achievement students 14 and 15 years old. A regression analysis was done with family income and parents' education used as independent variables. Masters found that for two youths having similar abilities and goals, the difference in their estimated probabilities is a measure of their educational opportunities. For a student in a family having less than $3000 income where parents have limited education, the probability of the student's being a poor educational achiever (assuming he or she was in school at age 14 or 15) was estimated at .47. At 16 or 17, the student's chance of being a dropout was estimated at .33. In contrast, the probability that an average student would drop out was estimated at .12 and .11, respectively.[2]

An earlier study, which supports Master's findings, estimated that

2. An average child is one whose family income is $5000 to $10,000 and whose parents have completed 9 to 11 years of school. For a child whose parents' income is over $10,000 and whose parents are high school graduates, the probability of dropping out declined to .02 and .01.

the dropout rate for the nation (based on youths aged 16 and 17 not attending school) was higher for low-income families earning under $3000. The study took into account other factors such as sex, race, and residence; however, independent of these factors, the rate remained the same (U.S. DHEW, 1966).

Income, then, may be seen as a proxy for (a) the probability that parents will have more time to spend with their children, and (b) the probability that parents will purchase more of the educational materials and necessities of daily life that support educational achievement. The findings from several of the NIT experiments provide a unique opportunity to explore the role which stable and adequate income may have on the educational achievement of the children of participating families.

Analyses of the data on changes in educational achievement are available from studies done in New Jersey and in the rural areas of North Carolina and Iowa. The New Jersey study estimated the effects of the New Jersey NIT experiment on decisions of youths aged 16 and 17 to continue in school. The rural study focused on school attendance, comportment and academic grades, and the scores of standardized achievement tests. The results have indeed suggested that a national income maintenance program may, through provision of stable and adequate income, lead to improvements in school performance and levels of educational attainments. Analysis of the New Jersey data revealed that teenagers in the treatment families were 20% to 90% more likely to graduate from high school than their control counterparts. During the 3-year study, teenagers showed an increase of one-third to one-half of a year in educational attainment (Mallar & Maynard, 1976).

Children participating in the rural study showed improvements in attendance, comportment and academic grades, and scores on standardized tests. Absences fell by 30%. Those most positively affected were second through eighth graders in North Carolina. Neither the children of high school age in North Carolina nor any of the children in Iowa showed any change in school performance. Thus, the program appeared to be most effective for children in lower grades; their behavior was easier to modify. The analysis did not adequately explain the differences between the results of rural children in North Carolina and those of rural children in Iowa (Maynard, 1976). Nevertheless, the findings generally supported the importance of income. The short duration of the experiment does not permit an assessment of long-range or lasting impacts. In fact, changes that resulted during the first few years may be lost over a longer time period; conversely effects that could not be observed in the short run may be revealed over a longer period.

Masters' research (p. 232, reviewed above) indicated that a short-term increase in welfare payments to the poor would result in minimal changes in school achievement. Masters found that variables such as the ability and ambition of parents would be likely to alter both family income and children's educational attainment.

Much of the research indicates that an inadequate and unstable income can have some effect on the educational achievement of children from low-income families. Whether or not an increase in income *alone* can alter this situation has not been determined. Indeed, the research to date has not been able to capture the recursive nature of the process by which children achieve well in school. It remains somewhat unclear whether income is a significant causal effect or whether background factors result in higher income and higher school achievement.

HOME ENVIRONMENT

Poverty, disease, instability, and conflict often characterize the homes of children of low-income parents, as has been frequently confirmed. The impact of these problems upon the family is held to be such that parents find it difficult to provide the appropriate stimulus and support necessary for their children's educational achievement. Parents' cultural patterns and values are predicted to be reflected in their children's performance at school and to contribute to their own attitudes toward education. Whether or not the amount of support a poor family can provide is sufficient for good educational performance is questioned. The literature includes two major views: (a) Children of poor families are not provided with the appropriate stimulus and environment for learning in the home in order to achieve in school. (b) Poor parents, living under difficult conditions, would like to see their children succeed more than they themselves have. Aspirations are high but expectations are low because of the lack of support resources available to the children.

A case study of families from different social classes, all with children in the fifth and sixth grades, rated them on a variety of interactive processes going on between parents and children. Included in these were family emphasis on achievement and language development and provisions for general learning. Deficiencies in each of the family "process areas" were found among low-income families. Methods of general learning—books, travel and even household articles—were lacking. The effects of the home environment was characterized as a "stimulus deprivation" (Moles, 1965). Deutsch, Katz, and Jensen (1968), in a study of "disadvantaged children," concluded that in many localities, parents have to purchase books and supplies on a limited income. Other home learning tools, such as dictionaries, educational games, and story books, take second place to a concern for basic subsistence. Further evidence of these material deprivations comes from research on dropouts; they were less likely than middle-class students to possess reference books, newspapers, or a quiet place to use them (Kriesberg, 1970). The living space of many lower-income children limits their opportunity to study. (Moles, 1965; Masters, 1969). In many poor communities, overcrowding is worsened because several families may occupy a single dwelling unit out of economic necessity.

Bronfenbrenner (1974) reviewed a great number of studies on programs for early childhood compensatory education to determine whether or not such intervention techniques are successful in raising the achievement levels of disadvantaged children. In so doing, he developed a theory to explain the variations in success of different programs by the degree to which they resulted in substantial short-run improvements which were not eroded over some longer period.

Findings were reviewed from several studies of Headstart Programs and later from Follow Through programs that provided compensatory enrichment programs for disadvantaged children both prior to and concurrent with traditional kindergarten and early elementary school programs. The preponderance of the evidence indicated temporary gains in average I.Q. scores among children in these programs as compared to a control group not so exposed. Within several years, however, as the programs continued and children terminated, initial gains declined. Bronfenbrenner argues that even well-conceived compensatory programs are unable to immunize children against the profound disadvantages that are characteristic of the environments to which they must return.

Evaluations were made of smaller experimental programs that involved earlier contact with children. Mothers were the critical agents interacting with children between 2 and 3 years old, and they were aided by a "trained" visitor in the home. Significant and lasting I.Q. gains among participating low-income children were demonstrated. Bronfenbrenner concludes that the critical element in raising the abilities of low-income children is very early intervention that concentrates on developing and strengthening the precondition for learning, that is, the early development of an enduring one-to-one relationship between parent and child that involves the child in verbal interaction around cognitively stimulating activities. Children who participated in such "ecological intervention" showed dramatic gains far in excess of those shown in traditional Headstart and Follow Through programs.

Among the variations in the gains of the children exposed to such intervention it was found that those who did best were the ones who had less disadvantaged parents. Bronfenbrenner concludes that influencing the critical "dyad" of mother and child is dependent upon certain basic environmental conditions. Severely overcrowded homes with mothers away at work are not as successful as middle-class homes in building the supportive interaction between mother and child necessary for proper cognitive development. Bronfenbrenner concludes if the most disadvantaged children are to succeed in school, material deprivation, which results in poor housing, poor health, and absent mothers, must be eliminated.

His findings suggest the significance of changing arrangements for work and income maintenance in order to enhance the proper cognitive development of children. His theory, however, is heavily dependent on a number of extremely small studies where personalized strategies for home intervention have been used. Though it is unclear how successful such a program would be with a larger number of children, the results do support the view that material conditions hostile to optimal parenting may have a significant impact on the school achievement and cognitive functioning of poor children.

PARENTS' ASPIRATIONS AND EXPECTATIONS

Parents' aspirations for their children's education has been cited by several studies as having a meaningful effect on children's educational attainment. Herriott (1963) pointed out that two major influences bear upon the theory of aspiration: one's own level of aspiration, that is, the level of self-assessment relative to the assessment of others; and the perceived level of expectation that significant others hold for one's behavior. Soares (1970), in his many studies of self-concept and achievement, also concluded that the immediate family is the most significant influence on aspirations and achievement. An earlier study of AFDC mothers indicated that the educational *aspirations* of low-income parents for their children are often as high or higher than those of affluent parents. The *expectations,* on the other hand, were not high; nor did low-income parents see themselves playing an active role in helping their children to achieve (Herzog, 1969).

The Thompson and Miles (1972) study interviewed 6000 low-income people, including AFDC mothers, attempting to assess the degree of educational aspirations they had for their children. Most of the mothers interviewed stressed the fact that they wanted their children to have the same opportunities and advantages as other children, including a good education. They also felt that welfare payments should be large enough to provide these things. According to Kriesberg's study (1970), husbandless mothers do not differ from married mothers in aspirations. Nearly all would be disappointed if a son or daughter did not complete high school. From a survey testing the differences, he found that 8% would be disappointed if a son completed fewer than 11 years of school, 72% if he did not complete 12 years and 20% if he did not finish more years. The comparable percentages among the married mothers were 10, 60, and 30%, respectively.

Results of a study in a northern Appalachian community do not support the notion that parents uniformly have high educational aspirations for their children. Children of poorer educational, cultural, and economic backgrounds made up at least 25% of the total elementary school population. This study noted a great deal of variation among parents in the value placed on schooling. Some parents who worked in unskilled jobs were convinced that lack of education explained their own confinement to poverty and jobs with low pay; others did not see any real connection between education and life chances (Feldman & Feldman, 1972). Podell (1969), in his survey of AFDC mothers and expectations, found that 80% expected their children at least to finish high school, and 20% wanted them to go to college. About 50% wanted their children to enter professional occupations, but only about 30% expected them to do so. The more education the mother had, the further she wanted and expected her children to go educationally and occupationally.

The Greenberg and Davidson (1972) study (mentioned earlier) also investigated the home and family variables for fifth-grade black children, 80 of whom were high achievers, and 80 low achievers. Parents of the high achievers were found to have more of a concern for education, an awareness of the child as an individual, and a general social awareness; they were also found to use a rational discipline and structure in the home. The results of this survey indicated that lower-class children who achieve are subject to family influences similar to those usually ascribed to the middle class.

Many studies have discussed the relationship existing between socioeconomic status and aspirations for children's educational achievement. Kreisberg indicated that it was not clear whether parental aspirations resulted from current circumstances and general background factors or whether the abilities and interest of the children themselves affected the parents. However, mothers' aspirations involved greater consideration of what might be attained as against what was valued.

HEALTH FACTORS

As noted in the previous chapter, the children of poor families frequently suffer from malnutrition and inadequate medical care. These adverse factors put them at risk as learners, either by permanently impairing their capacity to learn or by interfering with the acquisition of knowledge (Birch & Gussow, 1972). In many schools, children who appear irritable, disinterested, and unmotivated are considered to have behavior problems. Several studies indicate that the single most common behavioral finding in malnourished children is apathy accompanied by irritability (Birch & Gussow, 1972). It must not be overlooked that hunger and illness in children immediately affects their attention level, interest, and motivation to learn—in short, their achievement in school.

Although health is a major determinant of ability and motivation to learn, psychological factors related to the physical and mental condition of poor children are often overlooked when their educational achievement is considered. (The many symptoms associated with inadequate nutrition and health care were discussed in Chapter 4.) It is well established that inattention, hyperactivity, inability, undue fatigue, and numerous other behavioral problems result from poor health and nutrition; the greater the deprivation, the more severe the subsequent impairment. Mental retardation and delays in cognitive development resulting from inadequate diet and health care may be far more critical factors in the failure to learn than has yet been documented.

INEQUALITY OF SCHOOL RESOURCES

Inequality in the distribution of educational resources is frequently cited in indictments of the present educational system. It has been shown that schools in well-to-do communities offer higher per-pupil expenditures than do schools in low-income communities. The result, critics claim, is that low-income communities have larger classes, inadequate physical facilities, less teacher training, and poorer libraries. These disparities in resources, critics contend, result in lower levels of educational achievement. Two research questions are posed: To what extent do low-income communities receive more limited school resources than well-to-do communities receive? Do disparities in school resources explain the profound variations in the achievement levels of students within and between schools and school districts of different economic status?

In many urban areas, litigation has followed the accusation that patterned inequalities in expenditures exist by income and race. Many studies have sought to evaluate claims of inequality in the allocation of resources. Results have varied considerably, both by location and by units of measurement. For example, Katzman (1971) found only weak relationships in Boston between the social characteristics of students and the allocation of resources, as measured by such factors as pupil–teacher ratio, age of building, number of teachers with master's degrees, teachers' experience, and current expenditures per pupil. Only expenditures and teacher turnover appeared to be related to the income level of the community in which a school was located.

Other researchers have found support for the claim that community income level can lead to systematic bias in the allocation of resources to schools (Michelson, 1972; Sexton, 1961). The results of various studies tend to be extremely sensitive to the selection of variables. Many research findings demonstrate a positive relation between income and some measure of resource allocation, and a negative relation for other measures (Martyn, 1965). Several studies of neighborhoods in Oakland, California, and in New York City revealed a systematic bias in expenditure levels *in favor* of low-income and upper-income districts (Levy, Meltsner, & Wildavsky, 1974; Sanger, 1976). These findings did not support the contention that the allocation of resources disadvantaged low-income schools or districts; indeed, they demonstrated that allocations were systematically biased against middle-income districts.

Several research efforts have attempted to assess nationally the extent of unequal allocation of resources. A study by Owen (1972) reevaluated data from the Coleman report, *Equality of Educational Opportunity* (1966). Coleman found little variation in resources and a generally insignificant impact of resources on students' educational achievement. Using an alternative methodology, Owen reported that an analysis of the data from school districts in nine cities revealed significant discrimination against poor and nonwhite schools in the allocation of expenditures for instruction. The effect personal income levels in different neighborhoods had on expenditures for salaries is illustrated in Table 5.1 for a typical city in the sample. According to Owen, the distribution of expenditures per pupil is of interest in itself as a measure of inequality in the allocation of resources. However, it also reflects differences in educational quality because salary costs rise with student–teacher ratios and with the average experience level of the faculty.

Although most studies evaluated allocations within a school system, a national study compared a survey sample of 4404 public elementary and secondary schools representative of the nation's 81,000 local public

TABLE 5.1
*Average Family Income by Neighborhood and
Expenditures per Pupil on Teachers' Salaries.*

Average family income in school area	Expenditures per pupil on teachers' salaries
$4000	$158
6000	193
7500	219

Source: From "The Distribution of Educational Resources in Large American Cities" by J. Owen, *Journal of Human Resources*, 1972, 7, p.33

schools (Borinsky, 1975). The analysis compared schools in poverty and nonpoverty areas on a large variety of resource variables, including pupil–teacher ratio, percentage of certified teachers, central library, teacher turnover, special instruction, and teachers' starting salary. The results did not support the claim of widespread inequality. For example, in comparison to nonpoverty schools, poverty schools had (a) nearly equal pupil–teacher ratios (20 pupils per teacher for poverty schools, 21 pupils per teacher for nonpoverty schools and not significant at the .05 level); (b) about the same percentage of teacher turnover (21% compared to 19% for all teachers); and (c) about the same percentage of schools with noncertified teachers (59% compared to 62%) [Borinsky, 1975].

Many studies, using a variety of measures, have indicated the presence of inequality in the allocation of resources, although there is no clear picture of the degree. In some school systems, court-ordered equalization has been implemented. Differing survey methods, analytic techniques, and measurements of variables seem to result in different findings, even in a single site. Nevertheless, many researchers have argued that even if inequalities in resources exist between poor and nonpoor schools, they may not have any meaningful relationship to educational opportunity. To assess the impact of educational resources on the educational achievement of students has been a major research task.

EDUCATIONAL RESOURCES AND ACHIEVEMENT

Commonly, researchers interested in measuring the impact of school resources (input variables) on student achievement (output variables) have used what is known as a production function approach; a method that approaches education as a production process and attempts to evaluate the role school resources play in producing student outcomes. The value of this methodological technique depends strongly on the specification of variables. For example, the outcome of the educational process is usually measured by the performance of students on standardized achievement tests. Many critics argue that test scores do not reflect values, ambitions, and subsequent occupational status which are important dimensions of the outcome of education; nor are test scores valid measures of school achievement (outputs), even in the narrowest sense. Nevertheless, lack of more pertinent data has dictated the frequent use of such less-than-ideal measures.

Most models have attempted to control for characteristics of student backgrounds by including variables of home and community measures, such as socioeconomic status, parents' education or occupational status, and peer-group influences as measured by the presence of college-bound classmates and similar variables. To these control variables are added a number of relevant school resources. A multiple regression then produces the relative weight of school inputs in explaining the variation in school achievement.

Few of the studies using this "production function" methodology have produced consistent or strong results indicating any significant explanatory power of school resources after background factors and peer influences have been taken into account (Bowles & Levin, 1968; Coleman, 1966; Smith, 1972). One fundamental difficulty arises when background factors are considered in the model with resources. Earlier studies indicated some degree of variation between resources and income, but variables that measure resources and background factors are collinear. Indeed, background factors may be picking up the effects of unequal resources, as well as the converse. Nevertheless, even accounting for these joint effects, estimates of the impact of resources have at most been shown to predict between 1% and 5% of the variation in students' educational achievement (Mayeske, Wisler, Beaton, Weinfeld, Cohen, Okada, Proshek, & Tabler, 1972). Variations in these estimates are explained by the specific resource variables selected and the sample chosen for analysis.

Additional studies using this methodology have generally been forced to conclude that the level of school resources, in general, is relevant only weakly in explaining variations in student achievement, and that background and community variables (including peer influences) consistently remain most important (Thomas, 1963; Perl, 1973). Among a vast number of studies, a number of variables pertaining to school resources often do result in statistically significant coefficients; however, seldom are the same resources found to be significant in all, or even some studies. Variables related to the quality of teachers are those most commonly found to be significant. The level of physical resources rarely appears to have any impact at all. The absence of consistently important resource variables should not be taken as proof that the level of resources a school has does not make a difference (Averch, Carroll, Donaldson, Kiesling, & Pincus, 1974). The resources that do make a difference may not have been selected for analysis; the variables chosen in most studies may not have been appropriately measured. Further, most research is dependent upon aggregate data in which the school or district is the unit of analysis. It is indeed quite possible that disaggregated data, where the student is the unit of analysis, may show important differences lost in aggregate data. In addition, absence of experimental research in which longitudinal data are available and control groups are present makes it difficult to conclude with any degree of certainty that the proper resources over an appropriate time frame are not important in explaining variations in students' educational achievement.

INSTITUTIONAL DETERMINANTS

One of the criticisms of the research on the effect of school resources on students' achievement was that aggregate data do not permit an assessment of the impact of *specific* resources on a *given group* of children. Many researchers have claimed that the behavior and attitudes of teachers and staff members have important and direct effects on the achievements of individual students with whom they interact in the classroom. A most important factor is the degree to which teachers have positive expectations of students. If teachers do not expect lower-class students to perform as well as middle-class students, they behave in ways which communicate this bias to lower-class students: the students, in turn, behave to fulfill the expectations (Wilkerson, 1970).

Many attempts have been made to ascertain the derivation of teachers' biases against lower-class children and to evaluate what role these biases play in explaining the variation in individual performance among students. A recent monograph devoted to this subject summarized the major reasons for teachers' low expectations for such children. First, teachers have certain personality traits predisposing them to have lower expectations for certain children; they are exposed to certain socializing experiences and societal prejudices that shape their perceptions of students. Secondly, I.Q. scores and cultural deficits influence teachers' expectations. Thirdly, educational structures affect teachers' expectations (Persell, 1977).

MIDDLE-CLASS TEACHERS AND LOWER-CLASS STUDENTS

Many authors attribute much of the failure, hostility, and apathy of lower-class students to the clash of middle- and lower-class values, racial bias, and the general inability of teachers to communicate with students who are poor (Goodwin, 1977). Coleman (1966) also questioned the ability of schools to equalize social-class differences in cognitive achievement. It is argued that a "cultural gap" exists, whereby teachers who are middle-class in origin and values are unable to appreciate the particular educational problems of poor children; the social attributes of these teachers (race, sex, and upbringing) do not provide them with essential skills and sensitivities for meeting the needs of poor children (Goodwin, 1977). Negative attitudes may also prevail among middle-class teachers who have little choice in school placement or who may feel frustrated at having to handle situations with which they have not been adequately prepared to cope (Wilkerson, 1970). Such teachers may see a kind of "moral unacceptability" in the actions or appearance of lower-class children. Goodwin, however, could not demonstrate in his Baltimore study that school systems hire more middle- than lower-class teachers or that educational practices come to reflect the bias of the teacher's background.

TEACHER TRAINING AND SOCIALIZATION

The type of socialization or training middle-class teachers encounter in low-income children also affects their expectations (Persell, 1977). Stein (1971) and Hill (1971) support this notion. For example, most teachers are likely to see in the "culturally deprived child" those characteristics identified in the clinical literature, emphasizing deficiencies in the child and/or the child's environment and placing very little emphasis on the school system. Other critics have suggested that prejudice is an important factor affecting teacher expectations for children. Teachers of different races may be reared in different social contexts and hold different expectations for students (Krupczak, 1972; Pugh, 1974).

Silberman (1970) contends that expectations of success and accountability for failure are built into the school structure so that teachers are very much influenced by the atmosphere of the school. Havighurst (1964) argues that the difference between a successful and unsuccessful school in a culturally deprived neighborhood depends to a very high degree on the attitudes and morale of the teaching staff.

TEACHER EXPECTATIONS AND BEHAVIOR

Several investigators have shown that the expectations of teachers significantly influence a student's academic performance. One cannot fail to detect the pervasiveness of low expectations among professionals in ghetto schools (Wilkerson, 1970). A few of the common variables thought to influence the teacher expectations are pupils' I.Q. ratings, test scores, appearance, language, and socioeconomic class (Persell, 1977). The results of a study that followed a class of ghetto children from kindergarten through first and second grade (Rist, 1970) revealed that in kindergarten the teacher's expectations from and identification of "slow" and "fast" learners was based on social-class status.

Teachers' expectations have been found to function as self-fulfilling prophecies (Rosenthal & Jacobson, 1968). In support of this conclusion were the findings of Brophy and Good (1970) from a study in a small Texas school district that served a generally rural and lower-class population. The observation included four first-grade classrooms and 45% of the students from a higher socioeconomic background who were living on a nearby military base. The question the study posed was how teachers' expectations are communicated so as to cause children to produce reciprocal behavior. The study revealed that teachers demanded better performance from students they felt would be more likely to achieve, and were more likely to accept poor performances from students for whom they had low expectations. The authors also found that teachers were less likely to praise good performances and that good performances occurred less frequently when expectations were lower.

The expectations and behavior of teachers and the self-expectations of students may interact in their effect on student achievement. Peng (1974) found that when both teachers' expectations and self-expectations were high, students were high achievers. The results of his study indicate that the positive behavior of teachers may be related to student gains only when the preconditions for a positive situation exist, with respect to teacher expectation and self-expectation. Rosenthal (1974) concluded that school achievement was most affected by the amount of material taught and the amount and type of interaction between teachers and students. After reviewing the literature on this subject, Persell found that out of 44 induced-expectancy studies he reviewed, there were 18 in which both the behavior of the teacher and the outcome for the student were measured. In most of these studies there were consistent relationships between the behavior of teachers and cognitive outcomes. In 8 of the studies, the behavior of teachers changed in the direction of the induced expectations, and students changed as well. In 5 studies, the behavior of teachers was modified in a way that was consistent with the induced expectations, but students showed no change. Persell concludes that where induced expectations appear to approximate natural ones, both in credibility and behavioral manifestations, they are most likely to affect students. Baker (1973) also suggests that because of their less powerful position in society, lower-class students are more vulnerable to teacher expectations than are middle-class students.

Fleming and Anttonen (1971) did a study challenging the phenomenon of the self-fulfilling prophecy. The study attempted to examine the effects of teachers' expectations on intellectual growth when the teachers were informed and misinformed of the students' I.Q. levels. Data were recorded for students of both sexes. The sample consisted of the second-grade classrooms of 22 schools; 11 had high poverty indices and 11 low poverty indices. The total sample consisted of 1087 students. Students within each classroom were randomly assigned to one of four treatment conditions. Under the experimental design, the teachers received one of four different types of test information for each student: (a) traditional I.Q. scores as actually tested; (b) no I.Q. information; (c) primary mental abilities percentiles; and (d) I.Q.s inflated by 16 points.

In contrast to the studies just reviewed, these results were unable to support contentions that the self-fulfilling prophecy is applicable to all educational settings. No significant differences were found among the groups; that is, the inflated group did not gain more I.Q. points than any of the other groups tested. The expectancy effect was not demonstrated, either as an overall effect or for any of the different ability groups (Fleming and Anttonen, 1971). Other studies have supported these findings (Grieger, 1970; Schain, 1972; and Spielberg, 1973); but most studies indicate that students' educational achievement strongly relates to their teachers' expectations. Evidence supports the view that teachers, in general, have lower expectations for students from low-income homes and that this has a negative effect on achievement.

CONCLUSION

So convinced were most social scientists and policymakers that education was a critical determinant of future economic status that the War on Poverty placed educational programs at the center of policy strategy. Theories of poverty prevalent in the years immediately preceding the poverty program legislation stressed the importance of individual incompetence as a fundamental cause of poverty. Compensatory education and other programs were intended to address the special needs of the poor in an effort to prepare them to enter the competitive job market with background characteristics more desirable to employers.

Rather than seeking fundamental institutional explanations, researchers and policymakers pursued an approach that stressed the individual and centered on improving the qualifications of the poor themselves. The strategy was consistent with much research on the correlates of poverty and also with the nation's prevailing cultural philosophy. Though many of the programs of the War on Poverty were successful with small numbers of individuals, they failed to alter fundamentally the observed incidence of poverty.

Two interrelated results are apparent. First, the alleged progress resulting from educational programs was minimal and often of short duration. People who did complete the programs for education job training often remained poor. Abandoning the singular importance of training and education as critical determinants of economic status, opposing views have explained poverty in terms of institutional and labor market factors. The primary significance of educational attainments is hotly debated; there is no consensus that improving the educational attainment of the poor will result in the substantial reduction of poverty.

Nevertheless, the inadequate educational background of the welfare poor serves as an additional impediment when seen in the contexts of their other significant labor force disadvantages and of institutional factors which further (or primarily) alter their life chances. Education does appear to have a variety of indirect effects on the status of the poor through its influence on their use of health care and family planning services; and it does function to socialize and integrate people into the values and ways of participating in the larger society. The failure of education to provide these benefits to the children of the poor is therefore an important research and public policy question.

Though research has proliferated over the past 15 years, the state of knowledge remains disappointing. The findings of research offer few insights relevant to policies that might direct future initiatives. Background factors of the children studied tend to dominate all other variables used to explain failure in school. Nevertheless, since background factors are strongly correlated with other explanatory variables, such as resources, it is often not possible to separate out and measure the actual impact that any single variable may have in explaining variations in achievement.

Variables used to measure achievement rarely capture the complex outcome of the educational process. They tend to measure only narrowly defined cognitive achievement. Standardized tests and grades are only one aspect of student learning. "Higher cognitive processes (abstract reasoning, problem solving, and creativity, among others) are obviously important educational outcomes as is noncognitive achievement [Averch *et al.*, 1974, p. 171]." Since research has been unable to measure a variety of educational outcomes, it has not been able to make conclusive generalizations about them. Studies which attempt to explain educational outcomes on the basis of input factors and institutional variables alone have been unsuccessful in explaining a significant amount of the variation. Part of the problem may be that in most samples there is not enough variation in the independent variables to clearly reveal the significant determinants. There is not enough significant variation in educational policies nationally to reveal an explanatory variant in the system that is consistently related to students' educational outcomes. Another possible explanation is that there is no single, consistent, and unambiguous determinant that has importance for all children in all educational settings (Averch *et al.*, 1974). However, there may be interaction effects among several variables when found together.

In other words, the marginal differences observed in national samples of the resources, organization, teachers, class sizes, and funding of school systems do not seem to have consistent impacts on student outcomes. Averch *et al.* (1974) conclude, after a thorough review of the literature, that the results may indicate that marginal changes in educational practices have little impact. They argue that research findings are implicitly indicating that only sweeping and dramatic changes in the organization, structure, and content of educational experiences are likely to result in significant decreases in students' failure rates.

What remains central in assessing the importance of research results and improving the mobility of the poverty population is that continued emphasis on the background factors of children to explain educational failure provides no policy-relevant insights to alter present configurations. Indeed, such an approach, while comforting to planners and administrators, does little to effect results. It is a case of "blaming the victim"; continuing to focus on these factors impedes the development of additional research approaches or policy options.

6

Welfare Research: Political and Methodological Limitations

The past 2 decades have witnessed tremendous activity in income maintenance policy and research. Though considerable resources have been devoted to the problems of poverty and dependency, researchers and policymakers alike continue to disagree about what constitutes an effective strategy toward the reduction of poverty. This monograph has demonstrated the degree to which differences in approach and methodology have resulted in a variety of often conflicting and contradictory policy prescriptions. Furthermore, even noncontroversial research findings are often excluded from practical policy application because of strong ideological attachments to certain problem solving frameworks held by both political decisionmakers and the constituents they represent. The dominance of issues relating to work and work incentives throughout all debates on income maintenance policy reflects the prevailing priorities and problem-solving frameworks. The strength of such issues is revealed by the way they dominate discussions of welfare reform, even during periods of high unemployment and declining demand.

Most social policy analysis concludes with prescriptions for further research. In that respect this monograph is no exception. In spite of the

145

growth in research activity in this area, many questions remain
unresolved—some due to legitimate value conflicts among and between
the research and the policymaking communities. Other questions remain unresolved due to the weakness of the state of the art or the
limitations of the research questions asked and the data available.
Clearly, based on the review of the literature in all the previous chapters, substantial gaps in knowledge remain, even while areas with substantial grounding in research knowledge continue to be debated on the
basis of values.

Disagreement about the nature of dependency and the policies necessary to address it in many respects reflects the different biases of the
"income maintenance establishment." The shifts in the character of
both research and policy initiatives reflect the changing nature of this
"establishment." Until recently, the dominant force in poverty policy
included the social welfare community. Representing largely service
providers, organized social work had considerable impact on problem
definition and policy prescription. The clinical orientation of the social
welfare community provided a framework which situated the problems
of the welfare poor in the casework paradigm. Thus, an emphasis on the
need for services dictated to a large degree the character of poverty
policy. The welfare poor were seen to be in need of counseling, training,
and more generally, help to increase their human capital. Emphasis on
social services follows logically from the treatment model that the social
work community holds; causality lies firmly within the individual.

The 1962 and 1967 legislative amendments to the Social Security Act
revealed the dominance of this paradigm through the liberalization of
federal financing arrangements for the provision of social services for the
former, current, and potential welfare recipient. Requirements for registration for work training, job counseling, and job placement through
the WIN program further supported this approach to the welfare poor.
Throughout the research community, emphasis was on the personal
characteristics of welfare recipients as an explanation of their status.
(Sociological approaches to research on poverty were presented in
Chapters 2, 4, 5, and 6.) In many respects the stylishness of this kind of
research, and the policy implications which flowed from it, can be seen
as a function of the professional dominance of the social welfare
establishment.

By the mid-1960s a competing paradigm began to emerge. The
liberal–activist orientation began to influence both policy and, to a les-
ser degree, research. It came to see the problem of poverty as caused and
reinforced by institutional rigidity and the poverty of *power* among the
poor. Such an approach required attempts to coordinate and redirect a

school achievement and health care utilization, that neglect the important and independent impact of institutional arrangements themselves, have not been very useful in providing models for reform.

This section sought to place the blame for the imbalance and limited range of research approaches firmly on the ideological bias of the prevailing policymaking environment. Nevertheless, the narrowness of research approaches represented in the literature also speaks to some important limitations in the state of knowledge within social science and to a variety of important technical considerations related to the cost of knowledge.

COST OF KNOWLEDGE

Much of the microsociological emphasis on the research on poverty has been reinforced by the availability of pertinent data and the consideration of the actual cost of acquiring other data. There has been substantial dependence on small population samples of families in poverty which lend themselves far more to a microsociological analysis than to dynamic, large-scale considerations of economic and institutional factors. The costs of acquiring large-scale survey data on a representative national sample of poverty families are quite substantial. Therefore, a large proportion of the available evidence of poverty and its correlates has been based on welfare department case records or local samples of families in a particular jurisdiction. Other evidence has been inferred from national data bases such as the census or current population surveys. Rarely do these data sources provide all the appropriate variables required (far less than measured in an optimal manner) for a full range of research approaches. The available data necessarily limit the form and nature of research questions asked and the adequacy of results generated.

More recently, a variety of larger, more representative data sources has become available. Longitudinal data from several income maintenance experiments have aided enormously the efforts to follow families over time and to monitor changes in their behavior and well-being. Nevertheless, data from these experiments are extremely expensive to acquire; therefore, only survey questions essential to the experimental purposes were asked. If a researcher were interested in specific information, for example, related to the health care behavior of experimental families or their experiences with health care professionals, the data might be useless. Likewise, 8 years of a panel study of income dynamics of 5000 American families have recently been completed by the Institute for Social Research at the University of Michigan. This comprehensive data base has been a critical source for much of the important new research on the dynamics of poverty and dependency. Nevertheless, the cost of acquiring data appropriate for a wide variety of research uses limited the range and nature of the questions asked. In any kind of survey instrument, consideration of a subject's time and privacy may be critical in determining both the response rate and the rate of attrition. Such considerations require that the survey instrument be quite selective in the number of answers sought. Thus, many variables important to some researchers may be sacrificed.

It is not surprising, therefore, that a variety of data have not been available for critical research analysis. For example, many of the important questions which might be answered concerning changes over time in the school achievement of particular student populations have been only inadequately measured, usually on the basis of point-in-time aggregate data. Similarly, changes in health status and health care behavior have been only poorly inferred on the basis of aggregate point-in-time national surveys. Longitudinal data sources on large representative samples have been conspicuously lacking for a variety of important research questions.

Not only have data sources been inadequate for research in the social sciences, but research techniques available to social scientists have many important weaknesses that limit the kinds of questions that can be asked and the usefulness of the resulting answers.

The technique used most widely (having been made popular by economists) is multiple regression analysis. A key requirement of multiple regression analysis for accurate estimates of the impact of a group of independent variables on a dependent variable is that the independent variables be truly independent of one another. This problem has been specifically mentioned in relation to the determinants of educational achievement where the model included student background characteristics as well as a variety of resource and institutional variables. One of the difficulties in interpreting the results of those models was caused by the multicollinearity of the independent variables. Since background characteristics of students were highly correlated with the distribution of school resources, it was impossible to know precisely how much of the explanatory power of student background characteristics was accounted for by the distribution of resources. This is a problem of considerable significance in most social science research. Rarely can models of human behavior find independent variables truly independent of one another. Multicollinearity, therefore, influences the confidence that can be placed in many of the predictive estimates resulting from multiple regression analysis.

Another problem with much of the research in this area has been the attempt by researchers to identify and control for all of the exogenous variables likely to influence a specific outcome (e.g., going on welfare, dissolving a marriage). The determinants of behavior are so complex and often so subtle that it is often impossible to consider all of them in a single model. In fact, statistical "laws" limit the number of independent variables that can validly be considered in a single model on the basis of the number of observations.

Furthermore, even if all relevant variables could be identified, many fall into the category of the unmeasurable. For example, some hypothesized that the "stigma" effect of the AFDC program constrains the otherwise strong impact of the female independence effect on marital dissolution. Nevertheless, the magnitude of this effect can only be inferred since there is considerable difficulty in quantifying a concept like "stigma." An abundance of important concepts and variables in the social sciences confront similar measurement problems. Since there is a strong bias in favor of quantitative analysis, variables that are difficult to measure are often dropped from analysis in favor of those more easily measured by interval data. The result is that important determinants may be abandoned in favor of those more easily measured. In addition, when variables of a qualitative nature are included, they are often measured inappropriately, therefore calling into question the validity of the results. Abandoning multiple regression analysis in favor of more qualitative techniques creates other serious problems of bias and interpretation.

A fundamental weakness of much of the research on poverty and dependency is the lack of a sound theoretical foundation when developing empirical models. Theory in the social sciences is in its infancy and that body of theory which does exist has not sustained general support over long periods of time. Part of the difficulty in the social sciences as compared with the physical sciences is the ability of human beings to learn from experience and history (knowledge) and alter their behavior in response to new knowledge. Thus, even a valid theory may not maintain its explanatory power over some longer time frame. This is the challenge of the social sciences, but it is also the difficulty in developing valid research findings capable of explaining behavior and directing public policy.

It was mentioned above that researchers often have difficulties in specifying all the possible determinants of a particular outcome. A firm theory would permit a systematic justification for the inclusion of any particular factor. Without it, the appropriateness of including any particular variables in an analysis is often called into question. Thus, much research becomes raw empiricism, trial and error. The lack of a firm, explicit theoretical basis to direct analysis also means that different researchers consider different factors in a similar analysis and that few research findings are ever replicated. Therefore, as has been shown throughout the preceding chapters, it is difficult to compare and contrast the findings of differing studies. Theory enters the research process implicitly through value screens, without attention to its underlying assumptions.

POLICY IMPLICATIONS AND FUTURE RESEARCH ON POVERTY

Giving begrudging acceptance to the limitations of existing knowledge for both ideological and technical reasons, what then can be concluded from a review of the literature on the welfare poor? Perhaps most startling has been the complexity of the determinants relating to their status. Although an attempt has been made throughout this monograph to separate the causes from the consequences of welfare status, it is clear that a satisfactory separation is not always possible, given the current state of the art. Indeed, though decades of policy have attempted to search for clean and simple answers to poverty and dependency, none exist. Neither the provision of social services, nor work training nor enforced work nor political participation are likely to address all facets of the problems of poverty. Even the provision of an adequate, equitable income support system is unlikely to provide a clean and simple solution for the welfare poor. It has been demonstrated that even thoughtful and effective policy usually carries with it unanticipated consequences that often make the cure worse than the disease.

The literature has shown that the status of the welfare poor is intimately related to a large range of institutional failures. Welfare, rather than being the cause of multiple handicaps, is better seen as the last receptacle for those who have been ill served by others of our important social institutions.

Though the literature has more often than not uncovered relationships between the human resources of the poor and their welfare status, the source of the difficulty has often been squarely placed on the individual. Less often has the literature looked to the major institutions charged with the responsibility of imparting human resources to the population as a fundamental cause of poverty. The dramatic evidence, for example, of poor health, school failure, and inadequate employment experience is too often accepted as a series of "givens" in models explaining welfare patterns. The failures of institutions to provide needed human resources has not been given appropriate attention.

Perhaps the most important recent research finding has been that the population at risk of poverty is larger than generally assumed. If poverty can no longer be seen as restricted to some stable entrenched group, and if the risk of poverty is substantial for some larger portion of the working population, the issue of personal inadequacy would appear to have weak empirical foundation. Nevertheless, the strength of operating value screens is unlikely to support a shift to a more fundamentally systemic analysis of the determinants of poverty.

Taking a systemic approach to poverty and dependency is not popular. It requires examining the most fundamental operating assumptions of the economy. Historically, social policy has restricted itself to altering marginally the outcomes of the economic system. More recent research may be indicating that a marginal adjustment of outcomes is not adequate for achieving many important social goals. It will be with great difficulty, however, that current decision makers alter their conceptions about the appropriate point at which public intervention ought to occur to confront poverty and dependency.

American social policy has fluctuated uneasily between the humanistic goals of the modern welfare state and the requirements of the free market. This tension has created fundamental contradictions between human and economic goals. Indeed, legislative debates about Nixon's Family Assistance Plan demonstrated dramatically the degree to which these basic contradictions constrain social policy. Southern senators, whose constituents stood to gain the most from Nixon's income transfer program, and whose economies would benefit most from increased demand, were those most adamantly thwarting legislative attempts for an income support plan. Though their conservative values were paramount in their objections, it was the fear of interfering with their low-wage labor markets which had an important impact on their positions.

Research may be very important in the long run in helping to resolve these fundamental contradictions. As old paradigms that direct social policy begin to be questioned because of their seeming inability to alter fundamental social problems, new paradigms, based on a preponderence of solid research evidence, may begin to influence the policymaking environment (Rein, 1976). This is, by definition, a long-term goal. Nevertheless, it argues for a new emphasis on paradigm-challenging research.

This monograph has indicated throughout the usefulness of research approaches that seek to explain the sources of poverty within an institutional framework. More concentrated attention to this direction in future research activity may provide the foundation for important and dramatic new social policy planning. During the period of projected declining national growth and growing conservatism about government spending, any fundamentally altered policy initiatives will require strong and convincing empirical support. In such an environment, the role of research may take on far more importance. It is for this reason that future social science research on poverty and dependency must question prevailing research concerns and begin to examine more fully the usefulness of approaches that ask more fundamental questions about the institutional causes of poverty.

References

Aaron, H. (1973) *Why is welfare so hard to reform?* Washington, D.C.: Brookings Institution.

Aaron, H. (1975) Alternative ways to increase work effort. In I. Lurie (Ed.), *Integrating income maintenance programs* (1st ed.) New York: Academic Press.

Abrahamse, A., de Ferranti, D., Fleischauer, P., & Lipson, A. (1977) *AFDC caseload and the job market in California: Selected issues* (Report No. R-2115-CDOBP). Santa Monica: Rand Corporation.

Aday, L. (1975) Economic and noneconomic barriers to the use of needed medical services. *Medical Care, 13*, pp. 447–456.

Allen, C. (1974) The health of the disadvantaged: a new attack on an old problem. *Public Health Reports, 89*, pp. 499–503.

Allen, J. (1973) *Designing income maintenance systems: The income accounting problem* (Studies in Public Welfare Paper No. 5, Subcommittee on Fiscal Policy, Joint Economic Committee, U.S. Congress). Washington, D.C.: U.S. Government Printing Office.

Alpert, J., Kosa, J., & Haggerty, R. (1967) A month of illness and health care among low-income families. *Public Health Reports, 82*, pp. 705–713.

Appel, G. (1972) *Effects of a financial incentive on AFDC employment: Michigan's experience between July 1969 and July 1970.* Minneapolis: Institute for Interdisciplinary Studies.

Averch, H., Carroll, S., Donaldson, T., Kiesling, H., & Pincus, J. (1974) *How effective is schooling?: A critical review of the research.* Englewood Cliffs, N.J.: Educational Technology Publications.

Baker, S. (1973) *Teacher effectiveness and social class as factors in teacher expectancy effects on pupil scholastic achievement* (doctoral dissertation, Clark University). *Dissertation Abstracts International, 34*, 2376A.

Bane, M. (1975) *Economic influences on divorce and remarriage.* Cambridge, Mass.: Center for the Study of Public Policy.

Barr, N., & Hall, R. (1975) The taxation of earnings under public assistance. *Economica, 42*, pp. 373–384.

Beaver, S., & Chapek, S. (1975) *Socioeconomic determinants of fertility of American women: A multivariate reanalysis of the 1965 National Fertility Study.* Paper presented at meeting of Population Association of America, Seattle.

Becker, G. (1964) *Human capital.* New York: Columbia University Press.

Becker, M., Drachman, R., & Kirscht, J. (1974) A new approach to explaining sick-role behavior in low income populations. *American Journal of Public Health, 64*, pp. 205–216.

Bellin, L., & Kavaler, F. (1969) *Policing publicly funded health care for poor quality, overutilization, and fraud: The New York City medicaid experience.* Paper presented to American Public Health Association, Medical Care Section, November 1969.

Bellin, S., & Geiger, H. (1972) The impact of a neighborhood health center on patients' behavior and attitudes relating to health care: A study of a low income housing project. *Medical Care, 10*, pp. 224–238.

Berkanovic, E. (1974) *Perceptions of medical care.* Lexington, Mass.: Lexington Books.

Berkanovic, E., & Reeder, L. (1973) Ethnic, economic, and social psychological factors in the source of medical care. *Social Problems, 21*, pp. 246–259.

Berkowitz, M., & Johnson, W. (1974) Health and labor force participation. *Journal of Human Resources, 9*, pp. 117–128.

Bernstein, B., & Meezan, W. (1975) *The impact of welfare on family stability* (Center for New York City Affairs). New York: New School for Social Research.

Bernstein, B., Shkuda, A., & Burns, E. (1973) *Income-related social benefits in New York: Adequacy, incentives, and equity* (Studies in Public Welfare Paper No. 8, Subcommittee on Fiscal Policy, Joint Economic Committee, U.S. Congress). Washington, D.C.: Government Printing Office.

Bernstein, G. (1968) *An analysis of private physician participation in N.Y.C. medicaid programs.* Report to New York City Health Services Administration, October, 1968.

Bettelheim, B., & Rainwater, L. (1971) Mental health in the slums. In P. Freeburg (Ed.), *The social impact of urban design.* University of Chicago Press.

Bice, T., Eichhorn, R., & Fox, P. (1972) Socioeconomic status and use of physician services: A reconsideration. *Medical Care, 10*, pp. 261–271.

Birch, H., & Gussow, J. (1972) *Disadvantaged children: Health, nutrition, and school failure.* New York: Grune & Stratton.

Bluestone, B., & Hardman, A. (1972) *Women, welfare and work* (Social Welfare Regional Research Institute Publication No. 9). Chestnut Hill, Mass.: Boston College.

Boaz, F. (1977) Fair share in health care. In A. Schorr (Ed.), *Jubilee of Our Times.* New York: Columbia University Press.

Bogue, D. (1975) A long-term solution to the AFDC problem: Prevention of unwanted pregnancy. *Social Service Review, 49*, pp. 539–552.

Boland, B. (1973) *Participation in aid to families with dependent children program (AFDC)* (Studies in Public Welfare Paper No. 21, Part 1. Subcommittee on Fiscal Policy, Joint Economic Committee, U.S. Congress). Washington, D.C.: U.S. Government Printing Office.

Borinsky, M. (1975) *Comparison of schools with high and low proportions of poverty pupils*

(U.S. Department of Health, Education and Welfare), (National Center for Education Statistics, Office of Education). Washington, D.C.: U.S. Government Printing Office.

Boskin, M., & Nold, F. (1975) A Markov model of turnover in aid to families with dependent children. *Journal of Human Resources, 10,* pp. 467–481.

Bowden, I., Haner, W., & Kerachsky, S. (1973) *The rural income maintenance experiment.* Madison: University of Wisconsin, Institute for Research on Poverty.

Bowles, S., & Gintis, H. (1976) *Schooling in capitalist America.* New York: Basic Books.

Bowles, S., & Levin, H. (1968) The determinants of scholastic achievement: An appraisal of some recent evidence. *Journal of Human Resources, 3,* pp. 3–24.

Bradbury, K. (1977) *The effects of welfare reform alternatives on the family* (Special Report Series). Madison: University of Wisconsin, Institute for Research on Poverty.

Brasel, J., & Winick, M. (1972) Maternal nutrition and prenatal growth: Experimental studies of effects of maternal undernutrition on fetal and placental growth. *Archives of Diseases in Childhood, 47,* pp. 479–485.

Bronfenbrenner, U. (1974) Is early intervention effective? In S. Ryan (Ed.), *Longitudinal evaluation of preschool programs,* Vol. 1. (Report No. OHD 74-24). Washington, D.C.: U.S. Department of Health, Education and Welfare, Office of Human Development.

Brook, R., & Williams, K. (1975) Quality of health care for the disadvantaged. *Journal of Community Health, 1,* pp. 132–156.

Brooks, C. (1973) Associations among distance, patient satisfaction, and utilization of two types of inner-city clinics. *Medical Care, 11,* pp. 373–383.

Brophy, J., & Good, T. (1970) Teachers' communication of differential expectations for children's classroom performance: Some behavioral data. *Journal of Educational Psychology, 61,* pp. 365–374.

Brown, P. (1976) Differential utilization of the health care delivery system by members of ethnic minorities. *Journal of Sociology and Social Welfare, 10,* pp. 516–523.

Bullough, B. (1972) Ethnic identity and preventive health care. *Journal of Health and Social Behavior, 13,* pp. 347–359.

Bumpass, L., & Sweet, J. (1972) Differentials in marital stability: 1970. *American Sociological Review, 37,* pp. 754–766.

Burgess, E., & Price, D. (1963) *An American dependency challenge.* Chicago: American Public Welfare Association.

Burlage, D. (1976) *A preliminary review of research and selected bibliography related to separated and divorced mothers.* Paper submitted to Women's Action Project, Office of Special Concerns, U.S. Department of Health Education, and Welfare, Washington, D.C.

Cain, G. (1974) *The effect of income maintenance laws on fertility: Results from the New Jersey-Pennsylvania experiment.* (Final report of New Jersey graduated work incentive experiment). Madison: University of Wisconsin, Institute for Research on Poverty.

Caldwell, S. (1975) *Marital dissolution in the United States: Combining evidence from Macro Time Series, 1949–1971, and Micro Panel Data, 1968–1972* (Working Paper No. 0980-7). Washington, D.C.: Urban Institute.

Carter, H., & Glick, P. (1970) *Marriage and divorce: A social and economic study.* Cambridge, Mass.: Harvard University Press.

Cherlin, A. (1976) *Economics, social roles, and marital separation* (preliminary draft). Baltimore: Johns Hopkins University, Department of Social Relations, 1976.

Child Development Group of Mississippi (1968). *Surveys of family meal patterns* (Nutrition Services Division, May 17, 1967 and July 11, 1967). Cited in *Hunger, USA.* Washington, D.C.: New Community Press.

Christakis, G., Miridjanian, A., Nath, L., Khurana, H., Cowell, C., Archer, M., Frank, O., Ziffer, H., Baker, H., & James, G. (1968) A nutritional epidemiologic investigation of 642 New York City children. *American Journal of Clinical Nutrition, 21,* pp. 107–126.

Churchman, A., Shuman, C., & Kogan, L. (1975) Health and welfare correlates of school achievement in New York City. *Urban Education, 10,* pp. 305–320.

Clark, K. (1972) *The educationally deprived: The potential for change.* New York: Metropolitan Applied Research Center.

Clarkson, K. (1975) *Food stamps and nutrition.* Washington, D.C.: American Enterprise Institute for Public Policy Research.

Cobb, C. (1974) Community mental health services and the lower socioeconomic classes: A summary of research literature on outpatient treatment. *American Journal of Orthopsychiatry, 44,* pp. 404–502.

Coburn, D., & Pope, C. (1974) Socioeconomic status and preventive health behavior." *Journal of Health and Social Behavior, 15,* pp. 67–78.

Coleman, J. (1966) *Equality of educational opportunity* (U.S. Department of Health, Education and Welfare, Office of Education). Washington, D.C.: U.S. Government Printing Office.

Conforti, J. (1969) Attitudes toward health and health care facilities among low income youth. *Social Science Quarterly, 50,* pp. 687–694.

Coombs, L., & Zumeta, Z. (1970) Correlates of marital dissolution in a prospective fertility study: A research note. *Social Problems, 18,* pp. 92–101.

Cowley, J., & Griesel, R. (1966) The effect on growth and behavior of rehabilitating first and second generation low-protein rats. *Animal Behavior, 14,* pp. 506–517.

Cutright, P. (1971) Income and family events: Marital stability. *Journal of Marriage and the Family, 33,* pp. 291–306.

Cutright, P. (1973a) *Illegitimacy and income supplements* (Studies in Public Welfare Paper No. 12, Subcommittee on Fiscal Policy, Joint Economic Committee of the U.S. Congress). Washington, D.C.: U.S. Government Printing Office.

Cutright, P. (1973b) Timing the first birth: Does it matter? *Journal of Marriage and the Family, 35,* pp. 585–595.

Cutright, P., & Scanzoni, J. (1973) *Income supplements and the American family* (Studies in Public Welfare Paper No. 12, Subcommittee on Fiscal Policy, Joint Economic Committee, U.S. Congress). Washington, D.C.: U.S. Government Printing Office.

Davidson, C., & Gaitz, C. (1974) Are the poor different? A comparison of work behavior and attitudes among the urban poor and nonpoor. *Social Problems, 22,* pp. 229–245.

Davis, K. (1977a) Achievements and problems of medicaid (General Series Reprint 318). Washington, D.C.: Brookings Institution.

Davis, K. (1977b) A decade of policy developments in providing health care for low income families. In R. Haveman (Ed.), *A decade of federal anti-poverty programs.* New York: Academic Press.

Davis, K., & Reynolds, R. (1977) *The impact of medicare and medicaid on access to medical care* (Technical Series Reprint T-0130). Washington, D.C.: Brookings Institution.

Davis, K., & Schoen, C. (1978) *Health and the war on poverty.* Washington, D.C.: Brookings Institution.

Deutsch, M., Katz, I., & Jensen, R. (1968) *Social class, race and psychological development: Environment, development and scholastic achievement.* New York: Holt, Rhinehart and Winston.

Dickerson, J., & McCance, R. (1960) Severe undernutrition in growing and adult animals. *British Journal of Nutrition, 14,* pp. 331–338.

Dodge, W., West, E., Holloway, J., Bridgforth, E., & Travis, L. (1970) Patterns of maternal desires for child health care. *American Journal of Public Health, 60,* pp. 1421–1429.

Doolittle, F., Levy, F., & Wiseman, M. (1977) The mirage of welfare reform. *Public Interest, 47,* pp. 62–87.

Duncan, G. (1974) Educational attainment. In J. Morgan et al. (Eds.), *Five thousand American families: Patterns of economic progress,* Vol. 1. University of Michigan, Institute for Social Research.

Duncan, G. (1976) Unmarried heads of households and marriage. In G. Duncan & J. Morgan (Eds.), *Five thousand American families: Patterns of economic progress,* Vol. 4. University of Michigan, Institute for Social Research.

Duncan, G. (1977) Paths to economic well-being. In G. Duncan & J. Morgan (Eds.), *Five thousand American families: Patterns of economic progress,* Vol. 5. University of Michigan, Institute for Social Research.

Duncan, G., & Morgan, J. (1976a) Family composition change and other analyses of the first seven years of the panel study of income dynamics. In G. Duncan & J. Morgan (Eds.), *Five thousand American families: Patterns of economic progress,* Vol. 4. University of Michigan, Institute for Social Research.

Duncan, G., & Morgan, J. (Eds.). (1976b) *Five thousand American families: Patterns of economic progress,* Vol. 4. University of Michigan, Institute for Social Research.

Duncan, O., Featherman, D., & Duncan, B. (1972) *Socioeconomic background and achievement.* New York: Seminar Press.

Duncan, T., Lord, F., Curtis, J., Rasor, W., Nicola, B., & Viken, R. (1971) Student clinic for migrant laborers. *Northwest Medicine, 70,* pp. 464–467.

Durbin, E. (1969) *Welfare income and employment: An economic analysis of family choice.* New York: Praeger.

Durkin, E. (1975) The vicious cycle of welfare. In C. Lloyd (Ed.), *Sex, discrimination, and the division of labor.* New York: Columbia University Press.

Elesh, D., & Schollaert, P. (1972) Race and urban medicine: Factors affecting the distribution of physicians in Chicago. *Journal of Health and Social Behavior, 13,* 236–250.

Elliott, D. (1966) Delinquency, school attendance and dropout. *Social Problems, 13,* pp. 307–314.

Fabrega, H., Jr., & Roberts, R. (1972) Social-psychological correlates of physician use by economically disadvantaged Negro urban residents. *Medical Care, 10,* pp. 215–223.

Fechter, A., & Greenfield, S. (1973) *Welfare and illegitimacy: An economic model and some preliminary results* (Working Paper 963-37). Washington, D.C.: Urban Institute.

Feldman, H., & Feldman, M. (1972) *A study of the effects on the family due to employment of the welfare mother,* Vol. 1. Ithaca, N.Y.: Cornell University, Department of Human Development and Family Studies.

Feldman, J. (1966) *The dissemination of health information: A case study in adult learning.* Chicago: Aldine.

de Ferranti, D., Leeds, S., Grundfest, J., Leach, V., Parker, P., & Prusoff, L. (1974) *The welfare and nonwelfare poor in New York City* (Report No. R-1381-NYC). New York: Rand Institute.

Filer, L., & Martinez, G. (1964) Intake of selected nutrients by infants in the United States: An evaluation of 4000 representative six-month-olds. *Clinical Pediatrics, 3,* pp. 633–645.

Fleming, E., & Anttonen, R. (1971) Teacher-expectancy effect examined at different ability levels. *Journal of Special Education, 5,* pp. 127–131.

Fox, P. (1972) Access to medical care for the poor: The federal perspective. *Medical Care, 10,* pp. 272–277.

Frieden, A. (1974) The United States marriage market. *Journal of Political Economy, 82,* Part 2, pp. 34–53.

Freidman, B., & Hausman, L. (1975) *Work and welfare patterns in low income families.* Waltham, Mass.: Brandeis University.

Fuerst, A. (1974) *Priority problems of urban minorities regarding health care needs and delivery.* Paper prepared for meeting of American Public Health Association, New Orleans, Oct., 1974.

Furstenberg, F. (1971) Birth control experience among pregnant adolescents: The process of unplanned parenthood. *Social Problems, 19,* pp. 192–203.

Furstenberg, F., Gordis, L., & Markowitz, M. (1969) Birth control knowledge and attitudes among unmarried pregnant adolescents: A preliminary report. *Journal of Marriage and the Family, 31,* pp. 34–42.

Garfinkel, I. (1973) On estimating the labor supply effects of a negative income tax program. In G. Cain & H. Watts (Eds.), *Income maintenance and labor supply: Econometric studies* (Chicago Institute for Research on Poverty monograph series). Skokie, Ill.: Rand McNally.

Garfinkel, I. (1974) Income transfer programs and work effort: A review (Studies in Public Welfare Paper No. 13, Subcommittee on Fiscal Policy, Joint Economic Committee, U.S. Congress). Washington, D.C.: Government Printing Office.

Garfinkel, I., & Masters, S. (1978) *Estimating the Labor Supply Effects of Income Maintenance Alternatives* (Institute for Research of Poverty monograph series). New York: Academic Press.

Garfinkel, I., & Orr, L. (1972) *Welfare policy and the employment rate of AFDC mothers* (Discussion Paper No. 133). Madison: University of Wisconsin, Institute for Research on Poverty.

Garfinkel, I., and Orr, L. (1974) Welfare policy and the employment rate of AFDC mothers. *National Tax Journal, 27,* pp. 275–284.

Glick, P., & Norton, A. (1977) *Marrying, divorcing, and living together in the U.S. today.* Washington, D.C.: Population Reference Bureau.

Goode, W. (1965) *Women in divorce.* New York: Free Press.

Goode, W. (1971) Family disorganization. In R. Merton & R. Nisbet (Eds.), *Contemporary social problems.* New York: Harcourt Brace Jovanovich.

Goodrich, C., Olendzki, M., & Reader, S. (1970) *Welfare medical care: An experiment.* Cambridge, Mass.: Harvard University Press.

Goodwin, D. (1977) *Delivering educational service: Urban schools and schooling policy.* New York: Teachers College Press, Columbia University.

Goodwin, L. (1972) *Do the poor want to work?* Washington, D.C.: Brookings Institution.

Goodwin, L. (1973) Bridging the gap between social research and public policy: Welfare, a case in point. *Journal of Applied Behavioral Science, 9,* pp. 85–114.

Graham, G. (1966) "Growth during recovery from infantile malnutrition." *Journal of American Medical Women's Association, 21,* pp. 737–742.

Greenberg, D. (1971) *Income guarantees and the working poor in New York City: The effect of income maintenance programs on the hours of work of male family heads* (Report No. R-658-NYC). New York: Rand Institute.

Greenberg, J., & Davidson, H. (1972) Home background and school achievement of black urban ghetto children. *American Journal of Orthopsychiatry, 42,* pp. 803–810.

Greenleigh Associates, (1969) *A pilot study of intergenerational dependency in New York City.* New York.

Greenlick, M., Freeborn, D., Colombo, T., Prussin, J., & Saward, E. (1972) Comparing the use of medical care services by a medically indigent and a general membership population in a comprehensive prepaid group practice program. *Medical Care, 10* pp. 187–200.

Greenlick, M., Freeborn, D., Gambill, G., & Pope, C. (1973) Determinants of medical care utilization: The role of the telephone in total medical care. *Medical Care, 11,* pp. 121–134.

Grieger, R. (1970) *The effects of teacher expectancy on the intelligence of students and the behavior of teachers* (doctoral dissertation, Ohio State University). *Dissertation Abstracts International, 1970, 31,* 3338A.

Grove, W. (1970) Who is hospitalized? A critical review of some sociological studies of mental illness. *Journal of Health and Social Behavior, 11,* pp. 294–303.

Haber, Z. (1969) Implementing head start health goals in New York City. *Medical Care, 7,* pp. 134–138.

Hampton, R. (1975) Marital disruption: Some social and economic consequences. In G. Duncan & J. Morgan (Eds.), *Five thousand American families: Patterns of economic progress,* Vol. 3. University of Michigan, Institute for Social Research.

Haney, C., Michielutte, R., Vincent, C., & Cochrane, C. (1973) The value stretch hypothesis: Family size preferences in a black population. *Social Problems, 21,* pp. 206–220.

Hannan, M., Tuma, N., & Groeneveld, L. (1977) Income and marital events: Evidence from an income maintenance experiment. *American Journal of Sociology, 82,* pp. 1186–1211.

Harrison, B., & Rein, M. (1976) *Some microeconomic relations between work and welfare* (Working paper No. 40). Cambridge, Mass.: Joint Center for Urban Studies, MIT & Harvard University.

Hausman, L. (1967) *The potential for work among welfare parents* (Manpower Research Monograph No. 12, U.S. Department of Labor). Washington, D.C.: U.S. Government Printing Office.

Hausman, L. (1970) The Impact of welfare on the work efforts of AFDC mothers. *President's Commission on Income Maintenance Programs: Technical studies.* Washington, D.C.: U.S. Government Printing Office.

Hausman, L. (1972) *Cumulative tax rates in alternative income maintenance systems* (Studies in Public Welfare Paper No. 4, Subcommittee on Fiscal Policy, Joint Economic Commitee, U.S. Congress). Washington, D.C.: U.S. Government Printing Office.

Havens, E. (1973) Women, work, and wedlock: A note on female marital patterns in the United States. *American Journal of Sociology, 78,* pp. 975–981.

Havighurst, R. (1964) *The public schools of Chicago.* Chicago Board of Education.

Herman, M. (1972) The poor: Their medical needs and the health services available to them. *Annals of the American Academy of Political and Social Science, 399,* pp. 12–21.

Herriott, R. (1963) Some social determinants of educational aspirations. *Harvard Educational Review, 33,* pp. 157–177.

Herzog, E. (1969) Facts and fictions about the poor. *Monthly Labor Review, 92,* pp. 42–49.

Hester, J., & Sussman, E. (1974) Medicaid prepayment: Concept and implementation. *Milbank Memorial Fund Quarterly, 52,* pp. 415–444.

Hill, R. (1973) The determinants of labor supply for the working urban poor. In G. Cain & H. Watts (Eds.), *Income maintenance and labor supply: Econometric studies* (Chicago Institute for Research on Poverty monograph series). Skokie, Ill.: Rand McNally.

Hill, S. (1971) *Race, class and ethnic biases in research on school performance of low-income youth.* Doctoral dissertation, University of Oregon.

Hoffman, S., & Holmes, J. (1976) Husbands, wives, and divorce. In G. Duncan &

J. Morgan (Eds.), *Five thousand American families: Patterns of economic progress,* Vol. 4. University of Michigan.

Hoffman, S., & Podder, N. (1976) Income inequality. In G. Duncan and J. Morgan (Eds.), *Five thousand american families: Patterns of economic progress,* Vol. 4. University of Michigan, Institute for Social Research.

Honig, M. (1973) The impact of welfare payment levels on family stability. (Studies in Public Welfare Paper No. 12, Subcommittee on Fiscal Policy, Joint Economic Committee, U.S. Congress). Washington, D.C.: U.S. Government Printing Office.

Hood, A. (1967) Educational and personality factors associated with unusual patterns of parental education. *Journal of Educational Research, 61,* pp. 32–34.

Hulka, B., Kupper, L., & Cassel, J. (1972) Determinants of physician utilization: Approach to a service-oriented classification of symptoms. *Medical Care, 10,* pp. 300–309.

Hunger, USA (1968) (report by Citizens' Board of Inquiry into Hunger and Malnutrition in the United States). Washington, D.C.: New Community Press.

Hurtado, A., Greenlick, M., & Colombo, T. (1973) Determinants of medical care utilization: Failure to keep appointments. *Medical Care, 11,* pp. 189–198.

Ireland, L., Moles, O., & O'Shea, R. (1969) Ethnicity, poverty, and selected attitudes: A test of the 'culture of poverty' hypothesis. *Social Forces, 47,* pp. 405–413.

Jaffe, F. (1972) Low-income families: Fertility changes in the 1960s. *Family Planning Perspectives, 4,* pp. 43–47.

Janowitz, B. (1976) "The impact of AFDC on illegitimate birth rates." *Journal of Marriage and the Family, 38,* pp. 485–494.

Jencks, C. (1972) *Inequality: A reassessment of the effect of family and schooling in America.* New York: Basic Books.

Johnson, S. (1976) The impact of women's liberation on marriage, divorce, and family life cycle. In C. Lloyd (Ed.), *Sex, discrimination, and the division of labor.* New York: Columbia University Press.

Kafatos, A., & Zee, P. (1977) Nutritional benefits from federal food assistance. *American Journal of Diseases of Children, 131,* pp. 265–269.

Kane, R., Kasteler, J., & Gray, R. (1976) *The health gap: Medical services and the poor.* New York: Springer Publishing Company.

Kaplan, H., & Tausky, C. (1972) Work and the welfare Cadillac: The function of and commitment to work among the hard core unemployed. *Social Problems, 19,* pp. 469–483.

Katzman, M. (1971) *The political economy of urban schools.* Cambridge, Mass.: Harvard University Press.

Kavaler, F. (1968) *Medicaid in New York City: People, providers, and payment, telling it how it is.* Report by deputy executive director, New York City Medical Assistance Program.

Kehrer, B., & Wolin, C. (1976) *The impact of an income maintenance experiment on low birth weight.* Paper for Conference on Social Sciences in Health, Miami Beach, Fla. October, 1976.

(Levy, F.) (1973) *Multivariate regression analysis of annual national turnover rates, using the 1969 and 1971 AFDC national surveys.* Wayne, Pa.: Ketron Inc.

Koos, E. (1954) *The health of Regionville: What the people thought and did about it.* New York: Columbia University Press.

Kosa, J., & Zola, I. (1975) *Poverty and health: A sociological analysis.* Cambridge, Mass.: Harvard University Press.

Kriesberg, L. (1970) *Mothers in poverty: A study of fatherless families.* Chicago: Aldine.

Krupczak, W. (1972) Relationships among student self-concept of academic ability, teacher

perceptions of student academic ability, and student achievement (doctoral dissertation, University of Miami). *Dissertation Abstracts International, 33,* 3388A–3389A.

Lane, S. (1975) *Food aid program effects on food expenditures and levels of nutritional achievement of low income households (unpublished manuscript).* Davis: University of California, Department of Agricultural Economics.

Langner, T., Greene, E., Herson, J., Jameson, J., Goff, J., Rostkowski, J., & Zykorie, D.
(1969) Psychiatric impairment in welfare and nonwelfare children. *Welfare in Review, 7,* pp. 10–21.

Leacock, E. (Ed.). (1971) *The culture of poverty: A critique.* New York: Simon & Schuster.

Leidenfrost, N. (1972) A nutrition education service for low income families. *Welfare in
Review, 10,* pp. 44–52.

Lejeune, R. (1968) *Illness behavior among the urban poor.* Doctoral dissertation, Columbia
University, New York.

Lerman, R. (1973) The family poverty and welfare programs: An introductory essay on
problems of analysis and policy (Studies in Public Welfare Paper No. 12, Subcommittee on Fiscal Policy, Joint Economic Committee, U.S. Congress). Washington, D.C.:
U.S. Government Printing Office.

Leveson, I. (1972) The challenge of health services for the poor. *Annals of the American
Academy of Political and Social Science, 399,* pp. 22–29.

Leveson, I. (1973) *The effect of abortion reform on AFDC caseloads.* New York City Health
Services Administration, Office of Program Analysis, Planning, and Budgeting.

Levinson, P. (1969) The next generation: A study of children in AFDC families. *Welfare in
Review, 7,* pp. 1–9.

Levinson, P. (1970) How employable are AFDC women? *Welfare in Review, 8,* pp. 12–16.

Levitan, S. (1977) *Work and Welfare in the 1970s.* Prepared for the Welfare Policy Project of
the Institute of Policy Sciences and Public Affairs (Duke University) & Ford Foundation, New York.

Levitan, S., Rein, M., & Marwick, D. (1976) *Work and welfare go together.* Baltimore: Johns
Hopkins University Press.

Levy, F. (1976) *How big is the American underclass?* Berkeley: University of California
Graduate School of Public Policy.

Levy, F., Meltsner, A,, Wildavsky, A. (1974) *Urban outcomes.* Berkeley: University of
California Press.

Lewis, O. (1963) The culture of poverty. *Transaction, 1963, 1,* pp. 17–19.

Lowe, C., & Alexander, D. Health care of poor children. In A. Schorr (Ed.), *Children and a
decent people.* New York: Basic Books.

Lowenthal, M. (1971) *Work and welfare: An overview* (Social Welfare Regional Research
Institute Publication No. 1). Chestnut Hill, Mass.: Boston College.

Lowery, J., Jr. (1967) *Study of the Current Status of Children Who Received Public Assistance in
Mecklenburg County, North Carolina, in January 1955* (mimeographed).

Lurie, I. (1973) *Legislative, administrative, and judicial changes in the AFDC program* (Reprint
No. 93). Madison: University of Wisconsin, Institute for Research on Poverty, 1973.

Lyon, D. (1977) *The dynamics of welfare dependency: A survey.* Prepared for the Welfare
Policy Project of the Institute of Policy Sciences and Public Affairs (Duke University)
& Ford Foundation, New York.

Lyon, D., Armstrong, J., Hosek, J., & McCall, S. (1976) *Multiple welfare benefits in New York
City* (Report No. R-2002-HEW). Santa Monica: Rand Corporation.

Macaulay, J. (1975) *Is welfare bad for children* (Paper No. 302-75). Madison: University of
Wisconsin, Institute for Research on Poverty.

MacDonald, M., & Sawhill, I. (1978) Welfare policy and the family. *Public Policy, 26,* pp. 89–119.

Mallar, C., & Maynard, A. (1976) *The effects of the rural and New Jersey income maintenance experiments on school performance and educational attainment.* Princeton, N.J.: Mathematica Policy Research.

Maloney, W. (1967) The Tufts comprehensive community health action program." *Journal of the American Medical Association, 202,* pp. 411–414.

Martyn, K. (1965) *A report on education to the Governor's Commission on the Los Angeles Riot.* Los Angeles.

Masters, S. (1969) The effects of family income on children's education: Some findings on inequality of opportunity. *Journal of Human Resources, 4,* pp. 158–175.

Mayeske, G., Wisler, C., Beaton, A., Weinfeld, F., Cohen, W., Okada, T., Proshek, J., & Tabler, K. (1972) *A study of our nation's schools* (U.S. Department of Health, Education and Welfare). Washington, D.C.: U.S. Government Printing Office.

Maynard, R. (1976) *The effects of the rural income maintenance experiment on school performance of children.* Princeton, N.J.: Mathematica Policy Research.

Mayo, J. (1975a) Patterns of mobility in the AFDC program. *Social Service Review, 49,* pp. 553–568.

Mayo, J. (1975b) *Work and welfare: The employment and employability of women in the AFDC program.* University of Chicago, Community and Family Study Center.

McKinlay, J. (1972) Some approaches and problems in the study of the use of services: An overview. *Journal of Health and Social Behavior, 13.*

Mechanic, D. (1973) *Politics, medicine and social science.* New York: Wiley.

Mechanic, D. (1974) *Health, medicine and society.* New York: Wiley.

Mechanic, D. (1975a) *Medical sociology.* New York: Wiley.

Mechanic, D. (1975b) *Mental health and social policy.* New York: Wiley.

Menchik, M. (1975a) *Hospital use under medicaid in New York City* (unpublished draft). Rand Institute, New York.

Menchik, M. (1975b) *Some aspects of ambulatory care under medicaid in New York City.* Unpublished draft, Rand Institute, New York.

Mermann, A. (1966a) *Lowndes County, Alabama, TICEP health survey.*

Mermann, A. (1966b) Statement prepared for U.S. Subcommittee on Employment, Manpower, and Poverty, Washington, D.C.

Meyers, S., & McIntyre, J. (1969) *Welfare policy and its consequences for the recipient population* (U.S. Department of Health, Education and Welfare). Washington, D.C.: U.S. Government Printing Office.

Michelson, S. (1972) For the plaintiffs: Equal school resource allocation. *Journal of Human Resources, 7,* pp. 283–306.

Miller, J., & Ferman, L. (1972) *Welfare careers and low wage employment.* Technical Report, Institute of Labor and Industrial Relations, Ann Arbor, Mich.

Miller, M. (1973) Who receives optimal medical care? *Journal of Health and Social Behavior, 14,* pp. 176–182.

Mincer, J. (1972) *Schooling, experience, and earnings.* New York: National Bureau of Economic Research.

Mincer, J. (1974) Education, experience and the distribution of earnings and employment. In F. Juster (Ed.), *Education, income and human behavior.* New York: National Bureau of Economic Research.

Moles, O. (1965) Training children in low-income families for school. *Welfare in Review, 3,* pp. 1–11.

Monteiro, L. (1973) Expense is no object . . . . : Income and physician visits reconsidered. *Journal of Health and Social Behavior, 14,* pp. 99–114.

Moore, G., Bernstein, R., & Bonanno, R. (1972) Effect of a neighborhood health center on hospital emergency use. *Medical Care, 10,* pp. 240–247.

Moore, K. (1978) Teenage childbirth and welfare dependency. *Family Planning Perspectives, 10,* pp. 233–35.

Moore, K., & Caldwell, S. (1976) *Out-of-wedlock pregnancy and childbearing* (Working Paper 992-02). Washington, D.C.: Urban Institute.

Moore, K., & Waite, L. (1977) Marital dissolution: Early motherhood or early marriage. Washington, D.C.: Urban Institute.

Morgan, J. (Ed.). (1974) *Five thousand American families: Patterns of economic progress,* Vol. 2. University of Michigan, Institute for Social Research.

Morgan, J., Dickinson, K., Dickinson, J., Benus, J., & Duncan, G., (Eds.). (1974) *Five thousand American families: Patterns in economic progress,* Vol. 1. University of Michigan, Institute for Social Research.

Mosteller, F., & Moynihan, D. (Eds.). (1972) *On equality of educational opportunity.* New York: Random House.

Myers, M., O'Brien, S., Mabel, J., & Stare, F. (1968) A nutrition study of school children in a depressed urban district. *Journal of the American Dietetic Association, 53,* pp. 226–242.

Myths about welfare are refuted. (1974) *Family Planning Digest, 4,* p. 3.

National Center for Health Services Research (1975). *Women and their health: Research implications for a new era.* Proceedings of conference, San Francisco, August, 1975.

Nelson, B. (1976) *On becoming a client: Authoritative help-seeking as dependent participation.* Paper prepared for World Congress of International Political Science Association, Edinburgh, Scotland.

Nelson, B. (1978) *Help-seeking from public authorities: Who arrives at the agency door?* Princeton: Woodrow Wilson School, Princeton University.

Olendzki, M., Grann, R., Goodrich, C. (1972) The impact of medicaid on private care for the urban poor. *Medical Care, 10,* pp. 201–206.

Opton, E., Jr. (1972) *Factors associated with employment among welfare mothers.* Berkeley, Calif.: Wright Institute.

Osborn, M. (1971) The impact of differing parental educational level on the educational achievement, attitude, aspiration, and expectation of the child. *Journal of Educational Research, 65,* pp. 163–167.

Ostow, M., & Dutka, A. (1975) *Work and welfare in New York City.* Baltimore: Johns Hopkins University Press.

Owen, J. (1972) The distribution of educational resources in large American cities. *Journal of Human Resources, 7,* pp. 26–38.

Palmore, E. (1963) *Factors associated with school drop-outs and juvenile delinquency among lower class children* (Social Security Bulletin No. 26). Washington, D.C. U.S. Government Printing Office.

Parker, P. (1975) *Comparison of hospital use rates for the welfare and non-welfare poor in New York City.* Unpublished draft, Rand Institute, New York.

Peng, S. (1974) *Expectations, instructional behavior and pupil achievement* (doctoral dissertation, State University of New York, Buffalo). *Dissertation Abstracts International, 35,* 1508A.

Perl, L. (1973) Family background, secondary school expenditure, and student ability. *Journal of Human Resources, 8,* pp. 156–179.

Persell, H. (1977) *Education and inequality: A theoretical and empirical synthesis.* New York: Free Press.

Peskin, J. (1975) *In-kind income and the measurement of Poverty* (U.S. Department of Health, Education and Welfare, Office of Income Security Policy). Washington, D.C.: U.S. Government Printing Office.

Placek, P., & Hendershot, G. (1974) Public welfare and family planning: An empirical study of the 'brood sow' myth. *Social Problems, 21,* pp. 658–673.

Platt, B., Heard, C., & Steward, R. (1964) Experimental protein-calorie deficiency. In H. Munro & J. Allison (Eds.), *Mammalian protein-metabolism,* Vol. 2. New York: Academic Press.

Plionis, B. (1975) Adolescent pregnancy: Review of the literature. *Social Work, 20,* pp. 302–307.

Podell, L. (1969) *Families on welfare in New York City.* City University of New York, Center for the Study of Urban Problems.

Podell, L. (1973) Family planning by mothers on welfare. *Bulletin of the New York Academy of Medicine, 49,* pp. 931–937.

Polgar, S., & Hiday, V. (1974) The effect of an additional birth on low-income urban families. *Population Studies, 28,* pp. 463–471.

Pomeroy, R. (1969) *Studies in the use of health services by families on welfare: Utilization by publicly assisted families.* City University of New York, Center for the Study of Urban Problems.

Pope, C., Yoshioka, S., & Greenlick, M. (1971) Determinants of medical care utilization: The use of the telephone for reporting symptoms. *Journal of Health and Social Behavior, 12,* pp. 155–162.

Presser, H. (1974) Early motherhood: ignorance or bliss. *Family Planning Perspectives, 6,* pp. 8–14.

Presser, H., and Salsberg, L. (1975) Public assistance and early family formulation: Is there a pronatalist effect? *Social Problems, 23,* pp. 226–241.

Pugh, L. (1974) *Teacher attitudes and expectations associated with race and social class.* Paper presented at American Educational Research Association, Chicago, April, 1974.

Quint, J., & Brown, D. (1974) *Welfare case turnover in 1972* (Report No. OPR-8857632-12). New York City Human Resources Administration.

Rainwater, L. (1968) The lower class: Health, illness and medical institutions. In I. Deutscher & E. Thompson (Eds.), *Among the people: Encounters with the poor.* New York: Basic Books.

Read, M. (1969) *Malnutrition and mental development: Needed research to clarify critical questions* (Special Report). U.S. Department of Health, Education and Welfare, Public Health Service Child Health and Human Development, Growth and Development Branch, Bethesda, Md.

Rein, M. (1974) *Work or welfare? Factors in the choice for AFDC mothers.* New York: Praeger.

Rein, M. (1976) *Social science and public policy.* New York: Penguin Books.

Rein, M. (1977) *Is there a welfare class?* (mimeographed draft paper). Cambridge, Mass.: Joint Center for Urban Studies, MIT & Harvard University.

Rein, M., & Rainwater, L. (1976) *Sources of family income and determinants of welfare.* Cambridge, Mass.: Joint Center for Urban Studies, MIT & Harvard University.

Rein, M., & Rainwater, L. (1977) *Patterns of welfare use* (Working Paper No. 47). Cambridge, Mass.: Joint Center for Urban Studies, MIT & Harvard University.

Rist, R. (1970) Student social class and teacher expectations: The self-fulfilling prophecy in ghetto education. *Harvard Educational Review, 40,* pp. 411–451.

Roe, D., & Eickwort, K. (1974) *Health and nutritional status of working and non-working mothers in poverty groups.* Ithaca, N.Y.: Cornell University Graduate School of Nutrition.

Rosenstock, I. (1966) Why people use health services. *Milbank Memorial Fund Quarterly, 44,* pp. 94–124.

Rosenthal, R. (1974) The pygmalion effect: What you expect is what you get. *Psychology Today,* Library Cassette No. 12. New York: Ziff-Davis.

Rosenthal, R,, & Jacobson, L. (1968) *Pygmalion in the classroom: Teacher expectations and pupils' intellectual development.* New York: Holt, Rinehart and Winston.

Ross, H., & Sawhill, I. (1975) *Time of transition: The growth of families headed by women.* Washington, D.C.: Urban Institute.

Rubenstein, A. (Ed.). (1970) *Schools against children: The case for community control.* New York: Monthly Review Press.

Rubin, R., Rosenblatt, C., & Balow, B. (1973) Phychological and educational sequelae of prematurity. *Pediatrics, 52,* pp. 352–363.

Ryan, W. (n.d.) Poverty, progress, and inequality. *Research utilization briefs,* Vol. 1. Community Council of Greater New York.

Rydell, C., Palmerio, T., Blais, G., & Brown, D. (1974) *Welfare caseload dynamics in New York City* (Report No. R-1441-N.Y.C.). New York: Rand Institute.

Saks, D. (1975) *Public assistance mothers in an urban labor market.* Princeton University Industrial Relations Section.

Salber, E., Feldman, J., Offenbacher, H., & Williams, S. (1970) Characteristics of patients registered for service at a neighborhood health center. *American Journal of Public Health, 60,* pp. 2273–2283.

Samora, J,, Saunders, L., & Larson, R. (1961) Medical vocabulary knowledge among hospital patients. *Journal of Health and Human Behavior, 2,* pp. 83–92.

Sanger, M. (1976) *Public services: An investigation of intra-city distribution patterns.* Ann Arbor, Mich.: University Microfilms International.

Santos, F. (1975) The economics of marital status. In C. Lloyd (Ed.), *Sex, discrimination, and the division of labor.* New York: Columbia University Press.

Satin, D., & Duhl, F. (1972) Help?: The hospital emergency unit as community physician. *Medical Care, 10,* pp. 248–260.

Sawhill, I., Peabody, G., Jones; C., & Caldwell, S. (1975) *Income transfers and family structure.* Washington, D.C.: Urban Institute.

Schain, S. (1972) *Learning of low ability children and tutor behavior as a function of the self-fulfilling prophecy* (doctoral dissertation, University of Illinois). *Dissertation Abstracts International, 34,* 642A.

Schiller, B. (1973) Empirical studies of welfare dependency: A survey. *Journal of Human Resources, 8* (Supplement), pp. 19–32.

Sciara, F., & Jantz, R. (1974) Father absence and its apparent effect on the reading achievement of black children from low income families. *Journal of Negro Education, 43,* pp. 221–227.

Sewell, W., & Hauser, R. (1975) *Education, occupation, and earnings.* New York: Academic Press.

Sexton, P. (1961) *Education and income.* New York: Viking Press.

Shapiro, S., Fink, R., & Rosenberg, C. (1972) A program to measure the impact of multiphasic health testing on health differentials between poverty and non-poverty groups. *Medical Care, 10,* pp. 207–214.

Shea, J. (1973) Welfare mothers: Barriers to labor force entry. *Journal of Human Resources, 8* (Supplement), pp. 90–102.

Shea, J., & Meyer, J. (1972) *Potential recipients of family assistance payments: Characteristics and labor market behavior.* Ohio State University, Center for Human Resource Research.

Silberman, C. (1970) *Crisis in the classroom: The making of American education.* New York: Random House.

Sklar, J., & Berkov, B. (1974) Abortion, illegitimacy, and the American birth rate. *Science, 185,* pp. 909–915.

Smith, G. (1967) *On the welfare.* Rutgers University Research Section, Institute of Management and Labor Relations, New Brunswick, N.J..

Smith, M. (1972) Equality of educational opportunity reconsidered. In F. Mosteller & D. Moynihan (Eds.), *On Equality of Educational Opportunity.* New York: Random House.

Smith, V. (1974) *Welfare Work Incentives* (Studies in Welfare Policy No. 2). Michigan Department of Social Services. Lansing, Mich.

Snyder, H., Nana, O., & Smith, P. (1968) The effect of medical facilities on use by the migrant workers in California. *Medical Care, 6,* pp. 394–400.

Soares, A. (1970) Self-concepts of disadvantaged and advantaged students. *Child Study Journal, 1,* pp. 69–73.

Soares, A. (1971) A study of the interpersonal perceptions of disadvantaged children. *Proceedings of American Psychological Association, 79th Annual Convention,* Washington, D.C.

Soares, A,, & Soares, L. (1969) Self-perceptions of culturally disadvantaged children. *American Educational Research Journal, 6,* pp. 31–45.

Sparer, G., & Johnson, J. (1971) Evaluation of OEO neighborhood health centers. *American Journal of Public Health, 61,* pp. 931–942.

Sparer, G., & Okada, L. (1974) Chronic conditions and physician use patterns in ten urban poverty areas. *Medical Care, 12,* pp. 549–560.

Spielberg, D. (1973) *Labeling, teacher expectation, pupil intelligence level and conditions of learning* (doctoral dissertation, Boston University). *Dissertation Abstracts International, 34,* p. 1716A.

Stein A. (1971) Strategies of failure. *Harvard Educational Review, 41,* pp. 158–204.

Stewart, J., & Crafton, L. (1975) *Delivery of health care services to the poor: Findings from a review of the periodical literature.* Austin: University of Texas, Center for Social Work Research.

Stewart, J., & Hood, W. (1970) Using workers from 'hard-core' areas to increase immunization levels. *Public Health Reports, 85,* pp. 177–185.

Stone, R., & Schlamp, F. (1965) Characteristics associated with receipt or non-receipt of financial aid from welfare agencies: An exploratory study. *Welfare in Review, 3,* pp. 1–11.

Stuart, B., & Bari, L. (1971) *Health care and income: The distributional impact of medicare and medicaid nationally and in the state of Michigan* (Research Paper No. 5). Michigan Department of Social Services, Lansing, Mich.

Suchman, E. (1965a) Social factors in medical deprivation. *American Journal of Public Health, 55,* pp. 1725–1733.

Suchman, E. (1965b) Social patterns of illness and medical care. *Journal of Health and Human Behavior, 6,* pp. 2–16.

Sumrall, J., Jr. (1976) *An overview of recent state AFDC benefits and caseload dynamics.* Chestnut Hill, Mass.: Boston College, Social Welfare Regional Research Institute.

Suttles, S. (1968) *The social order of the slum: Ethnicity and territory in the inner city.* University of Chicago Press.

Sweet, J. (1973) *Differentials in Remarriage Possibilities.* (Working Paper No. 73-29). Madison: University of Wisconsin, Center for Demography and Ecology.

Taubman, P. (1975) *Sources of inequality in earnings.* Amsterdam: North-Holland Publishing Company.

Thomas, A. (1963) Talent development and the national income. In H. James & H. Dyke (Eds.), *Wealth expenditures and decision-making for education.* Palo Alto, Calif.: Stanford University School of Education.

Thompson, D., & Miles, G. (1972) *Study of low income families.* North Star Research and Development Institute, Minneapolis, Minnesota. Washington, D.C.: National Technical Information Service.

Thurow, L. (1970) *Investment in Human Capital.* Belmont, Calif.: Wadsworth Publishing Company.

Torrens, P., & Yedvab, D. (1970) Variations among emergency room populations: A comparison of four hospitals in New York City. *Medical Care, 8,* pp. 60–75.

Tyler, R. (1974) The federal role in education. *Public Interest, 34,* pp. 164–187.

U.S. Bureau of the Census. (1971) *Social & Economic Variations in marriage, divorce, and remarriage: 1967* (Current Population Reports, Series P-60, No. 223). Washington, D.C.: U.S. Government Printing Office.

U.S. Bureau of the Census. (1972) *Marriage, divorce, and remarriage* by year of birth: June 1971 (Current Population Reports, Series P-60, No. 239). Washington, D.C.: U.S. Government Printing Office.

U.S. Department of Health, Education and Welfare, Office of Education. (1966) Task Force on Ecnomic Growth and Opportunity. *The disadvantaged poor: Education and employment.* Washington, D.C.: U.S. Government Printing Office.

U.S. Department of Health, Education and Welfare. (1972) *Health service use—national trends and variations, 1953–1971, United States* (DHEW Publication No. [HSM] 73-3004). Rockville, Md. National Center for Health Services Research.

U.S. Department of Health, Education and Welfare. (1973a) *Current estimates from the Health Interview Survey* (DHEW Publication No. [HSM] 73-105). Rockville, Md.: National Center for Health Statistics.

U.S. Department of Health, Education and Welfare. (1973b) *Health characteristics of low income persons* (DHEW Publication No. [HSM] 73-1500). Rockville, Md. National Center for Health Statistics.

U.S. Department of Health, Education and Welfare. (1974) *Findings of the 1973 AFDC study: Demographic and program characteristics* (DHEW Publication No. [SRS] 75-03766). Washington, D.C.: U.S. Government Printing Office.

U.S. Department of Health, Education and Welfare, Public Health Service. (1974) *Preliminary findings of the First health and Nutrition Examination Survey, United States, 1971–1972, dietary intake and biochemical findings.* (HANES Report) Rockville, Md.: National Center for Health Statistics.

U.S. Department of Health, Education and Welfare, Health Resources Administration. (1975) *Selected vital and health statistics in poverty and non-poverty areas of 19 large cities.* Rockville, Md.: National Center for Health Statistics.

U.S. Department of Health, Education and Welfare. (1976) *Health, United States, 1975* (DHEW Publication No. [HRA] 76-1232). Rockville, Md.: National Center for Health Statistics.

U.S. Department of Health, Education and Welfare (1976). *The Rural Income Maintenance Experiment.* University of Wisconsin, Institute for Research on Poverty.

U.S. Department of Health, Education and Welfare, Social Security Administration. (1977) *Aid to Families with Dependent Children: 1975 Recipient Characteristics Study.* Part 1

(DHEW Publication No. [SSA] 77-11777). Washington, D.C.: U.S. Government Printing Office.

U.S. Department of Labor & U.S. Department of Health, Education, and Welfare. (1978) *Employment and Training Report of the President*. Washington, D.C.: U.S. Government Printing Office.

U.S. Senate, Select Committee on Nutrition and Human Needs. (1969) *The food gap: Poverty and malnutrition in the U.S.* Washington, D.C.: U.S. Government Printing Office.

U.S. Senate, Select Committee on Nutrition and Human Needs. (1973a) *Hearings, part 2, governmental responses*. Washington, D.C.: U.S. Government Printing Office.

U.S. Senate, Select Committee on Nutrition and Human Needs. (1973b) *Hearings: Oversight on the WIC Program*, Washington, D.C.: U.S. Government Printing Office.

U.S. Senate, Select Committee on Nutrition and Human Needs. (1974) *To save the children: Nutritional intervention through supplemental feeding*. Washington, D.C.: U.S. Printing Office.

U.S. Senate, Select Committee on Nutrition and Human Needs. (1976a) *Medical evaluation of the Special Supplemental Food Program for Women, Infants and Children*. Washington, D.C.: U.S. Government Printing Office.

U.S. Senate, Senate Committee on Nutrition and Human Needs. (1976b) (Congressional Research Service). *The Role of the federal government in human nutrition research*. Washington, D.C.: U.S. Government Printing Office.

Venti, S. (1975) *The determinants of AFDC in Massachusetts: An econometric analysis* (Social Welfare Regional Research Institute Working Paper No. 25). Chestnut Hill, Mass.: Boston College.

Wan, T., & Soifer, S. (1974) Determinants of physician utilization: A casual analysis. *Journal of Health and Social Behavior, 14*, pp. 100–107.

Warheit, G., Holzer, C., & Schwab, J. (1973) An analysis of social class and racial differences in depressive symptomology: A community study. *Journal of Health and Social Behavior, 14*, pp. 291–298.

Warren, M., & Berkowitz, S. (1969) Employability of AFDC mothers and fathers. *Welfare in Review, 7*, pp. 1–7.

Weiss, J., & Greenlick, M. (1970) Determinants of medical care utilization: The effect of social class and distance on contacts with the medical care system. *Medical Care, 8*, pp. 456–462.

Wilkerson, D. (1970) The failure of schools serving the black and Puerto Rican poor. In A. Rubenstein (Ed.), *Schools against children: The case for community control*. New York: Monthly Review Press.

Williams, R. (1975) *Public assistance and work effort: The labor supply of low income female heads of household*. New Jersey: Princeton University.

Williamson, J. (1974) Beliefs about the welfare poor. *Sociology and Social Research, 58*, pp. 163–175.

Wilson, A. (1963) Social stratification and academic achievement. In A. Passow (Ed.), *Education in Depressed Areas*. New York: Columbia University Press (Bureau of Publications, Teachers College).

Winegarden, C. (1974) The fertility of AFDC women: An econometric analysis. *Journal of Economics and Business, 26*, pp. 159–166.

Wingert, W., Freidman, D., & Larson, W. (1968) The demographical and ecological characteristics of a large urban pediatric outpatient population and implications for improving community pediatric care. *American Journal of Public Health, 58*, pp. 859–876.

Winick, M. (1970a) Fetal malnutrition. *Clinical Obstetrics and Gynecology, 13*, pp. 526–541 (a)

Winick, M. (1970b) Nutrition and mental development. *Medical Clinics of North America,* *54,* pp. 1413–1429. (b)

Winick, M. (1974) *Nutrition and Fetal Development.* New York: Wiley.

Winick, M., & Coombs, J. (1972) Nutrition, environment, and behavioral development. *Annual Review of Medicine, 23,* pp. 149–160.

Winick, M., Rosso, P., & Brasel, J. (1971) Malnutrition and cellular growth in the brain: Existence of critical periods. Reprinted from *Lipids, malnutrition and the developing brain* (Ciba Foundation Symposium).

Wise, A. (1968) *Rich schools, poor schools: The promise of equal educational opportunity.* University of Chicago Press.

Wiseman, M. (1976). *Changes and turnover in a welfare population* (Working Paper No. 70). Berkeley: University of California, Department of Economics Income Dynamics Project.

Yedvab, D., & Schmidt, E. (1973) Patient identification with the I-spy health program (children and youth project). *Medical Care, 11,* pp. 52–58.

Young, L. (1966) Personality patterns in unmarried mothers. In R. Roberts (Ed.), *The Unwed Mother.* New York: Harper & Row.

Zelnik, M., & Kantner, J. (1972) Sexual experience of young unmarried women in the United States. *Family Planning Perspectives, 4,* pp. 9–18.

Zelnik, M., & Kantner, J. (1973) Contraception and pregnancy: Experience of young unmarried women in the United States. *Family Planning Perspectives, 5,* pp. 21–35.

Zelnik, M., & Kantner, J. (1974) The resolution of teenage first pregnancies. *Family Planning Perspectives, 6,* pp. 74–80.

Index

size
  labor supply and, 41
  unemployment and, 36–39
turnover, 3–15, 38
variations, 1–8
Child care
  employment and, 28, 46, 53
  health care utilization and, 110, 116
Children
  employment and, 28–29, 32, 34, 36, 54
  malnourished, 92–101
  marital instability and, 59, 61–62, 131
  remarriage and, 69
  welfare dependency and, 9–10, 13, 18, 24–25, 27, 30, 51–54, 62
Community Action Program, 147
Concentrated Employment Program, 33
contraception, *see* Family planning

D

Dependency, *see* Welfare dependency

E

Education, 7, 9, 18, 22–23, 29–30, 36–37, 48, 93, 103–107, 120–144
  employability and, 123
  employment and, 29–30, 36–37, 48, 123
  health and, 93, 98, 103–107, 120, 135
  human resources and, 121–126
  nutrition and, 93, 135
  policy, 123, 142–144
  welfare dependency and, 7, 9, 18, 22–23, 121–144, 150
Educational achievement
  determinants of
    institutional, 123–142
    socioeconomic, 123–135, 139–144
  expectations of
    parents', and, 131–135
    self, and, 141–142
    teachers', and, 139–142
  family background and, 123–126
  family composition and, 126–127
  health and, 86, 101, 135
  home environment and, 131–133
  income and, 128–131, 136
  inequalities in, 122–123
  institutional determinants of, 123–142

occupation and, 127–128
parents', effect on child's, 124–126
poverty and, 122–123, 131, 142–144, 151
school resources, distribution of, and, 122–123, 135–139
Resources, *see* School resources
Employability, 9, 17–22, 36, 85–86, 90, 121, 123
  education and, 123
  health and, 85–86, 90, 120
  measuring, 17–22
  predictors of, 18–19, 36, 121
  work experience, previous, and, 36
Employment, 7–10, 12–14, 17–49
  attitudes toward, 31–36
  benefit levels, welfare, vs., 43–47
  education and, 29–30, 36–37, 48, 123
  family head, of, 26–31, 37–40
  health and, 25–26, 28–30, 36, 48, 85–86
  obstacles to, 28, 31–36, 46–48, 53–54, 85–86, 90, 101
  personal resources and, 26–31, 36, 40
  race and, 28–33, 48
  research on, 150
  self-esteem and, 33
  welfare dependency and, 17–49, 150, 155

F

Family Assistance Plan, 148, 155
Family
  background, and educational achievement, 123–126
  composition, 11–14, 18, 24–26, 30, 48, 51–84, 110, 126
    educational achievement and, 126–127
  planning, 72, 75–76, 79–84, 106, 121, 123, 143
  size
    income vs., 54
    marriage/remarriage probabilities and, 54, 77, 82, 84
    preferred, 77
    welfare benefits and, 76
  stability, 8–10, 51, *see also* Marital instability
Fertility
  economic status and, 53
  income and, 77–80
  welfare system's effect on, 75–82

poverty and, 61–68, 82
predictors of, 56, 58–59, 62–63
pregnancy and, 13–14, 66–68, 72–75, 82
unemployment and, 60–61, 82
welfare
 patterns and, 53–57
 system effects on, 56–57, 61–68, 82
Marriage
 age at, 55–56, 61, 67–68, 82
 economic institution, as an, 57–59
 probabilities of, 54–55, 68–71, 77, 82, 84
 welfare system effects on, 54
Medicaid, 26, 46–47, 62, 89, 102, 109, 111–117
Medical education, 106; see also Health care services
Mental retardation, 93, 96, 98–99, 135
Michigan, University of, study; see Panel Study on Income Dynamics
Mortality
 infant, 90–92, 96, 98, 119
 rate, 90–92

N

Negative income tax, 42–46, 56, 68, 120, 130, 148
Nutrition, 86, 92–101, 120–121, 135

O

Occupation, 23–24, 39
 educational achievement and, 127–128
 unemployment and, 39–40
Office of Economic Opportunity, 33

P

Panel Study on Income Dynamics, 2, 5, 21–22, 29–30, 35–37, 39, 51–53, 56–58, 61, 67–71, 82, 124, 151–152
Parents' educational achievement, effect on child's, 124–126
Parents' expectations, effect on child's educational achievement, 131–135
Personal resources
 employment and, 26–31, 36, 40
 welfare dependency and, 7, 11, 18, 22–31, 48
Policy
 education, 123, 142–144

health, 93, 101, 119–121
welfare, 1–2, 18, 26, 49, 145–156
Poverty, 2, 13, 18, 147
 culture of, 2, 31
 determinants of, 147–148, 150–151
 educational achievement and, 122, 131, 142–144, 151
 family composition and, 51–53
 health and, 85–88, 92, 97
 marital instability and, 61–68, 82
 research on, 151–156
Pregnancy, see also Illegitimacy
 complications, during, 97
 marital instability and, 13–14, 66–68, 72–75, 82
 premarital, 72
 unwanted, 66–67, 73–74, 76–77, 81–84
Prenatal care, 91–92, 97, 112

R

Race
 education and, 123, 127–128, 136
 employment and, 28–33, 48
 female household headship and, 65–66
 health
  utilization of health care and, 105, 108, 114
 remarriage and, 69
 state of health and, 95
 welfare dependency and, 66
Remarriage
 determinants of, 54–55, 68–71, 77, 82, 84
 race and, 69
 welfare system effects on, 54, 68–71, 84
Resources, human
 education and, 121–126
 employment and, 36, 40
 welfare dependency and, 7, 11, 18, 22–31, 48, 147, 154–155
Resources, school
 achievement and, 122–123, 135–139, 143
 distribution of, 135–137
 inequality of, 135–139

S

School, see also Resources, school
 dropouts, 128–130, 132